Protestants in an Age of Science

Protestants
in an Age of Science

THE BACONIAN IDEAL
AND ANTEBELLUM
AMERICAN RELIGIOUS THOUGHT

by Theodore Dwight Bozeman

The University of North Carolina Press
Chapel Hill

Copyright © 1977 by
The University of North Carolina Press
All rights reserved
Manufactured in the United States of America
ISBN 0-8078-1299-4
Library of Congress Catalog Card Number 76-25962

Library of Congress Cataloging in Publication Data

Bozeman, Theodore Dwight, 1942–
    Protestants in an age of science.
    Bibliography: p.
    Includes index.
    1. Religion and science—History of controversy—
United States. 2. Bacon, Francis, Viscount St. Albans,
1561–1626. 3. Protestantism.
I. Title.
BL245.B7   261.5   76-25962
ISBN 0-8078-1299-4

To my Mother

Contents

Acknowledgments

I happily recall the kindness with which several historians assisted me in bringing this study to its final form. Stuart Clark Henry and Irving B. Holley, Jr., of Duke University wrested time from busy schedules to provide indispensable counsel at several stages of preparation. Martin E. Marty of the University of Chicago read and commented incisively upon the next-to-final draft. Several colleagues in the School of Religion and the Department of History at the University of Iowa generously shared ideas and criticisms. Much thanks also is due to the excellent staffs and holdings at the Perkins Library of Duke University, the Firestone Library of Princeton University, the Speer Library of Princeton Theological Seminary, the manuscript division of the Historical Society of Pennsylvania and the library of the Presbyterian Historical Society, both in Philadelphia, the South Caroliniana Library of the University of South Carolina, the Historical Foundation of the Presbyterian and Reformed Churches Library at Montreat, North Carolina, and the Main Library at the University of Iowa. Publication of the present work has been aided by a generous grant from the Graduate College at the University of Iowa.

Introduction

In the standard syntheses of American religious history to date, one will find little reference to the impact of natural science upon religious thought prior to the age of Darwin.[1] This neglect is symptomatic of a relative lack of interest among historians in science as it affected religion before the Civil War. Perry Miller and others have emphasized the high significance attributed to science by many Puritans, and everyone knows that young Jonathan Edwards conducted a brilliant research in the natural history of the spider; but few scholars have been interested in probing the relationship between science and religion throughout the long period in which American thinkers—despite the growing Transcendentalist challenge—operated predominantly within the intellectual framework fashioned by Newton and Locke. The present study will focus upon the later segment of this period, the troubled but reasonably unified epoch in American epistemological thought stretching roughly from 1820 to 1860. Churchmen of these decades commonly are represented as lacking serious interest in scientific issues. Sidney E. Mead has written that after about 1800 the evangelical reaction against the French Revolution stifled the outreach of intellectual concern among the American Protestant churches: "By and large, except perhaps for Unitarianism, the bulk of American Protestantism turned against the ethos of the Enlightenment and thereafter found itself indifferent to, or in active opposition to, the general spiritual and intellectual currents of modern Western civilization."[2] James Ward Smith, treating more broadly of "American philosophy" in the era, has argued that "during the first half of the nineteenth century science played a comparatively minor role in shaping the American mind. The age of romanticism did not take science seriously."[3] The research to be reported here will suggest grounds for qualifying these generalizations. It will describe science as a major and formative influence upon a central tradition in American religious thought during this supposedly antiscientific "age of romanticism."

In the chapters to follow, the spotlight will play upon a little-known yet prominent pattern of nineteenth-century thought termed —after Francis Bacon—"Baconianism." Partly because it came to primary expression among intellectual middlemen of the day —churchmen, professional orators, quarterly reviewers, pamphleteers, and the like, few of whom made original or lasting contributions to intellectual traditions—Baconianism generally has been disregarded by historians of thought.[4] Its proponents were Protestant Americans (and Britons) who subscribed without much qualification to the science-oriented empiricism of the Enlightenment as reorganized on the basis of Scottish Realism and for whom the newer antiempiricist chords being sounded by the various forms of romanticism in philosophy, religion, and even science were fundamentally repugnant. They, not the Transcendentalists, represented the broad foreground of Anglo-American intellectual leadership.

The Scottish influence, whose great impact upon the ideas here to be considered will oblige us carefully to examine the philosophical formulations of "Realism," also has suggested the feasibility of using the Old School branch of American Presbyterianism as the subject of a detailed case study in Protestant Baconianism. For within the Old School, theologically the most potent Protestant group outside New England before the Civil War, the Scottish strain in American Protestantism was at its strongest. Our procedure will be, first, to locate and characterize the roots of Baconianism within the Scottish Philosophy, and then to gauge its impact upon American ideas by means of a detailed study of Presbyterian literature.

Our study will reveal that the restrictive orientation to sensory experience characteristic of Scottish Philosophy did not exhaust the meaning of Baconianism for nineteenth-century Americans. A "Baconian"—whether scientist or not—was a man captivated by the ongoing spectacle of scientific advance. Although during the period in question specialization gradually was removing central areas of research from the ken of nonprofessionals, the process was slow and its results uneven. Its ultimate implications by no means had dawned upon the intellectual public. Hence in continuity with the tradition of the eighteenth-century "virtuoso," nonscientist thinkers of our period made a significant and fruitful effort to keep abreast of the literature of science and participated with a presumption of competence in debate of scientific issues of the day. Working scientists—men like Benjamin Silliman and Louis Agassiz—directed many of their publications to the general public and participated in organized efforts to imbue that public with an appreciation of the methods and fruits of research. Baconianism—resting on the assumption that all scientific method was a simple operation upon sense data—both presumed and reinforced the general assumption that the intelligibility sought by science did not exceed the reach of amateurs and laymen.

If churchmen were suitably endowed with intellectual ability and curiosity, they might aspire to real comprehension of existing science; but more, they might profess to discover and amplify significant correlations between natural science and Christian theology. "Baconianism" might become for them a symbol of the essential goodness and theological relevance of the scientific enterprise. Science, of course, had been known to wander into paths of infidelity, and nineteenth-century science was rife with heresies, with unbiblical formulations, with materialism and impiety. Hence churchmen also would have to find within Baconian perspective a guarantee of restraint, a criterion wherewith impious researches might be chastened as "unscientific." And indeed, the career of the Christian Baconianism to be chronicled below is heavily punctuated with conflict waged against scientific ventures at odds with Protestant belief. Hence one effect of a careful probing of the attitudes of antebellum churchmen toward the science of their day will be to enhance our awareness of continuity in nineteenth-century American intellectual life. The chapters to follow should establish that, within some sectors of American Protestantism, the emergence of the issue of science versus religion in the later debates over Darwinism represents not a sudden focusing of religious concern upon science, but rather a nasty turn in a preexisting and far more congenial pattern of interplay and skirmish. To neglect or minimize the scientific interests of many antebellum Protestant thinkers is to obscure this important prehistory.

As is well known, the postbellum decades were also a time of great debate within the American churches over the issue of "higher criticism" of the Bible. During this period conservative Protestants formed a huge phalanx of opposition to all efforts at dissolving or relativizing the literal truth of Scripture. A gathering emphasis upon the absolute "factual" veracity of the biblical text was to provide a main foundation both of the Fundamentalist movement of the early twentieth century and of the powerfully resurgent conservative evangelicalism of more recent times. If, therefore, as recently has been shown by Ernest R. Sandeen, the Presbyterian "Princeton Theology" provided a major "root of Fundamentalism," an analysis of the concepts of religious and biblical truth worked out by the early Princeton theologians and their colleagues within the conservative Old School church will clarify an additional stream of continuity in American thought.[5] Analysis will make evident that key attitudes nourishing later conservative biblicism had been elaborated prior to the Civil War and under the impression of a positive coordination between Protestant religion and that heavily empiricist, factual style in scientific inquiry of which Bacon had become the crucial symbol.

A final reason for undertaking such a study is to illustrate anew the explanatory power of a contextual approach to the history of ideas. Few historians of science have exhibited a sympathetic interest in the historical interplay of religious and scientific perspective. Indeed, in our secular age, intellectual historians in many fields often have pursued their work without much sympathy or regard for the impact of religious concern upon the life of the mind. "Church historians," on the other hand, have been known to proceed as if religious thought were a cloistered matter of specifically "religious" doctrines without much vital connection with issues in philosophy, science, sociology, and the like. Historians of whatever stamp, writing in a century in which religious issues have ceased generally to stir the public and to stimulate intellectual debate outside the camp of religion, and in which scientific and philosophical issues normally are handled in cool aloofness from religion, understandably have difficulty measuring the fabric of ideas in earlier periods of our nation's history. Certainly throughout the period covered here, religion—at least in its Calvinist and Unitarian forms—was a great nurturing agent of the American intellect. With few exceptions, nonclerical intellectuals —most often educated in a denominational college—paid significant homage to religious values. Professional religious thinkers, on the other hand, felt free and were expected to engage in the public discussion of currently moot issues in all fields. Nontheological journals such as the *American Quarterly Review* or the *Southern Literary Messenger* were filled with significant contributions by churchmen. Many theological journals, such as the *Bibliotheca Sacra* or the *Princeton Review*, for their part, maintained a level of intellectual sophistication and a breadth of coverage not inferior to the best "secular" journals.[6] Given these conditions, the reader of the following study will not be surprised to learn that antebellum America, marked by a lively and growing interest in natural science *and* evangelical Protestantism, widely nurtured the comfortable assumption that science *and* religion, Baconianism *and* the Bible, were harmonious enterprises cooperating toward the same ultimate ends.

Protestants in an Age of Science

1.

The Source and Rise of Baconianism in America

In 1823, Edward Everett gave utterance to a trend currently pervasive among Anglo-American thinkers when he declared, "At the present day, as is well known, the *Baconian* philosophy has become synonymous with the true philosophy."[1] Any cross-sectional reading in representative British and American literature of the day—college and university addresses, scientific and philosophical essays and addresses, quarterly reviews, theological journals—will reveal the prevalence of a configuration of thought often labeled "the Baconian Philosophy." This pattern generally was equated with the "inductive" methodology of current science, which, it was held, was careful to root its depiction of the general laws of nature in a meticulous survey of particulars. Yet it also evoked a cluster of related ideas: a strenuously empiricist approach to all forms of knowledge, a declared greed for the objective *fact*, and a corresponding distrust of "hypotheses," of "imagination," and, indeed, of reason itself. The entire complex was ascribed ultimately to Francis Bacon.

How is this remarkable Baconian vogue, appearing nearly two centuries after Bacon's death, to be explained? To the small but growing corps of seventeenth-century "moderns" who worked out a program of "experimental science" in dissent from the established Aristotelianism, "Bacon" was a magic name; his writings seem particularly to have inspired several of the men who founded the Royal Society.[2] Yet at no time during the eighteenth century could it be said that an overt "Baconianism" — in the sense described in this study — played an extensive role in Anglo-American intellectual traditions. Sir Isaac Newton himself, the greatest figure of British science and the idol of the Enlightenment, scarcely mentioned Bacon in his published writings, and not a single reference to Bacon appears in Locke's *An Essay on the Human Understanding*, which set the tone for most subsequent philosophical developments in both Britain and America. An examination of other characteristic intellectual productions of the eighteenth century reveals a similar picture. Such prominent figures as George Berkeley, David Hume, Adam Smith, Joseph Butler, Jonathan Edwards, John Wise, Benjamin Franklin, and William Paley occasionally referred to Bacon, at times with marked admiration. Most accepted complacently the current assumption that Bacon was the originator of scientific method, the "Legislator of Science," as William Whewell later remarked; but they knew nothing of the explicit and ardent Baconianism that emerged shortly.[3]

One significant exception to the preceding generalization supplies a vital clue to the popularity of a "Baconian Philosophy" after the turn of the nineteenth century: the philosophical work of Thomas Reid and of the emerging Scottish School of common-sense Realism to which his thought gave rise. The initial purpose of this chapter will be to examine the possible significance of Scottish Realism for nineteenth-century Baconianism. Only those features of the original Realism that have direct bearing upon a later consideration of Baconianism in American thought will be considered. In the subsequent portion of the chapter, the rapid absorption of the Baconian pattern by American thinkers will be traced.

Realism and Natural Science

Although the Scottish School comprised several figures, two were of central importance. Thomas Reid (1710–96), Adam Smith's successor in the chair of moral philosophy at Glasgow University, was clearly the chief architect of the Realist position.[4] Reid developed a cautious "scientific" epistemology that proved so attractive and accessible it became the basis, as Rudolf Metz has indicated, of the first "real school of philosophic training" in British thought since the Cambridge Platonists.[5] Of the several figures who became identified as leading Realists in the following generation, clearly the most important, and the most influential in America, was Dugald Stewart (1753–1828), who held the chair of moral philosophy at Edinburgh University from 1785 to 1809. Stewart's philosophy was largely a more elegant restatement and embellishment of Reid's, and he devoted a long career in his influential Edinburgh post to the consolidation and promulgation of what already had become known as "the Scottish Philosophy." Reid and Stewart comprehend between them the essential range of early Scottish Realism insofar as it is pertinent to the present study, and attention, therefore, will be limited primarily to their formulations.[6]

In a grateful memoir of the man whose intellectual labors so extensively undergirded his own, Stewart observed accurately and with keen approval that the influence of "Lord Bacon" upon Reid "may be traced in almost every page."[7] Reid's plentiful virtues as a "scientific" thinker, thought Stewart, owed specifically to his undeviating "Baconian" discipleship. As for himself, Stewart professed faithful devotion to Baconian principles. The intellectual historian Robert Blakey accurately noted in 1850 that "Mr. Stewart was an enthusiastic admirer of Lord Bacon. . . . Indeed, his enthusiasm on this point seems to have been . . . intense and indiscriminate."[8]

The seldom-qualified veneration in which Reid and Stewart held the name of Bacon appears to be the effectual root of the Baconian Philosophy. For their estimation of Lord Bacon was not unfocused. It was not Bacon the moralist, nor Bacon the elegant English stylist, nor Bacon the subtle statesman who elicited their zeal. The Bacon who stood forth in their works was supremely the creator of the inductive method and, hence, the father of modern science.

Few of the scholars who in recent years have given attention to Scottish Realism have amply recognized the extent to which it was shaped by the powerful stimulants of Enlightenment natural science. In the memoir of Reid, Stewart laconically observed that Reid had been "familiarized from his early years . . . to experimental inquiries"; he evidently thought it gratuitous to add that scientific enthusiasm for "experimental inquiries" in many ways had dominated Reid's philosophical development from the beginning and thus supplied several of its nucleating concerns.[9] Dazzled both with the fresh intellectual grandeur and the stunning practical achievements of Newtonian science, Reid had acquired a devoted mastery of its basic methods and principles. His correspondence reflects a day-to-day preoccupation with the latest writings, apparatus, experiments, and findings of natural philosophy. It was therefore fitting that his first university position was a chair of philosophy comprising mathematics and physics as well as logic and ethics.[10] Stewart's involvement with natural science was only slightly less extensive than Reid's. As a student at Edinburgh at a time when intellectual life at the university was "nourished in great measure by the writings of Bacon and Newton," Stewart acquired a lifelong attachment to science in a course in natural philosophy presided over by an infectious Newtonian, James Russell.[11] Stewart succeeded his father in the chair of mathematics at Edinburgh in 1775; here he handled a course in astronomy and may have dealt at least nominally with the algebraic methods of recent physics.[12]

Thus it is no surprise that Reid and Stewart frequently coupled the name of Bacon with that of Newton, whose scientific achievements had established him as a national hero and as the most potent symbol of the triumphant enterprise of natural science.[13] But the Newton who came to voice in the works of Reid and Stewart was preeminently the apostle of Bacon. Both attributed Newton's huge accomplishments in science not primarily to genius but to method, that is, to his dogged adherence to the "rules of philosophizing" laid down by Bacon and summarized in the critical formula of "induction." They acknowledged that Bacon himself had performed little inductive research of value. A far-seeing pioneer, he had merely charted the way into the scientific future. It had remained for Newton to enflesh the bones of right method, to give "the first and noblest examples of that chaste induction, which Lord Bacon could only delineate in theory."[14]

The Realists' appeal to science and to Bacon as the author of scientific method suggests a number of fresh clues for the study of the Scottish Philosophy and of its subsequent massive impact upon British and American intellectual life. Existing analyses of Realism concentrate upon its constructive, positive philosophical basis as formulated by Reid: the replacement of the Cartesian and Lockean theory of "ideas" with a doctrine of intuited "first principles," and the resulting accommodation of basic epistemology to the "commonsense" of mankind. This approach is deficient on two vital counts. First, it does not adequately accent the profound concern for the state and course of the natural sciences which conditioned most Realist thought; and, second, it fosters neglect of a closely associated current of skepticism and restraint which, no less than the positive doctrine of "first principles," shaped the full contribution of the Scottish School to Anglo-American intellectual culture. An analysis of the factor of Baconianism integral to Realist perspective will make it possible to bring these often disregarded but important considerations into proper view; they, in turn, will contribute to an explanation of the broad popularity of Realism in nineteenth-century America.

Both Reid and Stewart considered their entire philosophical program to be an enactment of the inductive plan of research set forth in Bacon's *Novum Organum*. Their appeal to Bacon meant in the first place a conviction that the fortunes of scientific discovery had been overwhelmingly dependent upon a right grasp of *methodology*. "Taught by Lord Bacon," declared Reid, men at last had won release from the treadmill of medieval "deductionism," at last had been set unerringly on "the road to the knowledge of nature's works."[15] Highly impressed, in the manner of the "moderns," with Bacon's frequent and slashing attacks upon the abstract "whirling about" of Aristotelian orthodoxy, Reid set the new measures of induction sharply over against the scientifically barren syllogistic exercises of the Schoolmen. Bacon first had laid bare the sham of fruitless inquiry, had bridled the wandering intellect of the classical and medieval centuries with a simple yet infallible procedure for disclosing the concrete structure and laws of the universe, namely "the slow and patient method of induction."[16]

This centering of science upon inductive methodology allowed the Realists easily to make the characteristic Enlightenment leap from natural philosophy to a "science of man." Reid and Stewart spent their mature university careers in chairs of moral philosophy, which in the Realist version meant an extension of scientific method to mind, society, and morality.[17] In this trio of concerns, the study of "mind," which in the eighteenth century had come to be known as "mental philosophy" or "psychology," had priority; for through an "inductive" analysis of the faculties and powers by which the mind knows, feels, and wills, Realist moral philosophers hoped to establish scientific foundations for existing society and morality. What is important, however, is that underlying the heavy emphasis on "psychology" that characterized all Realist thought was also an acutely felt need to supply a fitting philosophical foundation for the scientific practice of induction itself.

A certain circularity was involved in the effort to validate the inductive method by means of induction, but the Realists seriously attempted to do so, and their effort amounted finally to an identification of the human mind as a structure "designed" explicitly and solely for an inductive style of knowing.

Ideas, Objects, and Intuition

The philosophical occasion for Reid's first efforts in mental philosophy was his startled realization, while perusing Hume's *Treatise on Human Nature*, that currently accepted assumptions about the knowing facility of the mind were woefully deficient.[18] Much of his work is to be understood as an effort to parry the Humean challenge to traditional certainties with a new epistemological formula more capable of meeting the conceptual needs of inductive science.

Reid began by acknowledging that the notorious mind-body problem bequeathed by Descartes to the Enlightenment had not yet been satisfactorily resolved. The conceptual point of departure for the Scottish Philosophy—and a basic point in all Baconianism

—was a resolution of the natural order into "two great kingdoms," a "system of bodies" and a "system of minds." This formulation, however, posed for philosophy and for natural science the acute difficulty of negotiating the "vast interval between body and mind" which it assumed; for all "knowing," and especially the analysis of nature propounded by natural science, plainly presupposed an intimacy of connection between the two disparate "kingdoms."[19] Into the original Cartesian breach Locke had insinuated an epistemology of "ideas," itself derived partly from Descartes, according to which a knowing mind perceives "ideas" assumed to represent objects in the material world. Reid recognized this attempt to stop the gulf between nature and mind as ingenious but ultimately futile. For Hume had now demonstrated, and with an awful cogency, that "the common [Lockean] philosophy," when driven to an ultimate conclusion, supplied a sandy foundation for such crucial premises of inductive science as the actual "existence" of an external world of objects or the operation of causes in that world. The difficulty was that, if the immediate object of perception was not a thing itself, but solely an "idea" thereof, then any affiliation of that idea with an actually existing object was an inference devoid of perceptual support.[20] Scanning the realm of ideas closely, Hume also had failed to find confirmation for the common assumption that "causation" is an object of experience and therefore of knowledge. Causation implies an active transaction between objects or events, but men have and can have no "idea" of the intangible and therefore imperceptible element of "power" which it assumes. Thus the manifest premise of the scientific movement, that there is an actual "system of bodies" governed by causal relations and accessible to the inquiring mind, had ceased to be philosophically intelligible.[21]

Reid shuddered at the intellectual danger into which Hume had thrust "the whole fabric of natural philosophy,"[22] and he determined to meet the emergency head-on. Precisely the assumption that the objects of perception were "ideas" obliquely related to things-in-themselves appeared to him to account for the discord in the Lockean logic that finally had provoked the disastrous speculations of Hume. He therefore scuttled the "unwieldy hypothesis" of ideas altogether and devised a fresh account of perception more congenial to the philosophical requirements of inductive science.

In Reid's system, taken over by Stewart and by innumerable Americans, perception was construed as a dynamic activity in which sense seized immediately on the thing and established a continuous contact between mind and nature. What is actually perceived, that is, is no longer an idea of a thing but the real empirical lineaments of the thing itself: "Perception . . . hath always an object distinct from the act by which it is perceived." It was, echoed Stewart, "the external objects themselves, and not any . . . images of these objects, that the mind perceives."[23]

The voice of skeptical philosophy, however, would promptly demand to know the means by which such unruffled assurance was obtained. How could one know that the apparent dimensions of normal perception are authentic—that external objects, bound within a web of causal relationships, have a real existence and that they are perceptually available? Reid insisted, and Stewart was quick to agree, that the event of perception is an organic complex of image and "belief." The image or "conception" of an external object that forms in the mind during perception cannot be scaled down to a mere subjective flicker, for it is inevitably accompanied by an intuitive belief or "judgment" as to the objective existence both of that object and of its field of causal relationships. The senses instinctively receive nature as real in its presented forms. "Judgment" was not to be understood as a datum transmitted to the mind by the senses, but as an a priori enrichment and validation of sensory information, evincing itself by "a strong and irresistible conviction and belief."[24]

This, in brief, was the new psychology of intuitive realism with which Reid hoped to armor the great tradition of Newton and Locke against the blitz of skeptical philosophy. In both Britain and America, it was to become the base upon which, in the period following, the supreme Baconian confidence in the senses and in inductive reasoning would rest. By thus securing the veracity of the normal deliverances of perception, as that word was understood in common parlance, Reid and his followers had readjusted

British empiricism to accord more faithfully both with the common-sense assumptions of the day and with the more rigorous inductive procedures of science. Now it was possible to buoy a philosophically vexed world with word that "the evidence of sense is a kind of evidence which we may securely rest upon."[25] This emphasis upon "trust in the senses" and their factual content, which implied a sharp reaction against the confidence in "pure reason" marking several directions of thought in the seventeenth and eighteenth centuries, became an important refrain in the works of the Scottish School generally.[26]

Hume and the Limits of Knowledge

To assume, however, that Reid merely had restored scientific epistemology and method to the relative confidence they had enjoyed before the philosophical sabotage wreaked by Hume would be a grave misrepresentation. For if Reid had stuffed the loopholes of skepticism with new doctrines of perception and judgment, he had been forced simultaneously to embrace major conclusions of the Humean critique. The appeal to intuition implied a number of specific retrenchments in the already cautious Lockean description of epistemological operations. High across the chasm between mind and nature the Scottish Philosophy had hoisted a delicate construction of perceptions undergirded by judgments, but the tiers upon which it ultimately rested disappeared without visible foundations in the "darkness" below: "We know, that when certain impressions are made upon our organs, nerves, and brain, certain corresponding sensations are felt, and certain objects are both conceived and believed to exist. But in this train of operations nature works in the dark. We can neither discover the cause of any one of them, nor any necessary connection of one with another."[27] Reid's doctrine of intuition had restored a basic intelligibility to perception, but key dimensions of its operation now would remain irrecoverably "hid in impenetrable darkness." He had in effect been compelled to acknowledge the truth of Hume's sober words, that "nature has kept us at a great distance from all her secrets."[28]

Francis Bacon himself had projected his hopes for a "Great

Instauration" (renewal) of empirical science partly in reaction to the strong movement of philosophical skepticism that marked the latter sixteenth century.[29] He often complained of the intellectual insolvency of "those who deny that we can know anything, and so introduce a wandering kind of inquiry that leads to nothing."[30] Such desolate counsel Bacon branded as "by far the greatest obstacle to the progress of science," and, partly with the desire to restore a strain of confidence and "hope" to philosophy, he propounded the gains to human knowledge and power that would ensue if men would thrust away the alluring abstractions of scholasticism and learn to dwell "purely and constantly among the facts of nature."[31] Despite this surge of optimism, however, Bacon's thought was heavily marked by the skeptical currents against which he struggled. He never tired of reminding his readers of "the dullness, incompetency, and deceptions of the senses" and urged that the human intellect is "far more prone to error than the sense is."[32] Bacon's famous analysis of the "idols" that block pure perception and understanding is a profound study of the weakness and inconstancy of the mind.[33] He hoped, through a programmatic immersion in concrete fact, to restore both sense and intellect to efficacy, but his acute appreciation of their innate deficiencies lent a dark and sober hue to his assessment of human cognition.

This sobering note of limitation and caution yoked Reid warmly to his inductivist mentor. Each had confronted and overcome a vigorous skepticism, but each in turn was fundamentally chastened by the experience. Each found it impossible to reestablish confidence in knowledge without first conceding and clearly marking out the acute defects that circumscribed the human understanding in its drive for knowledge.

A severe amputation of the apparent certainties of Lockean epistemology was reflected, for example, in Reid and Stewart's candid admission of Hume's doctrine that "causation is not an object of sense."[34] The Realist's resort to intuition mirrored a conviction that, precisely as Hume had claimed, it is impossible to apply scientific reason to the impalpable elements of experience represented in the concept of active causation. "Judgment" fills the gap and confirms the existence of a causal agency, but it provides no empirical information about that agency. Cause has been reinstated, but its status is now openly that of an inexplicable *presupposition*, and in no sense a *result*, of empirical analysis. The notion of gravity, for instance, considered as an active force, "gives us *no conception of what the thing is*, but of what relation it bears to something else." And the same, of course, held true for all the "first principles" supplied by intuition. Stewart observed that "abstracted from other *data*, they are perfectly barren in themselves."[35]

This move had significant consequences for natural science. Reid's new "realism" was intended to enable scientists confidently to proceed with empirical investigation, but by distinguishing and segregating sensed and intuited elements of experience, he had etched narrowly the boundaries of feasible empirical inquiry. To employ again the example of causation, if efficient causal agency in nature is beyond sensory reach, then the scientific investigator properly may deal only with its visible effects, that is, with the pattern or sequence of physical events he can actually observe. He may view, with his telescope, a comet surging through space, but he cannot view the power by which it is impelled:

We are very much in the dark with regard to the real agents or causes which produce the phenomena of nature. . . . [For example] A Newtonian philosopher inquires what proof can be offered for the existence of magnetic effluvia, and can find none. . . . He confesses his ignorance of the real [efficient] cause of [magnetically induced] motion, and thinks, that his business, as a philosopher, is only to find from experiment the laws by which it is regulated. . . . What has been said of this, may be applied to every phenomenon that falls within the compass of natural philosophy. We deceive ourselves, if we conceive, that we can point out the real efficient cause of any one of them.[36]

This abrupt contraction of the aims of science, which exempted not only efficient causation but all intuited "first principles" from inductive inquiry, heavily conditioned the account of scientific induction which Reid and his followers were prepared to give. An intensified accent upon the limits of knowledge lay at the core of Realist perspective. For within the Scottish School, scientific method always was to be construed in predominantly negative terms. Despite the generous enthusiasm for science evinced by the leading Realists, they consistently laid more stress upon the austere limits than upon the expansive possibilities of inductive research. The total weight of evidence for any scientific proposition now must rest upon the spare frame of fact grasped by sense. This delimitation could be received by scientists with partial satisfaction because facts, at least, were utterly reliable: "What can fairly be deduced from facts, duly observed, or sufficiently attested, is genuine and pure."[37] But at the same time, the absolute dominion granted to facts sharply abbreviated the field of inquiry. Dugald Stewart thought that a primary virtue of Reid's philosophy was "to remind us of the limited powers of the human understanding" and insisted that the leading tendency of Baconian science was not to "flatter the pride of man" but to "lead to a confession of human ignorance."[38]

Eschewing intellectual pride, then, the natural scientist would restrict his function to a processing of the admittedly cramped range of information yielded by the senses, for this was the sole resource from which scientific concepts might be fueled:

Natural philosophy must be built upon the phenomena of the material system, discovered by observation and experiment. . . . [If] all the length men can go to in accounting for phenomena, is to discover the laws of nature, according to which they are produced; [then] the true method of philosophizing is this: from real facts ascertained by observation and experiment, to collect by just induction the laws of nature, and to apply the laws so discovered, to account for the phenomena of nature. Thus the natural philosopher has the rules of his art fixed with no less precision than the mathematician.[39]

As applied to the "law" of gravity, for instance, induction could reveal solely that nature "works" in accord with the pattern to which Newton had assigned the name "gravity."[40] The scientist may deal exhaustively with the observable "what" of nature's operations, but all considerations as to *why*, as to the hidden impulses underlying the gravitational effect, belonged emphatically "not to the province of physics, but to that of metaphysics."[41] Stewart made the point clearer by speaking of "a line, which no industry or ingenuity can pass . . . between that field which falls under the survey of the physical inquirer, and [an] unknown region. . . . It was . . . chiefly by tracing out this line that Lord Bacon did so much service to science."[42]

It was, in fact, doubtful whether Bacon could be claimed as a guardian of the "unknown region" of efficient causes. Reid had read the master more attentively at this point and acknowledged unhappily that he had assumed causes as legitimate objects of empirical research.[43] Yet Stewart clearly had in mind the original Baconian repudiation of nonempirical techniques in science, and the issue here set forth distinctly indicates the extent to which the Baconian version of inductivism raised upon the foundation of Realist psychology had become identified, in the words of Whitehead, with an emphatic and even authoritarian "recurrence to concrete fact."[44] The assignment of the first principles of knowledge to the scientifically inaccessible realm of metaphysics meant that all the resources of inquiry must be concentrated in the explication of sensed *fact*. In this way, the addictive appeal to Bacon, which marks the writings of Reid and even more so of Stewart, became a striking index of the restraining fixation upon direct empirical data quickly being established as a leitmotiv of the Scottish School.

Yet this was not to say that scientific work must be restricted to a gullible reading of empirical surfaces. In Reid's discussion of scientific methodology the keynote of "patient observation" was refined and extended by "accurate experiments" and by "conclusions drawn by strict reasoning from observations and experiments."[45] Dugald Stewart frequently observed that scientific experiment and induction were sophisticated techniques that pierced far beyond "mere observation" and the discernment of obvious relationships.[46] To "collect" by "just induction" the "laws of nature" implied a sensitive thrust of reason, inducting from facts underlying patterns of order; Newton's "collection" of the universal law of gravitation thus could be celebrated as a feat of the highest genius.[47]

The claim was ambiguous, however, for the acid test of any scientific explanation, in the view of Reid and Stewart, was not its ingenuity, but its footing in evidence. And to achieve adequate mastery of a body of facts sufficiently large and complex to establish a law of nature required prolonged and painstaking effort.

Accordingly, Realists regularly stressed that induction is but a "*slow* and *gradual* ascent in the scale of natural causes," thus deliberately echoing Bacon's oft-repeated admonition to "proceed regularly and gradually from one [inducted] axiom to another."[48] Induction, in short, was understood primarily as a *technique of restraint*, providing for a sluggish, methodical, but sure march toward generalization. The aim of scientific inquiry, on this model, was nothing less than a patient and precise fitting of the mind to the concrete pace and contour of nature. Scientific explanation was to be, for the Scottish Philosophy as for Bacon, literally a "grammar of the language of nature"; a scientific "law" was merely the individual fact writ large.[49] A curious but revealing corollary of this emphasis was that no law could be completely final because it could not represent literally the sum total of pertinent facts. Always there existed the possibility that continuing research might turn up an exception to the rule. Reid even deliberated the contingency that a tireless investigator eventually might turn up "a kind of matter in some bodies which does not gravitate," and thus "limit" the law of gravitation.[50]

The taut empirical limitations that Reid and Stewart, following Bacon, had assigned to knowledge made absolutely necessary a critical reconsideration of the role of imagination and of its offspring, "hypothesis," already a term of reproach in Britain by virtue of its association with the "fantastic vortices" of Descartes. Reid obviously felt that, next to the invention of the inductive method itself, Bacon's major contribution to scientific knowledge had been his emphatic exclusion of hypotheses, or "anticipations," as a legitimate tool of scientific research.[51] Armed with this conviction, Reid entered with all the zeal of a combatant in the famous debate between Newtonians and Cartesians about the status of a priori methods in scientific investigation.[52] Convinced, moreover, that the task set by Bacon and Newton was far from accomplished, that "the world" continued to be much "befooled by hypotheses," he launched an energetic campaign against these "reveries of vain and fanciful men."[53] In so doing he touched upon the most problematic feature of Baconian perspective.

Bacon himself appears not to have understood the vital role

played by abstract concepts in the creative science of his own era.[54] His outline of inductive procedure must be read in part as a sweeping critique of the scholastic methods that dominated current philosophy and placed a premium upon abstract and logical "wit." The mode of research he envisioned would supplant logic with fact, forcing a "chaste . . . and legal wedlock with things themselves." It was designed specifically to minimize the unruly and individualized factor of "genius."[55] In his system, "induction" was identified with an elaborate pattern of step-by-step procedures for monitoring the idol-ridden intellect. It was best, he felt, that "the strength and excellency of the wit [be given] but little to do in the matter" and that the entire process of inquiry "be done as if by machinery."[56] The scientist, then, need be capable only of winnowing his senses for factual raw material and of performing a set of quasi-mechanical operations upon it.[57] Here was no place for the unsystematic lurchings of reason and imagination beyond the immediately presented evidence; in order to meet the test of sense, an explanatory concept must represent something that had been experienced directly.

This single-minded empiricism was what the Scottish Philosophers found most compelling in the heritage of Bacon and Newton, and they sought faithfully to represent it in their assault upon hypotheses and "conjectures."

Like Bacon, Reid detected within the human mind an expansive and troublesome capacity for imaginative "invention," an outthrusting "power," which, even among children, "like the bud of a tree, is ready to burst its integuments."[58] The unruliness suggested by this image is an accurate reflection of the generally suspicious attitude of the Scottish School toward inventive reason.[59] Invention irked the inductivists because it was not safely bound to the senses and could operate beyond and in excess of nature. Having virtually defined induction as a programmatic fidelity to empirical restraints, Reid obviously was hard pressed to give a consistent account of a faculty, to which he could not deny the marks of "nobility" and "superiority," but which appeared exasperatingly eager to sully the empirical chastity demanded of the faithfully inductive scientist. In a discussion explicitly adapted from Bacon's "idols of the tribe," Reid lamented the futile cleverness of those "ingenious men" who have "invent[ed] hypotheses to explain the phenomena of nature; . . . Instead of a *slow* and *gradual* ascent in the scale of natural causes, by a just and copious induction, they would shorten the work, and, by a flight of genius, get to the top at once."[60]

The hypothetical reveries in which men, under the abstractive spell of imagination, apparently loved to indulge were dangerous not only because they made a reckless detour around the right avenues of perceptual commerce, but also because they assumed an easy congruence between mind and nature not confirmed by patient observation. Bacon had taught that "the universe to the human understanding is framed like a labyrinth," and the lesson was not lost upon his Scottish admirers.[61] In Reid's view, nature was the product of Divine ingenuity. It represented an incredibly expert capturing of diversity within a single plan, and it mirrored in every sector the fathomless complexity and "subtlety" of the Divine mind. To imagine, therefore, like the Cartesians, that through the power of his own reason one might reconstruct the inventive intricacy of Divine thought underlying the Creation would be a summit of human conceit; for it must presume a power of understanding "equal or superior" to that of God himself![62] Thus the pattern of nature's workmanship could not be deduced by an effort of intellectual cleverness, however prodigious; it must be "discovered" piecemeal by arduous research. Not even "the most sagacious physiologist" could ever foresee the principles of construction and function displayed in the human body; until he dissects, observes, and tests he can understand nothing.[63] Nature only discloses her secrets to the humble observer willing to forego "reveries" and acquiesce completely in the sensory messages of concrete factuality.[64]

The issue of hypothesis, in fact, came close to summing up the meaning of the Realists' intellectual allegiance to Bacon. What they found cogent in Bacon was his restrictive planning of research. The apostolate of the Scottish Philosophers to natural science was here digested into a concept of *restraint*. It was precisely the empirical "severity" of the method of induction which disjoined empirical truth from "inventive" fallacy and thereby generated reliability in scientific knowledge. If loose hypothesizing tendencies in science and philosophy had been responsible for the catastrophic notion of "ideas," the absurd vortices of Descartes, the unsavory materialism of associations in David Hartley's psychology, and many other serious errors—none of which referred to anything that can be experienced directly—it seemed exigent to prove once and for all the treacherous issue of roving from fact.[65]

Reid and Stewart, unlike Bacon, did not dismiss hypotheses altogether. They appeared willing to affirm responsible "queries" intended to guide empirical research and thus specifically designated for experimental testing and correction. If these queries were employed with due circumspection and advanced with the tentativeness befitting conjecture, they might facilitate investigation by suggesting new experiments and by guiding the discipline of observation in new and fruitful directions; but they were never to be confused with the hard currency of "law."[66] Fortunately the great Newton himself, who had framed a number of fascinating "conjectures," had known where to draw the Baconian line. Impeccably schooled by Lord Bacon, Newton was wonderfully purged of dogmatism in hypothetical matters. "His conjectures he put in the form of queries, that they might not be received as truths, but be inquired into, and determined according to the evidence to be found for or against them."[67]

Yet for Reid, at least, even this limited concession to the spirit of hypothesis was little more than an equivocation, for in further remarks he repeatedly emptied it of significance by underscoring the almost uniform futility that had attended the use of the most sober "queries." The obdurate complexity of nature joined with the unreliability of the intellect to render nonempirical researches simply fruitless. Newton's most brilliant hypothesis, the "ether," had come to nothing, for no evidence had ever been found to sustain it.[68] Again, of all the discoveries made concerning the structure and operation of the human body, "never one was made by conjecture." And what was true of the human body was equally true of every part and process of nature: actual "discoveries," made by properly inductive methods, "have always tended to refute, but not to confirm, the theories and hypotheses which ingenious men had invented."[69] What Reid seemed to offer with one hand, therefore, he snatched away with the other. Induction not merely disqualified, it systematically humiliated the imaginative intellect; for to subject one's most ingenious and subtle conjectures to the "fiery trial" of empirical test, in which "the greatest part, if not the whole, will be found to be dross," could only work upon it a stunting embarrassment.[70]

Stewart, not quite so radically absorbed in the spirit of empiricism, was willing to grant more constructive leeway to the abstractive tactic embodied in hypothesis. He refused to adopt completely Reid's supposition that hypotheses were "wholly arbitrary and gratuitous" and insisted that Bacon himself had recognized a need for conjecturing "a little farther" than the immediately available evidence. Yet for him as well as for Reid, the overwhelmingly important desiderata of research were delay and restraint. Explicitly renouncing any desire to transgress "the severe rules of the Inductive Logic," Stewart agreed with Reid that the sole function of hypotheses was instrumental, that they must be presented in a "modest and diffident manner," and that they must conform rigidly to all known facts and be tested ruthlessly against further observation and experiment.[71]

With imagination scolded thus supine, Reid and Stewart had made a close approach to the mechanical ideal of induction set forth by Bacon. Scientific concepts were to be forged directly and solely from observations. The superstructure of scientific laws built upon this foundation was secure, "immoveable," and permanent; all "opinion," contradiction, and sectarian foolishness were at last abolished.[72] But the impact of Hume was evident. Little could now be found for the once-proud intellect to perform save the essentially pedestrian operations of observation, experiment, and "*strict* reasoning" from facts to laws. This was the spartan and mechanical core of that "chaste induction" so circumspectly "delineated by Lord Bacon."

Summary of the Scottish Pattern

These, then, are the principal elements of "Baconianism" as elaborated by the Scottish School:

1. A spirited enthusiasm for natural science.

2. A scrupulous empiricism, grounded upon the confident "trust in the senses" and in the reality of the outer world supplied by the Realist doctrine of "judgment."

3. A sharp accent upon the limits of scientific method and knowledge, directed to the inductive control of generalizations by continuous reference to "facts." Abstract concepts not immediately forged from observed data have no place in scientific explanation.

4. A celebratory focus upon "Lord Bacon" as the progenitor of inductive science; a flat identification of Newtonian methods with Bacon's "induction."

This pattern, quickly dubbed the "Baconian Philosophy," was to be engrafted wholesale into the main structure of nineteenth-century American ideas. If Edward Everett, whose thought is an especially effective mirror of his times, was prepared by 1823 to equate the "Baconian philosophy" with "the true philosophy," and if its point of origin lay indeed in Scottish Realism, then it is evident that an important migration and extension of ideas had taken place. In what follows, the transfer of Baconianism from Scotland to America will be depicted.

Transition to America: The Rise of Realism

Recent study in the history of American ideas has made it clear that the Scottish Philosophy did not remain long cloistered in its homeland. There is now little doubt that for several decades after about 1800, Realism exerted a master influence upon American thought. From the mid-1820s, its preeminence was challenged increasingly by various and mushrooming forms of romantic idealism, but it remained the single most powerful current in general intellectual and academic circles until after the Civil War.[73]

Many scholars have observed the pervasiveness of Realism during this period of the nation's life. Howard Mumford Jones has called it "the official academic belief of the period"; Perry Miller has spoken of the "American ideology."[74] The evidence seems to indicate that Realist influence began trickling into the country shortly before 1800. Researchers have generally agreed that the first significant influx was marked by the accession of Edinburgh-trained John Witherspoon to the presidency of the Presbyterian College of New Jersey in 1769.[75] Finding a strong interest in Berkeleyan idealism entrenched on the campus, he routed it with a heavy application of Realist doctrine. With the efficacy and safety of the new ideas thus proved, the takeover thereafter was swift. Reid's philosophical reconstruction admirably suited the intellectual needs of the moment. Sydney Ahlstrom has described how Americans, and especially Calvinist and Unitarian churchmen, now seized greedily upon the resources the Scottish Philosophy offered for countering the "metaphysical heresies" of Hume and Berkeley and subduing the postwar challenge of French "infidelity."[76] Realism, in short, supplied a renewed foundation for intellectual endeavor in a time when the old Lockean ground seemed crumbly and insecure. Thus, after 1800 Realist texts were gradually introduced into the curricula of American colleges, most of which were church sponsored. Reid and Stewart, together with George Campbell and James Beattie, facile but effective popularizers of Reid's philosophy, quickly became well known to thinking Americans. Thomas Brown, an acute thinker who departed from the basic doctrines of the original school at a number of points, but who nonetheless must be considered an important mediator of Realist psychology, also was widely read.[77]

During the decade of the 1820s, just as Edward Everett and others were heralding the rise of Baconianism, Realism consolidated its hold upon the country. Herbert Schneider has noted that "a significant revolution" now took place in American colleges. Scottish texts, often adapted specifically for American use, quickly and decisively replaced the older eighteenth-century texts and were established as the center of the philosophical portions of the curriculum.[78] Stewart was apparently the most esteemed. By 1821 the *North American Review* could declare that his popular *Elements of the Philosophy of the Human Mind* "has passed . . .

through as many editions in the United States as in Great Britain."[79] Nine years later, A. H. Everett, now editor of the *North American Review*, observed that Stewart was "on the whole, at present, and will probably long remain, among English authors, the most popular professor of moral science."[80] And in 1833, Emma Willard, founder of the Troy Female Seminary, enriched the chorus of praise by affirming Stewart as "the most celebrated pneumatologist of our times."[81] In the general praise of Stewart, Reid was not forgotten; the difference was, as A. H. Everett nicely explained, that Reid was "deficient in the graces of manner."[82] Judge Joseph Story, for one, proclaimed in a popular oration his veneration for "the incomparable elegance of Dugald Stewart," yet he was plainly well read in Reid and Brown as well.[83] By 1828 the *American Quarterly Review* was announcing its delight with the achievements of Reid and Stewart, and of Brown insofar as he adhered to the baseline laid down by Reid.[84] And sometime later, Unitarian minister Andrew Preston Peabody summarized a great and undiminishing body of sentiment as he underscored the place of Reid in his list of "great names in intellectual science."[85] Further to recount the plentiful evidence of Realist hegemony would be redundant. It is evident that by early in the century the body of thought often labeled "Scotch metaphysics" had coursed into a central position in American thought.

Locke, "Lord Bacon," and Inductive Science

Without doubt it is more than a coincidence, in the same period when Realist influence was pervading the country and thousands of Americans were reading the encomiums of Bacon with which the writings of Reid, Stewart, and their followers were copiously seeded, the name and prestige of "Lord Bacon" were rapidly rising into prominence. Merle Curti has argued, and the evidence is overwhelming, "that Locke was America's philosopher during the Revolutionary period."[86] His was, until perhaps shortly after the end of the eighteenth century, the most potent name to be reckoned with in politics and philosophy. Yet, after the Revolution, with new philosophical challenges emerging, and with the gory culmination of the French Enlightenment helping to cast the older foundations of thought into doubt, the "great Mr. Locke" appeared to be stalemated. It was in this rapidly changing philosophical situation, as we have seen, that Realism found its firm footing in the American scene. The Scottish doctrine, in its turn, was openly rooted in the judgment that the philosophical troubles of the age were due to a radical defect in Locke's concept of "idea." The once-invincible vessel of Locke's psychology now seemed reduced to a leaky hulk on darkening waters. It was to be expected, then, that the luster surrounding him would be diminished, and indeed it was. Frederick Beasley, provost of the University of Pennsylvania and staunch Lockean resister of Scottish pretensions, was forced to admit in 1822 that Locke stood "degraded" in current opinion. George P. Schmidt, a close student of primary sources pertaining to collegiate education in the growing republic, has concluded that Locke had discernibly "lost caste."[87] Arguing for the continuing influence of Locke throughout the period, Curti has admitted that much of it was indirect, and has perhaps not made it sufficiently clear that the "Locke" invoked in the period after 1800 was most often being viewed through a Scottish lens. The reverent intonation of the name of Locke that one encounters so frequently in materials from the Revolutionary era generally declines into a whisper around the turn of the century. By about 1820, Locke was scarcely being taught in American colleges, having been crowded out by the new Scottish texts.[88]

But the retreat of praise for Locke had left a vacuum—a vacuum that now, under the stimulus of the explicit Baconianism proclaimed by the Scottish Philosophers, could be filled with a name equally British, and apparently, equally grand. It is difficult to recapture the grateful urgency with which many Americans now turned to Bacon. By 1860, his name had been invoked to bless and harmonize nearly every cause in the republic. Poetry, science, philosophy, religion, psychology, medicine, law, agriculture—all found plenteous use for the quickly formulized magic of the name "Lord Bacon." "Bacon," proclaimed Book the Ninth of Joel Barlow's near-ecstatic *The Columbiad*, was master of

All that is yet and all that shall be known,
. . . .
[He] Bids men their unproved systems all forego,
Informs them what to learn and how to know.[89]

The works of "Lord Verulam" were, according to Virginia politician and novelist William Wirt, "filled with pure and solid golden bullion." As "father of experimental philosophy" he had "rescued and redeemed the world from all . . . darkness, jargon, perplexity and error" and had "straightened the devious paths of science" for all posterity.[90] Stephen Simpson, an avid Jacksonian theorist whose *New Theory of Political Economy* appeared in 1831, thus could commend the work to his readers with the claim that "according to Lord Bacon's rule of philosophizing, I have drawn my theory from facts, and not deduced facts to suit my theory."[91] In 1844 the *American Agriculturalist* laid claim to Bacon as the patron of progress in American farming.[92] The "rule" of Bacon proved highly attractive to professional men. Lawyers and doctors, jockeying for position and stature in the growing and fluid nation, were happy to avail themselves of Bacon's rocketing prestige. In 1801, doctor of medicine David Ramsay declared that his profession was determined to overcome the vagaries of the past and to assume the full honors of "science" by consolidating about the inductive program of Bacon, "the father of all modern science." Others followed suit.[93] Francis Andrew March's 1844 offering on "The Relation of the Study of Jurisprudence to the Origin and Progress of the Baconian Philosophy" indicated that some lawyers too had been stepping to the Baconian tune. March argued that Bacon had originally imbibed the spirit of induction from his lawyer-father and his colleagues and that law is therefore the archetypically inductive and Baconian science.[94]

A name so potent could be turned to many uses. When, in 1836, the *American Quarterly Review* needed a figure to compare with William Wordsworth as men "before their age," Bacon was the automatic choice.[95] A Calvinist theologian in 1848, somewhat puzzled by Samuel Taylor Coleridge's fondness for aphorism, remembered that Bacon, too, had employed the form, and thereupon granted his stamp of approval.[96] A substantial contribution to proslavery thought during the 1840s was Natchez physician Samuel A. Cartwright's *Essays, Being Inductions from the Baconian Philosophy, Proving the Truth of the Bible and the Justice and Benevolence of the Decree Dooming Canaan to be Servant of Servants.*[97] And the practitioners of phrenology, who from the beginning of the American campaign during the 1820s were forced to defend their new "science" against the assaults of clergy, doctors, and other scientists, uniformly sought to break into the accepted circle of the sciences by enlisting under the banner of "the philosophy of Bacon."[98] An enthusiastic contributor to a Baltimore religious magazine in 1841 even found "the noble spirit of the Baconean [*sic*] philosophy" ultimately responsible for "the sacredness of the marriage tie, the purity of private life, the sincerity of friendship, charity towards the poor, and general love of mankind" in Anglo-Saxon countries![99]

But if the mere name "Lord Bacon" could convey authority to almost any cause, most of the ardent invocations were focused, in accord with the Realist example, on Bacon the architect of scientific induction. In both Britain and America, Bacon the "father of science" was the rage. Baltimore attorney and amateur philosopher Samuel Tyler, who in 1844 presented to the world a euphoric *Discourse of the Baconian Philosophy*, remarked with accuracy that "the great periodicals" of the Anglo-American scene "have been for a long time teeming with commentaries and expositions of the Baconian philosophy."[100] Already by 1823, Edward Everett found "the name of Lord Bacon, with the single exception of that of Sir Isaac Newton . . . the first in the modern philosophical world."[101] The London Society for the Diffusion of Knowledge, whose activities and publications were well known to Americans, published two volumes of an *Account of Lord Bacon's Novum Organum* in 1827 and 1828; the work soon was republished in the American Library of Useful Knowledge.[102] Soon thereafter, a prominent American orator announced his pleasure at being alive in an age when "the *Novum Organum* is read in the original by undergraduates."[103] By 1831 the American edition of the London *Quarterly Review*, which was one of the few opponents of the growing Baconian movement, snarled impotently that "the whole atmosphere rings with the name of 'Lord Bacon,' and with the paeans of 'Inductive Philosophy.'"[104] But a few words from an angry Tory could scarcely break the tide. The *Princeton Review* in 1844 greeted Tyler's effort in the *Discourse of the Baconian Philosophy* to "clarify" the meaning of induction by complaining that Baconianism had become a virtual fetish for Americans, a seldom-examined formula: "In these days . . . Bacon's name is in everybody's mouth, and every sciolist prates about the principles of the inductive philosophy."[105]

There can be little doubt, then, that throughout the antebellum decades, the prestige once associated with Locke and natural rights was gravitating massively toward Bacon and the inductive philosophy. There were, of course, some murmurings of discontent with the din of generally uncritical praise now afforded the Baconian Philosophy. The eminent Scottish scientist and mathematician John Leslie had argued in the *Edinburgh Review* as early as 1812 that Bacon's relative disregard of mathematical techniques in science disqualified him for the title of father of inductive natural philosophy.[106] Thomas Babington Macaulay, in a typically brilliant essay on "Lord Bacon" also published in the *Edinburgh Review*, underscored an already popular objection by arguing that "induction" had not been invented by Bacon at all. For Macaulay, induction was the common-sensical procedure adopted by all men in search of truth and had been practiced by scientists in all ages prior to Bacon.[107] Similar sentiments were echoed elsewhere, in both Britain and America.[108] Potentially the most damaging assault of all was launched upon the common assumption that Newton, idolized by all Baconians as the definitive practitioner of the master process of induction, actually had heeded the elaborate and puzzling obsolete inductive rules laid down by Bacon in the *Novum Organum*.[109]

But more than enough champions were always waiting to fend off such arrant affronts to "the unparalleled glory of Bacon."[110] For every attack, however measured, there were a hundred shocked disclaimers and defenses. About 1820, the respected Scottish geologist John Playfair defended in the *Encyclopaedia Britannica* the claim that Bacon was the architect of science. With several other defenders of the Baconian faith, he acknowledged that the *Novum Organum* was marred by traces of outmoded medieval and Renaissance conceptions. He was confident, however, that these did not compromise the excellence of the central concept of induction. Playfair then spoke for thousands of educated Britons and Americans, as he concluded that Bacon "is destined . . . to remain an *instantia singularis* among men, and as he has no rival in the times which are past, so is he likely to have none in those which are to come."[111]

Baconian forces received a significant accession when, in 1830, Sir John F. W. Herschel published his *Preliminary Discourse on the Study of Natural Philosophy*. Herschel, whose name reverberates through American intellectual literature in the 1830s and beyond, was at the time perhaps the most distinguished figure in Anglo-American science. His *Discourse*, which carried a bust of Bacon on the title page, was unquestionably the most discriminating formulation of the philosophy of science that yet had appeared in the nineteenth century. Herschel added fuel to the claims of the Baconian movement by styling Bacon—with evident enthusiasm— "the great reformer of Philosophy." Induction is the nucleus of scientific endeavor, he said, and assured a flattered Anglo-American audience that "it is to our immortal countryman Bacon that we owe the broad announcement of this grand and fertile principle." He also anticipated the spate of answers that Macaulay's 1837 article would elicit, by acknowledging that Bacon did not "invent" induction, but adding that the point was irrelevant: "It is not the introduction of inductive reasoning as a new and hitherto untried process, which characterizes the Baconian Philosophy, but his . . . spirit-stirring . . . announcement of its paramount importance, as the alpha and omega of science."[112]

Nothing seemed to slow the Baconian juggernaut. The Disciples of Christ erected Bacon College in Kentucky in 1836, "in honor of Lord Francis Bacon, father of the inductive method of reasoning and the new science."[113] By 1820 the *American Journal of Science* had pressed upon its subscribers the view that Newton's scientific work had been "incomparably the greatest" exemplification "of the excellency of the Baconian system"; small wonder that the young Ralph Waldo Emerson could tell his eager listeners on the lyceum circuit of the 1830s that Newton, Sir Humphrey Davy, even the envied Pierre Laplace, "have put in execution the plan of Bacon. The whole history of Science since the time of Bacon is a commentary and exposition of his views."[114] Ubiquitous Edward Everett told an Amherst College audience of his immitigable delight when he considered "how, from the master-principle of the philosophy of Bacon . . . has flowed, as from a living fountain, the fresh and still swelling stream of modern science."[115] "Where," queried Judge Story before the Harvard Phi Beta Kappas in 1826, "shall we find the true logic of physical science so admirably stated, as in the *Novum Organum* of him, who more than two centuries ago saw, as in a vision, and foretold, as in prophecy, the sublime discoveries of these latter days?"[116] So much for the frivolous suggestion that Newtonians were not Baconians! No one rose to protest when, shortly after its opening in 1836, Bacon College students organized the Newton Philosophical Society.[117]

There seemed little doubt, then, that the once-mighty Locke was being outclassed in the first decades of the nineteenth century. It remained for Samuel Taylor Coleridge, who was being widely read in America, to say outright what most people appeared to be thinking: "I suspect, that we should give the name of Newton a more worthy associate—instead of Locke & Newton, we should say, BACON & NEWTON."[118]

And if the pitiful contingent of Bacon's enemies only served to goad Baconians on to more extravagant praise of their "immortal countryman," they also provided the most explicit evidence that the Scottish Philosophy was indeed the vehicle mediating and inflaming the Baconian vogue. Between 1817 and 1856 four articles appeared in major American and British quarterly reviews in which the intimate association between Realism and the inductive philosophy was a topic of surly discussion. In a typical gesture, the *Quarterly Review* glowered angrily at Dugald Stewart for "perpetually talking of the *Baconian School*, the *Baconian logic*, and describing his own particular doctrines in philosophy as modelled upon Bacon's precepts." The gentlemanly reviewer was not above suggesting "that he and Dr. Reid were merely availing themselves of Bacon's venerable name."[119] The other reviewers reacted with similar umbrage to the Realists and "their prototype and idol, · Lord Bacon."[120] The Baconians, for their part, did not hesitate to acknowledge the connection. To Samuel Tyler, perhaps the most avid of all, Realism and Baconianism by 1843 had come to seem inextricably mutual: "The psychological theory, that all our ideas are founded in experience and are acquired through sensation and consciousness, . . . is the psychological correlative of the Baconian method of investigation."[121]

Conclusion

In this chapter an effort has been made to establish two primary points. First, it has been argued that the configuration, "Baconianism," was incubated in the formative writings of the Scottish Philosophy. Second, it has been shown that through the mediating influence of the Scottish Philosophy, Baconianism became a conspicuous and generally lauded factor in American (and British) intellectual life in the antebellum period. That the American version of the Baconian Philosophy did reproduce the militant empiricism of its Scottish progenitor will be demonstrated in later chapters.

Despite the breadth and significance of its American appropriation, Baconianism has not received much attention from historians of ideas.[122] This neglect can no longer be warranted. The recent growth of interest in the history of science has supplied an already productive stimulus to the study of science in its "cultural relationships." The impact, however refracted, of scientific ideas upon other realms of thought is more clearly seen today as an essential part of the story intellectual historians must tell; and surely the Baconian Philosophy, so promptly and widely adopted, must contain essential clues to the broad meaning of "science" in the antebellum era. But more, the receptivity of other areas of culture to scientific influence is an essential theme of their history. Thus, for instance, an examination of the response of religious thinkers in the period to then prevalent scientific doctrines would cast a welcome additional spotlight upon the nation's religious life. These considerations, indeed, are suggestive of an agenda for the remainder of our study. We will now turn to investigate in detail what a prominent group of antebellum churchmen made of Baconianism. The following chapter will present Old School Presbyterianism, centered at the Princeton heartland of Realism, as an ideal subject for an American case study in the Baconian ideal.

2.

The Presbyterian Old School: A Case-Study Profile

A vital development in American historical scholarship of recent decades has been the "recovery of American religious history" first announced in 1964 by Henry F. May.[1] Today there is wide agreement among historians that religious factors have played a fundamental role in American life and thought throughout most of our history. This chapter and those following affirm the general impression of close interaction between religion and other cultural concerns. They assume, first, that historical American religious thought cannot be understood in isolation from then current philosophical and scientific traditions of ideas, and second, that an examination of religious ideas will elucidate significantly the larger patterns in what Perry Miller has called "the life of the mind in America." Since the Reverend John Witherspoon usually is regarded as the significant pioneer exponent of Scottish Realism in this country, and Princeton College (and later Princeton Seminary) were highly active radii of Realist influence, we shall now investigate Baconianism in the context of the conservative "Old School" type of Presbyterianism for which by 1837 Princeton had become a byword.

A Concise Profile of the Old School

Old School Presbyterianism, like Baconianism, has been generally neglected by historians. As a representative of a conservative and often doctrinaire version of Calvinism, this wing of the American Reformed tradition more often has been castigated than investigated.[2] Many scholars have given attention to the remarkably outsized contributions made in the period by Presbyterians to American education.[3] Yet very few studies of the general intellectual interests and contributions of nineteenth-century American Calvinists of any stamp have been made.[4] At least one prominent church historian has suggested that the vein of religious intellect after about 1800 had run so thin as to be little worth the working.[5] Old School Presbyterianism was the branch of the antebellum Presbyterian church that refused to acquiesce in the rising current of optimism about man and his capacities, which Methodists, Baptists, and liberal Presbyterians had fused with the Great Revival and which Unitarians had domesticated into a pattern of genteel self-indulgence for the upper classes. Throughout the 1820s and 1830s, as more and more Presbyterians, allying with the more exuberant expressions and "new measures" of liberal revivalism, began to dilute the traditional Calvinist stress upon human corruption and inability, the stage was set for a serious intramural schism between conservatives and the liberal "New School" party.[6] When, in 1837, the Old School party gained control of the church's governing General Assembly, they abruptly exscinded the liberal sections, reaffirmed the church's allegiance to the older Westminster doctrines, and thereafter pursued an independent and vigorous course as critics of the dominant religious Zeitgeist.[7] In this study, the term "Old School" is not limited to the reorganized church of the period after 1837, but occasionally will refer to those conservatives of preceding decades whose thought afforded essential background for its development.

It would be misleading to construe the Old School in any simple sense as heirs of the eighteenth-century "Old Side" Presbyterian resistance to the Great Awakening, although there were important lines of continuity.[8] The major difference lay in attitudes toward revivalist evangelicalism. Whereas the Old Side had been unfriendly to the whole idea of revivals and was not prepared highly to appraise the formative evangelical doctrine of the "new birth," the Old School had accepted both. Their differences with the New School men hinged not upon the use but rather the abuse of revivalism. Although they attacked arminian and "enthusiastic" forms of revivalism, Old Schoolers repeatedly insisted that their fervent attacks on "revivalism, falsely so-called" had misfired if an impression of general hostility to the spirit of revival had been given.[9]

Bolstered by its identification with revivalism, the Old School regarded itself as a full participant in the Protestant evangelical front that was aggressively extending the reach of religion in American life. Emphases upon the "strong confessionalism" that characterized the church tend to obscure this important point.[10] The fact is that, whereas the earlier Old Side had demonstrated its lack of the spiritual capital necessary to compete with the openly evangelical New Side, conservative Presbyterianism in the succeeding century was a part of conquering Protestantism, on the march, militant, and expanding. A scant decade after the break, Robert Jefferson Breckinridge, prominent Kentuckian and a leading figure in the Old School, could review with evident pleasure the church's rapid and remarkable growth:

Her growth in members, ministers, and churches, has been steady and immense. . . . As it regards the *power* with which the Church has acted since 1838—compared with her previous movement—and the manifestations of her rapidly increasing efforts, in every good and every great enterprise—the indications are such as ought to fill our hearts with joy. How many churches have been built—how many souls converted—what a vast increase in numbers—what a prodigious extension of her borders —what immense sums collected to endow schools, colleges, and seminaries —to print books—to educate ministers—to spread the Gospel through the earth![11]

Such a church, animated by the high respect for learning characteristic of Calvinism, could have little place for intellectual indifference to the general currents of thought then abroad in the Western world.

During the period 1838–60, the Old School developed effective organizations for missions and education, equipped its Board of Publication to flood the country with tracts and books, and launched a remarkable experiment in parochial school education.[12] In addition, by means of a spate of publications that only Unitarians and Congregationalists could rival either in quality or in sweep, Old School churchmen unremittingly campaigned both to promulgate and to defend their characteristic theological positions. A leading design of this effort was to sophisticate and edify the evangelical mentality, to humiliate evangelical Protestantism out of its easy acquiescence in "Methodist" anti-intellectualism.[13] Despite its oft-remarked "failure" to compete numerically with Baptists and Methodists, the Old School easily qualified as "the most influential and theologically powerful body south of New England" and as a potent leaven in American intellectual culture.[14]

Within the Old School, Princeton was clearly the most important center of influence. It was, according to Thomas Smyth of Charleston, "the very seat and centre of Presbyterian orthodoxy and learning."[15] The influence of the college and, after 1812, the seminary, was ramified especially through the work of their graduates in education. Princeton men established academies and colleges in numbers out of all proportion to Presbyterian representation in the general population. The intellectual influence of Princeton also was radiated to all corners of the denomination through the pages of Charles Hodge's well-edited and sophisticated *Princeton Review*, which fittingly has been designated "the [then] strongest theological journal in the English-speaking world."[16]

Yet it is also essential to note that the Old School was heavily represented in the South. Archibald Alexander, the first professor of theology in Princeton Seminary and in whom, according to Lefferts Loetscher, "is to be found, in germ, the entire Princeton Theology," was "decidedly a Southern man."[17] His son and biographer, James W. Alexander, remembered that his father, "a Virginian to the last," seized "any opportunity for vindicating the honour of 'the old colony and dominion.'"[18] Alexander's southern proclivities were not uncharacteristic of the Old School as a whole, which both before and after 1837 attempted as rigorously as possible to exclude debate on the subject of slavery from its courts and took a conciliatory position in its periodicals and other publications toward this divisive question.[19] Nathan L. Rice, eminent Cincinnati pastor and well-known debater and polemicist, averred in 1853 that despite the large southern presence within the church, "ours is now the most united, homogeneous Church in the world; whilst Abolitionism . . . continue[s] to agitate the New School."[20] The southern wing of the church had thriving seminaries in Hampden-Sydney, Virginia, and Columbia, South Carolina; a group of its ministers established in 1847 the *Southern Presbyterian Review*, which after the failure of the *Southern Quarterly Review* in 1857 rivaled *DeBow's Review* as the most significant remaining intellectual organ in the South.[21]

Perhaps most significant of all, in determining the southern bias of conservative Presbyterianism, was the emergence in the South of a group of gifted and powerful leaders. To match Hodge, the South had James Henley Thornwell, "the Calhoun of the [southern] Church," probably the most intellectually gifted Presbyterian of his day.[22] And in such men as William S. Plumer, Robert Jefferson Breckinridge, Benjamin Morgan Palmer, John B. Adger, Stuart Robinson, George Howe, and others, the South had a phalanx nearly equal to the Alexanders, Hodge, Nathan L. Rice, Gardiner Spring, Lyman Atwater, and other mighties of the North and West.[23]

That the Old School did not in general pretend to court the basically lower-class constituencies of the Methodists, Baptists, and related groups should be clearly understood. Thornwell was pictured by President W. C. Preston of the South Carolina College as "representative of the Presbyterian Church, which embraces the bone and sinew of the state"; and Breckinridge boasted to a Scottish visitor in 1843 that "the great preponderance of the talent, education and wealth of Kentucky is Presbyterian."[24] These comments are typical, and evidence abounds to show that the Old School church was oriented toward the educated, professional, and prosperous classes and that their efforts both in missions and in edification were directed largely toward these groups. The unbending stand of the church in the matter of clerical education, its steadfast refusal to dilute educational requirements even when other denominations with fewer or no such standards were making comparatively huge gains on the frontier and among the lower classes elsewhere, cannot be fully understood apart from this explicit leadership-class orientation. John Holt Rice, founder of the seminary in Virginia and an Old School man long before 1837, regarded it "as a matter of very great importance, that as Science advances, and the range of human thought is extended, the ministers of religion should be able to keep an even pace, with the best-taught of their fellow citizens," and the "Report" that outlined for the church Rice's plan for the seminary insisted upon the need for thorough educational preparation in ministerial candidates on the ground that "christianity will suffer just in proportion as its teachers fall in intellectual attainment and mental power below other professional men."[25] Old School literature is heavily laced with such remarks, which often focus on strategy for the frontier. The highly respected Ashbel Green, who served a decade as president of the college at Princeton and became perhaps the most radical leader of the forces that precipitated the schism in 1837, was insisting even before 1820 that the prime target of missions in the West was men "of prime sense and considerable improvement, who . . . [have] great influence in directing the popular sentiment . . . and that if the missionary is not able to meet and cope with these, he nearly lost [sic] his whole influence."[26] Several historians who have spoken of the Presbyterian "failure of adjustment to the frontier milieu" have failed to take seriously the stated Presbyterian tactic; quality, not quantity, was the reiterated principle guiding Old School leaders seeking to missionize the intelligent leadership of American society.[27]

Finally, an abundance of evidence shows that Presbyterians had joined with a will in the general and perfervid American adoption of Scottish Realism. The philosophical initiatives taken at Princeton by Witherspoon were to prove decisive for subsequent generations of Presbyterian thinkers. Mediated primarily as an academic ideology through the curricula of denominational higher education, Realism was quickly established as a "vast subterranean influence" in Presbyterian life.[28] From the dawn of the century, it was evident in the literature that conservative Presbyterianism was committed virtually en bloc to the Scottish Philosophy. Samuel Miller was professing as early as 1802 a grateful attachment to the "modern metaphysicians of Northern Britain" who had refreshed belief in normal perception and restored confidence in a common-sense and orderly world. To men like Archibald Alexander, Miller's seminary colleague, the writings of Reid and Stewart were second nature. Alexander's course in "mental science" at the seminary was virtually a transcript of their thought embellished with more specifically theological concerns.[29] Orthodox zeal for "the incomparable Dr. Reid" knew few bounds and showed no signs of diminishing before 1860.[30] The extent of Scottish influence upon the generation following Miller and Alexander can be fairly indicated by Thornwell's remark that he had always venerated Stewart "as 'a very brother.'"[31] If Baconianism indeed was promulgated through the literature of Scottish Realism, surely no group in antebellum America was more subject to its influence than the orthodox Presbyterian church.

This, in brief, was Old School Presbyterianism: aggressively confessional, yet firmly evangelical; militantly on the move, out to prove it was no *"dead orthodoxy"*; intellectually centered at Princeton, yet with a large and powerful southern wing; equipped with a brace of prominent, gifted, and highly educated leaders; materially prosperous and predominantly oriented toward the economically and intellectually dominant groups in society. Moreover, the emphatic interests displayed by the church in higher education and in relating to the interests of the more literate portion of the population suggest an intimate involvement with intellectual issues of the day. Remarkably alive to current developments in literature, philosophy, and science, and prolific with voice and pen, they present a more than adequate subject for a study in American ideas. And in view of its intimate connections, through the lineage of Witherspoon and Princeton, with the Scottish Philosophy, the Old School is a highly suitable choice for a case study of the Baconian impact on American ideas.

Presbyterians and Science: Personal Involvements

If a fundamental element of Baconianism was zeal for natural philosophy, and if Scottish Realism was truly the mediating field of Baconian influence, then a close review of Old School literature could be expected to reveal a church open and hospitable to the fast-moving scene of science. So bold, indeed, was the enthusiasm for science manifested by conservative Presbyterians that even a cursory check will suggest its weight and impact. A remarkable number of church leaders displayed personal and often intense interests in the unfolding panorama of natural science; numerous individuals made careers in science in the denominational colleges; Presbyterian periodicals gave issues of science and religion detailed and lively coverage. These interests, moreover, substantially affected theology. The Old School leadership, no less than their Calvinist forebears, saw it as their duty to construe the Christian message in harmony with existing assumptions about the nature of the world and the human mind. The written remains of Presbyterian religious thought bear so clearly the marks of scientific influence as to require of their interpreter a respectable acquaintance with trends in nineteenth-century science.

Modeled to a substantial degree on the English Dissenting academies with their marked friendliness to the new science, the Presbyterian college at Princeton had displayed from the first a keen interest in natural philosophy.[32] With the accession of Witherspoon to the college presidency in 1767, this thrust was visibly accentuated. Samuel Miller noted in the *Brief Retrospect* that Witherspoon had "introduced into the course of instruction on Natural Philosophy, many improvements which had been little known in most of the American colleges." Witherspoon had gone to considerable effort to purchase and install new scientific apparatus, which, he boasted, "will be equal, if not superior, to any on the continent."[33] Succeeding administrations at Princeton also stressed natural science. Samuel Stanhope Smith, president from 1794 to 1812, who was to distinguish himself in scientific circles with an original treatise on physical anthropology, professed "so high an opinion of the usefulness of chemical philosophy" that in

1795 he arranged at Princeton for the first chair of chemistry in any American college. Smith also designed a short-lived curricular innovation whereby some students were admitted to study the sciences alone, circumventing the normal classical curriculum.[34] Smith came under fire from ministers who resented dilution of the traditional classical emphasis but was succeeded by Ashbel Green, also a scientific enthusiast. Green, who in later decades was to emerge as leader of the extreme wing of the Old School, had been elected in 1789 to the American Philosophical Society. At the college in 1818 he organized a chair of chemistry and experimental philosophy and staffed it with his son, Jacob Green. When a year later the Princeton trustees acted to abolish the chair, President Green was so vexed that he resigned.[35] Despite such occasional setbacks, the sciences continued to be strongly represented in the Princeton curriculum throughout the antebellum period. From about 1830, "there was no more distinguished group of scientists in the country than was embraced by the Princeton faculty," and the Princeton record in science was reflected in the curricula of other Presbyterian colleges and academies throughout the country.[36]

Among conservative Presbyterian leaders active in science, Samuel Miller, Ashbel Green, and Archibald Alexander were prominent. Prior to his presidency at Princeton, Green had served there in a chair of mathematics and natural philosophy (1784–85); and after the Revolution he contributed materially of time and energy to restoring the experimental apparatus damaged or destroyed during the conflict. Green also kept a personal notebook of observations in natural history. Miller's fascination with science was amply demonstrated in the celebratory *Brief Retrospect*; to the end of his life he was urging Princeton graduates to keep up their "collegial attainments" in "Natural Philosophy, Astronomy and Chemistry." Alexander had been tutored during his early teens by William Graham, an amateur scientist who conveyed to his young pupil an enduring ardor for "the Newtonian system." For a time Alexander taught science at Hampden-Sydney College in Virginia; an autobiographical sketch shows that he read constantly in scientific materials of the day. His biographer bragged that "throughout his whole life he retained a lively interest in mathematics and physical investigation . . . keeping himself acquainted with the course of discovery to an extent which was surprising to all around him." After Alexander's death, Joseph Henry, founding director of the Smithsonian Institution, who had served several years previously as professor of natural science at Princeton College, remembered that "he was much interested in all questions of physical science, and participated in the researches [in electromagnetism] in which I was engaged."[37]

Presbyterian interest in science could be documented massively. Charles Hodge was no less interested in Henry's epoch-making researches than Alexander and remained until his death a close personal friend of Henry. After his graduation from Princeton Seminary, Hodge had "widened his education by attending upon lectures in anatomy and physiology, delivered in connection with the medical department of the university."[38] Cortlandt Van Rensselaer, driving force behind the Old School parochial school movement of the 1840s, accompanied Amos Eaton, the well-known chemist and geologist, on geological field trips during the 1820s and later appears to have attended for a time the science-oriented Rensselaer Institute.[39] George Baxter, professor of theology in Virginia's Union Theological Seminary from 1831 to 1841 and a leader in the 1837 excision, had been professor of mathematics, natural philosophy, and astronomy in early Washington College; while John Matthews, a professor of theology in the theological seminary connected with Hanover College, Indiana, from 1831 to 1848, was remembered for his "aptitude for the study of the sciences. He was especially delighted with Astronomy; and he even formed an Orrery."[40] While a student at the University of Virginia in the early 1840s, Old School stalwart Robert Lewis Dabney grumbled that "the natural sciences are worth all the others put together, and yet not a sixth of the whole college time is devoted to them."[41]

Another register of Old School interest in science may be found in the few remaining records of presbyterial examinations of candidates for the ministry. Candidates often were examined directly on scientific subjects. This was sometimes a special measure for candidates judged to have inadequate college preparation. An aspirant in a Texas presbytery in 1853 and 1854 thus was "required to pass comprehensive examinations on 'the arts and sciences'" before being allowed to demonstrate his theological and homiletical capabilities.[42] Some presbyteries employed examination questions in the sciences for all candidates. Orange Presbytery announced in 1857 that its candidates thenceforth would be examined upon "the elements of the Physical Sciences, viz. Astronomy, Geology, etc.," as well as upon theological subjects. Perhaps the most interesting extant account of an actual examination is William S. Plumer's report of his examination in South Carolina in 1861: "In November he passed the terrible ordeal of Presbytery after Dr. Howe had proposed his name. His college examination was the thing he most feared. Dr. Leland gave him the first paragraph of Cicero against Cataline. After this followed such searching questions as 'What is Natural Philosophy?' 'What is Astronomy?' 'What is the Solar System?'"[43]

Further suggestive of Presbyterian scientific interests is the special coverage of publications and general information in science provided by several prominent journals. Green's *Christian Advocate*, for example, ran a regular feature of "Literary and Philosophical Intelligence," which reported such items as: "A foreign chemist has discovered that corrosive sublimate when mixed with gelatine is innoxious, the former to the latter being as one to twelve, in dry and 25 in fresh gelatine. Further researches on this subject, we think may result in a compound useful in medicine and the arts."[44] John Holt Rice's *Evangelical and Literary Magazine* also carried a section on "Literary and Philosophical Intelligence." Hodge's *Princeton Review* for April and July of 1852 published summaries of "Quarterly Scientific Intelligence"; the section was discontinued, perhaps because the regular review articles already provided frequent treatment of current literature in natural science.[45] Book reviews of scientific literature were also presented regularly by the *Southern Presbyterian Review*. Thus, Presbyterian journals contributed significantly to the general mediation of scientific information to the educated American public.

Old School Presbyterians, then, exhibited throughout the period of this study a pronounced and serious zeal for science. Historians of science should not be surprised to learn, for instance, that Benjamin Silliman's lectures on chemistry and geology in New Orleans in 1846 were presented in the First Presbyterian Church; or that the 1853 meeting of the American Association for the Advancement of Science was held in the Second Presbyterian Church in Cleveland.[46] The gravity and degree of interest indicated above suggest that the impact of natural science upon Presbyterian thought was anything but superficial. Somehow these American churchmen had found a way to evade the clever efforts devised in the preceding age of Enlightenment to transform the scientific revolution into an intellectual warfare against the "infamy" of religion. A more careful analysis of issues of science and religion within the context of the Old School will not only repay the researcher with fresh insights into the character of American thought in the nineteenth century; it will also expose an array of theologically strategic ways in which churchmen convinced that science could be held true to religion deployed the Baconian Philosophy in behalf of Calvinist orthodoxy.

3.

Christian Inquiry and Inductive Restraint

In a variety of ways conservative Presbyterianism served as a supportive context for the development of a Christianized Baconianism in antebellum America. In order to grasp the full skein of logic by which Calvinistic Christianity was correlated with Baconian inductivism, it will be necessary to probe in detail the intellectual needs and assumptions that made Baconianism appealing to keepers of Westminster faith.

To a significant degree, Presbyterian Baconianism may be understood as a counterthrust against the widespread effort in the eighteenth century to portray the scientific movement as innately hostile to traditional Christianity. Churchmen labored with angry energy to suppress this conception. An analysis of the basic approaches to the natural world, knowledge, and methods of scientific inquiry which they espoused reveals their firm conviction that modern science, correctly conceived, was directly correlated with Christian belief. Viewing nature as a Divine creation, they assessed scientific investigation as a potent aid to biblical piety. From this perspective, the leading problem of research was to assure that the scientist's quest would focus directly and faithfully upon the immediate, elevating truth of the Creation. At this point, the usefulness of Realist empiricism and of the strictly factual inductive philosophy identified with Bacon became apparent. Scientific explanation could now be equated with the immediate generalization of the facts of the Creation. A potential danger was posed by the requirement of then current scientific theory that some due be allowed for the deductive analysis of concepts once formulated inductively. Churchmen made certain that this usage could never admit a relapse into scholastic syllogism by depicting deduction as merely a secondary type of induction that must be verified in experience. Baconianism was, in short, an approach to the problem of science-and-religion that allowed Presbyterians to patronize science without approving speculative approaches that might neglect or distort the godliness of nature's truth.

The Enlightenment Challenge: Inquiry versus Religion

"The heart of the Enlightenment," Herbert W. Schneider has contended, "was the marriage of natural science with morals and religion."[1] Any broad acquaintance with the intellectual remains of eighteenth-century Britain and America will require this or a similar conclusion. However, a sharply contrasting viewpoint recently has been developed by Peter Gay in two brilliant volumes on *The Enlightenment*. Focusing his interpretation primarily upon the French scene and concentrating upon philosophical radicals— Voltaire, Diderot, Condorcet, d'Alembert, d'Holbach, Hume—Gay has presented a view of the century that emphasizes its growing and drastic alienation from the Western religious heritage and finds its most characteristic and culminatory expression in a frank "paganism." In Gay's view, the emergence of Newtonian science was in significant measure responsible for estranging the *philosophes* from their Christian tradition, for they found in the new science a force alien to and pitted against religion. Any "marriage" with religion into which it might enter must be adventitious, artificial, rooted in weak metaphysical nostalgia, and not in profound understanding of the inwardly secular character of the scientific movement itself.[2]

Gay's principal thesis, which clashes sharply with Schneider's, is that the essence of the Enlightenment was "criticism."[3] Gay's *philosophes* found the authentic expression of enlightened humanity in inquiring autonomous reason; their most basic commitment was to an acute rational probing of the issues of life. This position was formulated in explicit opposition to organized religion and the stunting restraints it was held to impose upon inquiry. Rooted in a perception of a "sacred" and "mythological" realm beyond the grasp of reason and sense, traditional religious perspective could only perceive inquiry as an enemy of faith, crushing it into compliance with myth. "Criticism," therefore, ultimately must set its face against Christianity, wielding philosophy and the scientific revolution as instruments for liberating the mind from its fettering hold. Not a marriage, but an embittered divorce of inquiry and science from religion, forms the heart of Gay's interpretation.[4]

Historians of the British and American Enlightenment well might feel uncomfortable with some features of this formulation. Gay's preoccupation with France, his concentration upon overtly anti-Christian radicals, his generalization of French hostility toward religion as a foundation principle of the Enlightenment as a total phenomenon, certainly are debatable.[5] Yet there can be little doubt that the themes depicted by Gay were prominent in the eighteenth century in all "enlightened" countries including America. If one focuses on the Anglo-American scene, it is hard to see that such radicals as Hume or Thomas Cooper were more authentic representatives of the spirit of the age than modernizing churchmen such as William Warburton or John Wise or pious natural scientists like John Winthrop of Harvard. Nevertheless, the critical secularist strain did help to shape trends of thought and gave rise to a number of militantly antireligious expressions that set inquiry and natural science squarely over against Christian tradition.

Unfortunately for its hopes of constructing a secular, scientific civilization, the critical enterprise centered in eighteenth-century France ran afoul of violent revolution. Among Western Christians, the terrible scenes of chaos and gore enacted in the years following 1789 evoked wholesale fright. While Britain, in reaction, was submitting to Edmund Burke and Tory rule, a mighty host of concerned American churchmen were frantically injecting the young United States with the potent antidote of revivalism. Their conserving mission met with broad success, and religious skepticism increasingly went out of style in the early decades of the nineteenth century. Despite all that evangelical zeal could accomplish in a relatively free society, however, the acrid voice of the anti-Christian Enlightenment was never completely stilled. Through the following decades, recognizable notes of "criticism" continued to emanate from a broad front of "infidels." Such enemies of traditional piety as William Maclure, Thomas Cooper, Frances Wright, and Robert Dale Owen came to be as much detested and feared by the defending faithful as were Voltaire and Hume.

The preoccupation of both orthodox and evangelical forces with the figure of the "infidel" in antebellum America has been traced and helpfully analyzed by Martin Marty.[6] Marty's work, however, does not touch upon one central issue: the significance of the infidel witness as a continuing and abrasive reminder to churchmen of the religious and moral dangers of secularizing inquiry and of the need to supply the nation with a rational and Christian alternative. Discernibly the central theme in the infidel message—in the best French tradition—was devotion to the omnicompetence of free inquiry. Its corollaries were, first, an insistence that the religious heritage is a manacle on the searching mind, and, second, a belief that the most liberating of critical activities was natural science, carefully dissected away from inherited "dogma."

"The times," argued Thomas Cooper in a blast in 1837 against mixing science and religion, "call for full and unlimited freedom of examination, in every department of knowledge without exception." Christian theology, he added, "renders impartial examination a crime."[7] The equally notorious Frances Wright, addressing standing-room-only crowds in "New York, Philadelphia, Baltimore, Boston, Cincinnati, St. Louis, Louisville, and other Cities, Towns, and Districts of the United States," summarized her message similarly: "All that I say is, examine; enquire. Look into the nature of things. Search out the ground of your opinions. . . . But your spiritual teachers caution you against enquiry."[8] Cooper himself was a professor of chemistry; he and Wright shared a basic belief that the focus of inquiry must rest upon the material order of nature. Inquiry and science formed the antithesis of religion and metaphysics.[9]

For the American Protestant intelligentsia, of which the Old

School was a major bulwark, these words formulated a principal intellectual challenge. In the secularization of inquiry and science touted by "philosophy, falsely so-called," whether by eighteenth- or nineteenth-century infidels, the Old School discerned the roots of social, mental, and spiritual chaos. There was a consensus within the denomination that the radical Enlightenment, especially in its French version, not only menaced religion but had been directly responsible for the French Revolution.[10] This explosive challenge was kept before the public by the infidel exhortations of the Wrights and Coopers. But more, in setting inquiry and science against inherited belief, the purveyors of secular enlightenment also had thrown down the intellectual gage to thinking Christians. Historians who have focused on revivalism as the American church's response to the French Revolution and to continuing infidelity have not told the whole story. In the decades after 1790, American Presbyterians set to work in a major and prolonged attempt to armor the Christian message against the damaging thrusts of "criticism." Their intention was twofold. First, they undertook to dissipate the supposed discord between intellect and orthodox belief and therefore to confute the equation of religion with unthinking myth and mental backwardness which lay at the heart of infidel doctrine. Second, they wished not to begin anew but to appropriate and strengthen the gains of the past. Their desire was to squelch the slander that the genius of the scientific movement, which in the preceding century had been brought to the fore, stood in essential opposition to Christian faith. They argued that the British and American Enlightenment had not dislodged science from biblical values and that one of its genuine achievements had been the merger of Protestantism with the new "natural Philosophy" in what Cotton Mather had called a "Christian philosophy."[11] The Old School, then, wished to sponsor a thoroughly "enlightened" version of Christianity, accepting as precious the heritage of intelligent inquiry and the zeal for science characteristic of the eighteenth century, but enfolding them within a frame of sound religious belief. In their drive to preserve concord between scientific inquiry and Christian tradition, orthodox churchmen were to find Lord Bacon a critically important schoolmaster and guide.

Samuel Miller's Brief Retrospect of the Eighteenth Century: A Summary of the Past and a Map of the Future

One of the most important American productions of the early nineteenth century was Samuel Miller's *A Brief Retrospect of the Eighteenth Century*. Together with Ashbel Green[12] and Archibald Alexander, Miller was one of the three archetypical Old School Presbyterians. As an ordained minister, later a founding member of the Princeton Seminary faculty, *and* a respected member of the American Philosophical Society, Miller was a living refutation of the central thesis of "criticism." His *Brief Retrospect*, basically an appreciative review of the scientific achievements of the century just ended, supplies an ideal short prospectus of the conservative Presbyterian answer both to the radical Enlightenment view of natural science and to the continuing pressures of infidelity.

Miller's argument may be reduced to five basic assertions. First, he agreed that free inquiry is a basic and meritorious achievement of the eighteenth century. "Never . . . was the human mind, all things considered, so much unshackled in its inquiries." He made short work of the popular charge that Christianity and inquiry were hostile: "It has often been objected to Christianity, that it is unfavourable to the progress of knowledge; that it discourages scientific enterprise; that it is inimical to free inquiry. . . . [But] the history of the last concurs with that of many preceding centuries, in demonstrating that the very reverse . . . is the truth. . . . In those countries in which Religion has existed in its greatest purity . . . literature and science have been most extensively and successfully cultivated." Here is the core of the Old School reply to secular views of science. Religion, far from being the implacable enemy of inquiry pictured by the *philosophes*, is in fact an indispensable nutrient medium for effective science and learning.[13]

Second, "the last century may be emphatically called the AGE OF PHYSICAL SCIENCE." Miller tirelessly rehearsed and celebrated the gains in knowledge and in "human comfort" attendant upon scientific research. Himself a member, he praised the achievements of the American Philosophical Society.[14]

Third, he made some critical distinctions. All that parades under the banner of science and inquiry is not authentic. Inquiry alone is fruitless groping; it must ally with right method. Scientific achievement rests solidly upon "Lord Bacon's plan of pursuing knowledge by observation, experiment, analysis and induction." Geologists, for instance, who "laboured rather to support a favorite hypothesis, than . . . patiently to consult the materials and structure of the fabric which they undertook to describe," had produced "visionary" and barren results.[15]

Fourth, the practice of right method depends upon a correct view of human cognitive operations. Miller was committed to the Realist revision, to "the principles and reasoning of certain modern metaphysicians of North-Britain." Of these, among whom he included Reid and James Beattie, the "most able" was Dugald Stewart.[16]

Finally, Miller was confident that science rightly pursued implies no hostility to Protestant religion; in fact, it reinforces belief. A painstaking Baconian style of investigation cannot fail to disclose "the agency of a divine Architect," the "wise design" everywhere displayed in nature. Science, moreover, provides confirmatory evidence for important portions of the scriptural account, such as the Deluge. Deviant theories were faulted, but not simply because of their variance with Scripture. Miller always found them hostile as well "to the results of the ablest observation . . . and to the dictates of rational philosophy." One might therefore assume a "perfect harmony between the RELIGION OF CHRIST and genuine Philosophy." At last, scientific endeavor was closely harmonized both with the inductive philosophy and with theological interest: to indulge in "fanciful speculation" was tantamount to "waging war against Nature's God!" The heart of the Enlightenment, then, was indeed a marriage of natural science with religion. The age of inquiry was simultaneously "THE AGE OF Christian SCIENCE."[17]

Miller's reconstructive backward look provides at the same time a rough blueprint of the general formulations with which the Old School was to meet the continuing challenge of the radical Enlightenment. Written during the period of intense American reaction to the French Revolution, the *Brief Retrospect* is very much a key document of the American Restoration. It developed a view of religion in which essential premises were coordinated positively with the Newtonian world-view and in which openness to science and learning was to shape the mind of conservative Presbyterianism from the dawn of the century until after the Civil War.

Adequately to understand the general intellectual formula with which Presbyterians baptized scientific inquiry, the philosophical commitments that underlay their work must be analyzed in some detail. Those scholars who have seen in the Old School little but obscurantism and "scholasticism" may be surprised to find many of its leaders immersed in the intellectual and scientific life of their time. Wilhelm Windelband long ago asserted that "the decisive factor in the philosophical movement of the nineteenth century is doubtless the question as to the degree of importance which the natural-science conception of phenomena may claim for our view of the world and life as a whole."[18] To a remarkable degree, this statement applies to the intellectual life of the Christian thinkers to be considered here.

The March of Mind

Conservative Presbyterians were zealous campaigners against the anti-intellectualism which Richard Hofstadter and others have found so pervasive in American life during the national period.[19] If intelligence was under fire in the land of Peter Cartwright, Natty Bumppo, and Andy Jackson, it was continually being retrieved from danger by churchmen who believed earnestly that piety void of learning and of disciplined ratiocination was a formula for cultural barbarism. If Methodists and Baptists felt it was necessary to scathe the head to save the heart, Presbyterians had a richer prescription: the head *and* the heart, symmetrically cooperating to the glory of *God*.[20]

One of the salient themes in popular intellectual literature of the antebellum period was the "march of mind." As Philadelphia lawyer and popular orator of the day William D. Kelley expressed it, "Ours is an age of intellectual progress . . . mind is on the march."[21] Obviously a version of the mounting and pervasive devotion to "progress" characteristic of the time, the march of mind regularly was coupled with the spectacle of expanding science and technology.[22] Old Schoolers, eager to demonstrate a hospitality toward science, chimed in. "In the nineteenth century," exulted John Holt Rice, "a mighty impulse has, assuredly, been given to the human intellect. There *is* a *march of mind.*"[23] Rice, who tirelessly breathed praises of intellect and science, was echoing the thoughts of colleagues like Ezra Fisk, who hailed "the march of intellect" exhibited in the headlong rush of the "Arts and Sciences."[24]

This meant, of course, a generous attitude toward freedom of rational inquiry. Presbyterians were incensed when antagonists like Frances Wright, in whom the critical spirit of the Enlightenment was still aflame, flatly associated American religion with the stifling attitudes that had persecuted Galileo.[25] One strategic response to this, as well as to the broader infidel argument pitting religion against learning, was to refer the charge to Rome. Presbyterians were agreed that Catholic Christianity, still cloaked in the dogmas of the Dark Ages, was a real foe of science. Wherever "popery" was established, "the mind became enchained" and a "ghostly tyranny" was asserted that simply ruled out of order the questing impulse upon which the edifice of science had been raised.[26] To apply the charge to Protestantism, however, was a blatant case of mistaken identity. Was not "the right and duty of free inquiry" one of the formative principles of Protestant faith?[27] Thus when, in the early 1850s, Old School theologians who entered the currently heated scientific debate about "the Unity of the human races" were met afresh with the cry of "Galileo," they set up an angry chorus of disavowals.[28]

Conservative Presbyterians, therefore, were not only willing but eager to set a high value upon the searching spirit of reason and the march of mind and science to which it gave rise. But it was not enough simply to laud the intellect. The restraining tenets of Scottish Realism made it impossible to regard reason as an autonomous power that could furnish its own norms of behavior. Moreover, as Reid sadly had observed, the eighteenth century, with its incessant acclaim of the force and reach of scientific reason, had lured many a speculative zealot into a cul-de-sac of chaotic and barren conjecture. The Old School therefore must discriminate between legitimate and illegitimate inquiry, between research and metaphysics.

Mind and Matter

The Old School clergy nowhere more distinctly revealed their allegiance to the world-view of Newton and Locke than in their conception of the elementary structure of nature. Newtonianism —and the eighteenth century—were built upon a dualism of mind and matter. As suggested already, the Scottish Philosophy completely absorbed this conception, lending it even further strength by presenting a more clearly etched picture of the relationship between the "two great kingdoms" of mind and object. And if Realism was the official academic philosophy of the national period, so the mind-matter distinction was everywhere, save in the slowly emerging Transcendentalist movement and related currents, a basic tenet of thought. Bellwether Edward Everett even capitalized the pair: "Mind and Matter."[29]

For reasons that will be stated later, there was notable concern in antebellum America about the intactness of this distinction. Presbyterians, at any rate, appeared ever anxious to proclaim and prove the difference as decisively as possible. Samuel Miller recorded in the *Brief Retrospect* that "at the close of the seventeenth century, the stupendous mind of NEWTON, and the penetrating genius of LOCKE, had laid their systems of *matter* and of *mind* before the world."[30] Three decades later, President Gilbert Morgan of the Western University of Pennsylvania decided that the branches of art and science in his curriculum could be, if somewhat imperfectly, "classified under matter and mind."[31] And in the South, the acute mind of Thornwell, soon to be president of South Carolina College and the South's leading theologian, was pinpointing the matter for the Euphradian and Clariosophic societies at South Carolina College: "Matter and mind are the categories, into which by the general consent of the nations, whatever exists may be classed."[32]

Much of the intellectual life of the Old School may be said to have consisted in demonstrating how knowledge, religion, and science are constructed out of the fundamental elements, mind and matter. In the purview of the Scottish Philosophy, the most immediate problem of knowledge had been the establishment of an effectual coupling between mind and matter, reason and fact. Accordingly, an emphatic and repeated refrain in Old School literature is the necessity to bind reason (mind) to fact (matter). "What is reasoning?" asked Archibald Alexander of his class in theology at Princeton Seminary in 1837. Diligent pupils recorded the urgent answer: "The exercise of comparing facts with each other and impressions with external things."[33] This definition, which was approximated dozens of times in Old School literature, evinced a determination to commit reason to a close operation upon the material world. Only from the "facts" of nature could scientific knowledge be derived. And if the task of research was to describe and explain the material world, then a strict conformity between the mental image of a natural fact and the fact itself must be assured. Gratefully following the Scottish lead, the Old School was convinced that the only way to accomplish this was to shape the operation of reason firmly to the configuration of sensory perceptions.

Presbyterians felt that they could rely upon the beefy firmness of *sense*. If they ever doubted, during the brief Princeton flirtation with Berkeley, the reality of material, their confidence had been completely recouped by the Realist doctrine of "judgment." For every perception was now seen to be accompanied with an inbred guarantee of objective verity. The senses, and not mind, established dependable linkage with the world. Nathan L. Rice, for one, suffered no qualms about the importance and validity of sensory experience. "All know that the human mind does, through the medium of the senses, perceive external objects; and the most sceptical philosopher cannot so far take leave of his common sense . . . as really to doubt the testimony of his senses."[34] This was, perhaps, the most salient note in what the Old School had taken from Reid and Stewart. Witherspoon had been copiously thankful for the assurance "that our senses are to be trusted in the information they give us,"[35] and his hearty appropriation of Scottish doctrine provided his successors with an inexhaustible confidence that science was in touch with a real world. Robert J. Breckinridge, the Presbyterian baron of Kentucky and moderator of the General Assembly in 1841, prevailed upon the country to acknowledge that "the truthfulness of our senses, and . . . of our consciousness [i.e., "judgment"], is for us the ultimate certainty upon which every other certainty rests."[36] And Thomas Smyth, whose name was synonymous with Presbyterianism in Charleston, did not hesitate to christen the senses as "pledges of God's veracity."[37] The senses, then, were an excellent and reliable apparatus with which reason might pair its skills and a voucher that one need not resort to speculation beyond the scope of sense in order to embrace the concrete truth of nature.

Truth: Objective and Subjective

The real stake in such discussions was not in the senses themselves, but in the objective tangibility of the Newtonian world. Assured that mind, through the senses, had direct access to matter, most nineteenth-century Americans suffered few qualms about the veracity of appearances. In normal and healthy operation, the perceiving mind was like "a clear mirror, which, when brought face to face with an external object . . . sees it *just as it is*."[38] A fact in science meant an actually existing, concrete, and immediately apprehensible phenomenon of material nature. Benjamin Silliman, the dean of American science, whose work was revered by Old School thinkers, knew that his investigations disclosed a "just and full comprehension of the real nature of things."[39] Medical students at the University of Pennsylvania were being told in the 1850s that chemical and physiological science required "the just perception and apprehension, by the senses and the proper faculties of the mind, of the positive truth of the phenomena . . . of the external world . . . as they really are."[40]

This ingenuous faith in objectivity was closely related to a key development in terminology. Antebellum America was overwhelmingly committed to a standard philosophical vocabulary. "Nature," "trust in the senses," "knowledge," "mind," "matter," and a host of related terms provided a broad ecumenicity of understanding in circles of learning. The most vivid term of all, as any scholar familiar with the sources will know, was the "sublime."[41] Yet a second term, which rivaled the sublime in frequency of appearance and is still more revealing of basic philosophical attitudes, was "truth." No intellectual historian of the period can avoid it; to have grasped its basic meanings is to have attained an important degree of literacy in the general philosophical motives and proclivities of the age.

The central meaning of truth was implanted precisely in the objective assurance that long had energized British empiricism that "philosophy . . . is nothing but the true knowledge of things."[42] Truth, as it related to science, incarnated the belief broadcast in the Scottish Philosophy that it was possible directly and innocent of any theoretical apprehension to seize upon the intelligible structure of the universe; it focused the attention of the beholder upon the palpable and accessible natural world. This concept underlay the most common understanding of natural science in the period and therefore provided essential background for Presbyterian ventures in scientific understanding. The well-regarded American naturalist, John D. Godman, in an essay on "The Beaver" published in the *Franklin Journal* in 1827, was perfectly clear that "truth" was his object, "alike the object and reward of all rational inquiry."[43] That monarch of nineteenth-century American science, Joseph Henry, outlining the plan of the Smithsonian Institution for the *American Journal of Science* in 1848, pledged his commitment to the "one great system of truth" which, in his view, defined the aim of scientific work.[44] Again, in the *Pleasures of Science* volume in the Family Library series which found its way onto many American shelves, the great professor Adam Sedgwick of Cambridge University invited interested young Britons and Americans into the temple of science to "study this language of pure, unmixed truth."[45] Hundreds of near-identical expressions may quickly be gleaned from scientific literature of the day.

Presbyterian writings reveal a wholesale and uncritical appropriation of the vogue of objective faith in truth. "The discovery of truth," decreed Archibald Alexander, is "the object of every science."[46] Every "conception" yielded by the senses was taken without question as "the image of something real."[47] And that vital "something real" given in perception was objective truth. To the generation of Presbyterian churchmen moving into active leadership around the turn of the century, Witherspoon had conveyed his conviction that human understanding has "truth for its object, the discovering things as they really are in themselves, and in their relations one to another."[48] A guarantee that scientific explanation can represent in the strictest sense a precise replica of the world—this was the happy issue of obedience to the senses.

Early in the nineteenth century, Ashbel Green's *Christian Advocate* was piping undisturbed to the crescendoing tune of confidence. "Truth," it announced, is *the real nature of things themselves.* . . . it is important to receive the truth of *things* on all subjects."[49] Perhaps never had there been a calmer faith in the objective reach of cognition. Men like Archibald Alexander tirelessly rehearsed their belief that "knowledge is the apprehension of truth," that the birds *do* sing and that honey *is* sweet.[50] "Knowledge," echoed Leroy Halsey of the University of Nashville, "is nothing but known truth."[51] Although, in the compound of knowledge, truth was the general structure of the material world, it rested upon a radically nominalist vision of singular material objects. Hence individual entities were to be grasped in truthful clarity of detail. According to the *Princeton Review*, "To know a truth precisely, is not only to apprehend it intelligently, but also to perceive just what it amounts to in itself, and how all its elements stand related to each other, and what its boundaries are . . . [as] a distinct, practicable entity."[52]

Further, the existence of so accessible a reality as truth in juxtaposition to a population of human intellects implied a special and providentially designed fittingness in their interaction. This was expressed most frequently with an image of ingestion. Declared George Junkin, "the mind of man is naturally adapted to the perception and love of truth. . . . Truth is . . . the food of the rational mind, by the use of which only, its powers are sustained and perfected." "Truth," agreed Leroy Halsey, "is the aliment of the mind, the food, the life of the soul." Hence truth was not merely a neutral congeries of matter; it was animated wonderfully to attract, fit, and nurture the mind; it was *meant* to be "known." "The mind of man," added Halsey, "was formed for knowledge."[53] All truth, Archibald Alexander had taught generations of students at the mother seminary, has "an imperative claim" upon the mind.[54] For the literary societies at Erskine College, Benjamin Morgan Palmer clarified the point with a fine image: "There is, so to speak, a polarity of the mind itself, by which, like the mariner's needle, it turns freely . . . and [comes to] . . . rest only on the magnetic meridian, pointing to truth as its pole."[55]

In order to understand the significance this age attached to the pursuit of natural science and the readiness with which it turned to the Baconian concept of method, it is essential carefully to understand and to underscore the point here being made. A massive literature from the period expresses the belief that the human mind ennobles and fulfills itself by a devoted "knowing" of "the truth of things." Green's *Christian Advocate* urged in 1828 that "the desire of knowledge is a distinct and original principle of our constitution."[56] The premise, not only that the mind is fundamentally commensurate with the Creation, that it has immediate access through the senses to reality, but also that it is poised and impelled by its very nature to embrace that reality, is deeply embedded in the thought-world in which the Old School participated. That the mind was meant to regale itself by studying the natural order and that nature was made for study were common refrains in Presbyterian literature. The *Southern Presbyterian Review* adjudged that "to know is the distinguishing characteristic of the mind. It may be said that the mind's existence consists in knowledge."[57] This was exactly the view implicit in Realism. Seen against the general background of evangelical anti-intellectualism, it is a helpful index of the intellectual mission upon which the orthodox Presbyterian church had embarked. An articulate summary of the pattern was provided by Thornwell: "The adjustment of his faculties to the objects by which he is surrounded is a command from God [to man] to exercise them . . . in the acquisition of knowledge. . . . These faculties evidently point to truth . . . and hence are a call of God through the essential constitution of the mind to know, as it is

of the eye to see, the ear to hear or the heart to feel. Every man is
. . . distinctly organized in reference to truth."[58]

Several commentators familiar to Presbyterians emphasized the role of curiosity in ensuring a zeal for the knowledge of nature's truth. Thomas Dick, Thomas Chalmers, and Henry Lord Brougham, British authors whose works in popular science and natural theology had an immense circulation in the United States, emphasized the importance of the providentially inlaid goad of curiosity.[59] Presbyterians found such doctrine highly congenial. Old Schooler John C. Young informed the senior class at Centre College in 1831 that "Our Creator has kindly and wisely implanted in every one of us a kind of appetite for information; and the gratification of the intellectual appetite is attended with great delight."[60]

Hence Presbyterians had every reason to believe that knowledge, or truth, was not merely a dead, huddled mass to be approached nonchalantly or with antiseptic detachment. Man's destiny somehow was bound up with his performance as a knower, with the adequacy of his response to the allure of truth. There it was, "the whole field of truth . . . spread out before the human intellect."[61] What was one to do with it? Truth was an invitation to participation, a challenge leveled directly at the questing instincts of the mind, a call to a grand search and mission. If man could find the key rightly with which to guide the mind, squinting through the senses, into an adequate knowledge of truth, he would achieve a principal end of his existence. Eloquent Benjamin Morgan Palmer provided the best synopsis of the Old School position:

Can it be doubted, that to learn is the province of a mind so constituted, and sustaining such relations to the outer world? . . . Here is the mind, destitute, at birth, of all knowledge, without power to create within itself a single material of thought, and depending upon experience for all dominion of an impetuous curiosity, which sends it forth. . . . It is furnished with the senses, the open avenues by which it enters the domain of nature. . . . It is endowed with certain fundamental and primary faiths [i.e., Reid's "first principles"]. . . . Over against the mind thus equipped God hath set the created universe. . . . Hath not God set the one against the other in the relation of subject to object, that the mind may know its mission to be the search for truth?[62]

"Truth," in fact, pointed to an important mode of religious experience in antebellum America. To know the truth of things was to taste "majesty and glory," for the massive panorama of nature was almost everywhere understood as an unfolding of Divine creativity. Sometime in 1830, William Ellery Channing crystallized the thought into a gemlike phrase: "Truth is an emanation from God, a beam of his wisdom."[63] Joseph LeConte, a rising young chemist and geologist from Georgia, in the early 1850s defined the ultimate function of natural science as a penetration into "the ocean of one infinite truth, which is God."[64] Here was a thought that provided a bridge from science to religion, one that Presbyterians were open and eager to traverse. A resounding acclaim from orthodox sectors of the country may be summarized in a succinct phrase from an address in 1858 by R. B. McMullen: "The Author of all unalloyed truth is God."[65] Here was a formula that fought fire with fire, that allowed churchmen to exploit the increasing magic of an appeal to science, yet at the same time to employ it as a weapon against those who saw in science merely the key to liberty and progress—in short, to the glorious secularism dreamed of in infidel philosophy.

Induction and the Art of Generalization

The Honorable Francis W. Pickens of South Carolina spoke the mind of an epoch from a podium at Erskine College in 1849: "The great foundation of general Truth is inductive reasoning."[66] Inductive reasoning was the great device of an era that had been to school to the Scottish Philosophy and to Lord Bacon for creating systematic rapport between mind and the truth for which it was made. As the Realists had taught, even from the encouraging realization that the senses were grand and trustworthy "open avenues" into nature, one could not construct a science of nature. For it was not self-evident how reason should operate upon received sensory information, nor how an immediate and unvarying application to the messages of sense was to be enforced. More-over, "science" was generally taken to imply that the intercourse between mind and matter must produce an ordered body of in-sights; truth was not a jumble but a subtly interconnected "sys-tem." To these related problems, Bacon's technique of induction was held to supply definitive solution.

The inductive philosophy thrived in the antimetaphysical at-mosphere of the national era. Its legion of advocates urged it upon the nation as a sorely needed discipline for compelling the mind from conjecture to fact. The leading merit of induction was said to be its explicit orientation to the solid currency of sensed fact, and this was something with which notoriously pragmatic Americans felt at ease. In strict accord with Scottish teaching, induction pictured observation and its extension in experiment as the initial step in every scientific inquiry. The famous jurist, George Tucker of the University of Virginia, applauded in 1835 the "steps by which man has passed . . . from rash hypothesis to theories founded on cautious observation and experiment."[67] The entire progress recorded by medical science since the Middle Ages was held by the *North American Review* in 1819 to be due to its ripening Baconian disposition "to see and observe, rather than to imagine and theorise."[68] Working natural scientists of the day gave general accord to the observational foundation of their work as prescribed by inductive reasoning. Benjamin Silliman, for ex-ample, could report by 1818 that the infant science of geology was "entitled to a rank among those sciences which Lord Bacon's philosophy has contributed to create" because it "has been reared upon numerous and accurate observation[s]."[69]

But observation alone did not constitute induction; it merely polled the senses for the materials—solid particles of truth—that might serve as the basis for an actual inductive inference. In common perspective, it was the high merit of "LORD BACON's plan" of induction "to present the truth in a simple form," to reduce the welter of data brimming from the senses to the sim-plicity of order.[70] And this implied the ability of reason to operate sensitively upon factual materials. Bacon had not abhorred reason; he had returned reason to itself by confining it to the sole appropriate task of "reasoning, founded upon careful observation." The important point, according to the great majority of commentators, was that the reasoning be "founded on *facts*."[71] But beyond this point, the consensus of understanding as to the explicit meaning of induction thins out somewhat. There is a degree of confusion in the materials of the day, both scientific and popular, about the content of an actual "induction." Two basic meanings, which frequently overlap, may be discerned. In the first case, induction was held to be synonymous, or nearly so, with classification. This involved little more than a categorizing of data into an array of congruent groupings and obviously was related to a pervasive current interest in natural history and mineralogy. Gulian Verplanck, for example, viewed "physical science . . . [as] the classification, under general rules and names, of multitudes of observations and experiments."[72]

Yet a second and vastly more important interpretation was widespread. In this view, inductive science was equated with what Francis Wayland of Brown University called "the glorious lessons of generalization." At this second level, induction meant, in the words of Alonzo Potter, that by "reasoning on particular facts . . . we gradually ascend to . . . [a] knowledge of general laws." "By induction," harmonized Judge Willard Phillips for the *North American Review*, "we infer general truths from particular facts."[73] The core of induction, that is, was now generalization in a much subtler sense than the construction of a taxonomic table of categories. The scientist's perception of initially grouped data was radically to be simplified through reference to unifying "laws" of behavior. This view eventually would prevail among a significant number of leading Old School Presbyterians.

The pervasive emphasis upon facts and the concomitant hostility to "excessive" reasoning in science obviously impeded antebellum efforts to transcend taxonomic views. To allow reason the rein to move beyond classification might seem to smooth the way for a relapse into the wanton abstractive tendencies abhorred by Baconians. And indeed, Presbyterian literature from the earliest decades of the century contains little evidence of interest in the scientific art of generalization. "Bacon and Newton," observed the

Presbyterian Magazine in 1821, "clearly understood that the . . . proper business of the student of nature, is to . . . ascertain its general laws."[74] But such expressions do not appear with either frequency or clarity until the 1840s. By that time, key Presbyterians were reading such treatises on the philosophy of science as Herschel's *Preliminary Discourse* and William Whewell's *The Philosophy of the Inductive Sciences*, which presented a sophisticated treatment of the derivation of laws and axioms in science; and a number now were prepared to accept a more generous interpretation.

Thus when a nervous Congregational minister in 1851 published an intemperate and ill-informed blast against geological "heresies," in which he suggested that the prerogatives of scientific geology stop with the grouping of facts concerning the earth's crust, Charles Hodge's *Princeton Review* published a scathing review: "What he describes as the legitimate province of geological science, is nothing more than the natural history of the subject. It is not science at all, in the true sense of the word. Science is not the simple knowledge and classification of . . . 'facts,' but the knowledge and classification of the *laws* to which those phenomena can be referred."[75] Herschel had described the procedure by which one arrived at the "universal laws" of nature as a "ladder" of inductions of increasing generalization. In a passage that reflects an explicit acquaintance with the *Preliminary Discourse*, Benjamin Morgan Palmer wrote that "Bacon . . . called men . . . to observe and to classify facts; to ascend carefully through more comprehensive generalizations, till the most general axioms are arrived at."[76] Palmer and his colleagues clearly pictured the aim of science as a decisive advance beyond the simple taxonomies of natural history. If the chaos of inarticulate phenomena were to be reduced to scientific order, there must be a classificatory simplification. The inference of "laws" from facts thus classified, however, represented a further and more decisive thrust of reason, and this was what induction actually consisted of. "Such is the great, leading aim of all sound and judicious investigation," wrote Thornwell, "to collect and arrange facts—to *generalize them* according to the uniformity of their successions. . . . When we proceed in this way . . .

we are said to proceed in the way of induction and to recommend and enforce this method was the great aim of the *Novum Organum* of Lord Bacon."[77]

If, however, this portrayal of "ascension" from particulars to generals clearly gestured beyond the crude additions of natural history, it did entail the assumption that the intellectual work performed by the scientist consists strictly in the simplifying summarization of observed data. Presbyterian pronouncements mirrored without qualm the Scottish view that generalization is the only legitimate type of explanation in science. Allegiance to the Baconian ideal of research rendered impossible more than a shadowy perception that explanatory concepts may involve more than a résumé of observations. Reid's notion of scientific discovery as the derivation of "general facts," which was aimed at sifting concepts entirely free from theoretic elements, was specifically invoked by a number of church intellectuals. This idea was widespread in literature in which the orthodox leadership was immersed. Thomas Chalmers, Thomas Dick, and John F. W. Herschel all maintained that a "law of nature" is "but the expression of *a general fact* grounded in the observation of particulars, and affirming within the limits of a brief and compendious utterance a something that was common to them all."[78] Determined to quash temptation to speculative reverie, Ashbel Green's *Christian Advocate* repeatedly stressed the "factual" character of generalizations, a proposition to which at least James W. Alexander gave specific approval.[79] But whether or not the term "general fact" actually was invoked, the stolid empiricism it represented was steadily in the forefront of Presbyterian thinking. And if concepts could be nothing but generalization, and generalization could be nothing but fact, little rein had been left for the vagrant play of theorizing reason.

Induction and Deduction in Baconian Perspective

Despite their considerable reverence for Herschel, theological leaders of the reorganized Old School church came to defer most often and most significantly in scientific matters to the writings of

Calvinist lawyer-philosopher Samuel Tyler. Tyler, whose work has only begun to receive attention from historians of ideas, was the most widely read and admired American philosopher of science from the mid-1840s until after the Civil War. George H. Daniels has observed that "throughout his lifetime he was highly acclaimed . . . as the greatest philosopher America had yet produced."[80] His most important work was *A Discourse of the Baconian Philosophy*, first published in 1844 and reissued in a revised and enlarged edition in 1850; an essay "On Philosophical Induction" appeared in the *American Journal of Science* in 1848.[81] His entire output reflects a passionate commitment to the Scottish Philosophy.

A fact of central significance for this study is that, during the 1840s and 1850s, Tyler served virtually as a house philosopher for the Old School Presbyterian church. In earlier years he had been a close personal friend of the respected orthodox leader John Miller. Later he engaged in frequent correspondence with both Hodge and Thornwell. In submitting the manuscript of the *Discourse* to a New York publisher in 1843, he volunteered Hodge as a reference "for my reputation for mental ability." Tyler once wrote to Hodge that "I consider you the greatest theologian of this age in the whole world." His work was so well known to Thornwell that the latter was able correctly to guess "on internal grounds" Tyler's authorship of an anonymous article in the *Princeton Review* for 1855.[82] The *Discourse* and a later production on *The Progress of Philosophy* (1858) were lauded unanimously by the leading Old School journals. The reviewers found in the volumes "an intellectual feast," a "masterly" performance, a "full evidence . . . of . . . thorough comprehension of the Baconian Philosophy." "Mr. Tyler," concluded the *Princeton Review*, "is second to no American metaphysical writer of the present generation," a sentiment shared by the *Southern Presbyterian Review*: "Mr. Tyler, we have no scruple in saying, is the first philosopher in America."[83] Even more significantly, most of Tyler's writings on philosophical induction, including the greatest amount of the material finally incorporated into the *Discourse*, appeared first in the form of articles in the *Princeton Review*.[84]

Two features of Tyler's interpretation of the Baconian Philosophy are of particular significance. First, relying heavily upon Herschel, he had a reasonably clear grasp of induction as an ascending and cumulative series of generalizations moving beyond mere classification. "Induction proceeds from particulars to a class of low degree, and from several classes of low degree to those of a higher, until we arrive at those of the highest degree."[85] The language of "classes" suggests taxonomy, but this was explicitly ruled out by Tyler.[86] Herschel, himself a sophisticated astronomer-physicist whose view of science certainly was not taxonomic, had spoken of "classification" in a similar sense. Induction required the scientist first to gather and organize empirical data, "and after diligently examining them in all possible lights, to educe some general principle from them which they clearly indicate."[87] This was the view of inductive generalization to which the Old School leadership in the later antebellum decades most readily subscribed.

Second, a fuller measure of Thornwell's—and the Old School's—grasp of the requirements of scientific method appeared in Tyler's discussion of the role of deductive reasoning in science. There was considerable confusion and contention in the period respecting the relative functions of inductive and deductive techniques in science. Important background for the discussion was provided by Reid's treatise on Aristotelian logic, which had interpreted Bacon's induction as a new and superior form of reasoning intended to supplant the syllogism. The scholastic program of reasoning from generals to particulars, wrote Reid, was precisely the error Bacon had set out to correct.[88] Reid's view greatly affected thought about science in the succeeding period, but became the object of a reaction in the 1820s. Mounting pressure for a more adequate view first found significant expression in 1826, with the publication of Anglican archbishop Richard Whately's immensely influential *Elements of Logic*. The volume quickly went through a multitude of editions and was widely discussed and generally praised in the great review periodicals.[89] Tyler's first important contribution to the philosophy of science was a review of a later edition of the *Elements* published in the *American Quarterly Review* in 1837.[90] Whately's principal point was a blunt denial that deduction was "a *peculiar* method of reasoning" which could be replaced by another. He appealed to Bacon himself in support of the contention that syllogistic reasoning was the normative and only possible type of reasoning. Bacon had not intended to dismantle the process of deduction from general ideas, but merely to direct it to its proper use, that is, as an interpreter of principles established inductively.[91]

Whately's attack on Reid, which was heavily reinforced by the appearance in 1830 of Herschel's *Preliminary Discourse*, cleared the way for a greater appreciation of deductive-mathematical methods in scientific research; it helped Tyler partially to avoid the meager empiricism with which Bacon was often identified.

Deductive reasoning, Whately had written, must assume the truth of the premises with which it begins; it is merely a drawing out of implications *already* contained in those premises. Therein Tyler found a formula for the assignment of induction and deduction to their respective places within the framework of scientific method. If deduction must begin with generalizations already formed, it cannot at the same time be a device for their formation. Induction, beginning with particular facts, refers them to general principles, or laws; these principles then become the premises for the additional procedure of deductive analysis. Tyler was perfectly clear that both induction and deduction are necessary to a complete conception of science: "The two together constitute one complete system of processes by which knowledge is acquired and perfected."[92]

An acknowledgment of deduction was, however, not to be taken as a lapse of Baconian regimen. Tyler's account deliberately captured the empiricist spirit at full tide. He wrote to George Frederick Holmes in 1854 that the *Discourse* had been specifically intended as a defense of Baconianism against the antiempiricist currents of romantic idealism which by 1844 had infected a number of Americans with a new zeal for "pure reason."[93] The *Discourse*, indeed, is punctuated with strictures against "a priorism"; and having admitted deduction into science, Tyler then set out to show that it in no sense stood above or beyond the government of fact. Every effort must be made to force it into correspondence with the tangible truth of things. Therefore Tyler now adroitly proceeded to define the interlocking processes of induction and deduction as simply a broader type of "induction." The inductive generalizations with which deduction must begin could not be equated with the infallible axioms of mathematics; the exhaustive and unerring analysis of all pertinent facts was a goal impossible to achieve. This was precisely why deduction had a role to play in science. Deduction, according to Tyler, is useful primarily as a means of checking and correcting inducted premises by testing their capacity to explain relevant phenomena. Thus Newton had established by laboratory experiment and inductive generalization the basic properties of light; these, reduced to mathematical formulas, then were employed deductively to explain the behavior of light in the rainbow. But the conclusive point was that the success of this endeavor had furnished additional verification of the original generalizations; even deduction involved a constant adjustment to experience. If the results of any deduction were found not to correspond with observed phenomena, then the premises must be reformulated. Since, then, scientific deduction "is conducted upon the . . . presumption merely, of the existence of the law or general principle, and not upon the absolute certainty of its existence," it is not a form of pure reasoning at all. It is governed not by the rules of mathematics but by evidence. In this sense, deduction was a fully Baconian device, an auxiliary type of the "induction in its largest sense" by which generalizations were extended.[94]

Conservative Presbyterians were predisposed by their abundant respect for rigorous and logical methods in theology to an appreciation of deductive analysis in natural science. Lyman Atwater, who was to succeed Hodge as chief editor of the *Princeton Review* in 1872, wrote that Whately's *Logic* "has done more than all else to restore this branch to its proper place in education," and he agreed wholeheartedly that the syllogism is "the form to which all reasoning may be reduced." To this view, Palmer also consented; he found syllogistic analysis to be "reasoning itself."[95] The admission was significant, for it underscored the necessity of abstract ratiocination in all inquiry. These Presbyterians would not lend their name to a version of empiricism that lightly stigmatized deduction as alien to a philosophy of "facts."

But the leader within Presbyterian ranks of the effort to rehabilitate deduction was James Henley Thornwell. Thornwell, who reveled in the rigors of logic and was reputed to have the largest collection of works in the field in the country, employed Whately's work as a textbook at the South Carolina College in the late 1830s.[96] Three manuscript lectures and various fragments now in the South Caroliniana Library deal primarily with "logic," attacking Reid's narrow view of induction and defending the worth of deduction in scientific research: "Dr. Reid and Mr. Stewart speak in high flown language of induction as the only effectual engine for the discovery of truth. They seem to think that syllogism and induction are enemies. The truth is induction is the stepping stone to syllogism." Thornwell exhibited an eagerness to "recover the syllogism from that general obloquy into which it has fallen." In a lecture almost surely written before the publication of Tyler's *Discourse*, he championed the use of deduction as a tool of discovery in total accord with inductive generalization. Even after an induction has been carefully performed, he argued, "there is yet ample scope for discovery in the countless multitudes of particulars included in our general species, which have been previously not noticed by the mind, and which would, forever, have remained so, if they had not been drawn into sight . . . by the power of analytic reasoning." Thus Thornwell also demonstrated a grasp of the important scientific role of deduction as a device of discovery. He affirmed, for instance, that "natural philosophy is contained in the doctrine of gravity and the laws of motion."[97]

Yet Thornwell, like Tyler, must remain rigidly true to the "school of experience" incarnated in the Baconian Philosophy. Fearful that a straightforward approval of deduction might be misconstrued as a departure from the Baconian rootage in particulars, he also devised a method of shaping deduction to the model of induction. To enforce the claim that the sole prerogative of deduction derives from previous induction, Thornwell maintained that the method of deduction itself originally had been inducted from facts. The syllogism had been developed and could be substantiated only "by a careful induction and scientific analysis from the actual laws which men do observe in every case of conclusive argument."[98]

With that, deduction simultaneously had been reclaimed from the disparagement suffered at the hands of Reid *and* thoroughly integrated with the empiricist tenets of Reid's Baconianism. Tyler, Thornwell, and others showed Presbyterians how to acknowledge the important function of deductive analysis in science without enfeebling the standard of experience. For all expositors were agreed that this, always, was the controlling factor determining the reach and validity of inquiry. Thus understood, there was nothing in the formula of fact, generalization, and deduction that finally exceeded the jurisdiction and restraint of sensory perception. The human mind might attain its cognitive destiny— apprehension of the truth of nature—and in accord with up-to-date techniques, but without falling to the snare of abstraction. To Presbyterian eyes, that was the beauty of the arrangement.

By embracing Baconianism, Presbyterians thus gave the lie to the thesis of "criticism" that inquiry could not fairly be sponsored by thinkers under the sway of religious belief. Since truth defined the providentially ordained aim of the cognitive powers, scientific research could be seen as an integral part of Christian perspective; intellect and belief were again happily joined. But this was only the first step of a much more ambitious engagement with natural science. Operating upon the philosophical premises outlined above, the Old School was prepared both to elaborate an extensive "doxological" view of scientific work and in the process to discover a range of additional uses for the Baconian Philosophy.

4.

Doxological Science and Its Enemies

Evidence is legion that the French Revolution provoked a reappraisal of the Enlightenment and the natural science it brought to the fore. The deistic and atheistic expressions to which the conflict gave vent inflamed awareness of the religiously destructive bent of "critical" science and philosophy. Many Protestant religious leaders now found fresh and burning reasons to distrust the scientific achievements of the Age of Reason. Forgetting for a moment the heavy religious admixture of the Anglo-American Enlightenment, Congregationalist Edward A. Washburn gave utterance to a widespread attitude when he wrote in the *Bibliotheca Sacra* in 1850 that "the eighteenth century saw revelation and science in direct hostility."[1]

While hewing as often to Samuel Miller's as to Washburn's assessment of the preceding century, thoughtful Christians throughout the country did feel acutely the dangers presented by the militantly secular version of science propagated by the Encyclopedists and, more recently, by such figures as William Maclure and Thomas Cooper. In the early portion of the century, the term "philosophy," which still incorporated the pursuits of natural science, had come to approach the status of an obscenity among many American churchmen.[2] The debacle in France had raised a serious question whether scientific inquiry could be safely domesticated to religious perspective. Many were tempted to confirm the thesis that religion and science were hostile by retreating altogether from modern learning and its manifest dangers. Against this temptation Old School leaders set a face like stone. Happily wedded to an affirmative view of the scientific movement, they engaged in an extensive campaign to restore science securely to a religious correlation.

A key element in this restoration was the belief, for which Presbyterians now mustered every possible ground of support, that Francis Bacon himself had been a paragon of Protestant piety. Underlying this construction was an urgent wish, nurtured by a long and still virile tradition of actual piety among working scientists, to conceive natural science as an essentially worshipful undertaking. Orthodox churchmen were happily aligned with existing patterns of scientific praise; crucial features of the natural world appeared unmistakably to point to providential origin and end. But doxology was not the only theme being expounded in the science of the day. Other and decidedly unworshipful tendencies also were making their mark among researchers who regarded mechanistic and naturalistic explanations of nature as superior to the Christian doctrines of Creation and providence. In response to this threat, Old School leaders contended that church intellectuals possess a right of scrutiny over reported scientific findings. This was not a relapse into dogmatism, for they insisted too that such review must be conducted in full accord with Baconian principles. The ground thus was cleared for a full-scale Baconian defense of pious perspective in science.

The Beatification of Bacon

Antebellum Americans, energized by the continuing surge of evangelicalism within their culture, devoted an immense amount of effort to the harmonization of science and religion. One of the more notable achievements of this effort was the transformation of Lord Bacon and his "follower," Newton, into exemplars of Protestant piety. Evangelical Christians inevitably would seek in their heroes a likeness of themselves, and to this development Old School Presbyterians contributed heavily. But to achieve the proper sanctification of Bacon, more than a daub of added cosmetic was needed. Unfortunately, the political career of this great father of science had ended in disgrace. During his term as lord chancellor of England (1618–21), Bacon had been accused and convicted of accepting bribes from persons engaged in important actions in his court. Thereupon divested of office and subjected to heavy fines, he withdrew from public life and spent the remainder of his days in shunned retirement. These events bespoke a character that pious admirers of Bacon could not bear lightly; and there were those who made matters worse by playing up the scandal. Macaulay's essay on Bacon had emphasized the morally dubious side of his career, relating in detail those "actions, which, if any man but Bacon had committed them, nobody would have dreamed of defending." Somewhat later, an unfriendly reviewer in the *Southern Literary Messenger* hoped that "his life may cool the ardor his philosophy has enkindled."[3] But admirers of Bacon could not allow his reputation to be tarred with impunity. Many participated in an effort to cleanse the record of stain and to present the genius of science to the world clad in the garb of moral rectitude and religious devotion. Everett's 1823 article on "Lord Bacon" was designed specifically to examine "the justice of the stigma left on his name" and to find it wanting. Everett and many others believed that Bacon's error had been exaggerated, that he had been used as a scapegoat by enemies in the king's administration, that he was, at most, guilty of impropriety.[4] Ralph Waldo Emerson presented a similar picture. However "dangerous," it had been nonetheless accepted practice to receive gifts from litigants. Bacon "was not himself corrupt. . . . His ruin was permitted [and encouraged] by King James" in order to distract attention from a current scandal.[5] The *American Biblical Repository* in 1847 published a full-scale defense, under the title "Religious Character of Lord Bacon," which presented a parallel account and concluded with praise for his "reverent study of the Bible" in retirement. Already by 1836 the *American Quarterly Review* thought it a sufficient refutation of Shelley's "godlessness" to quote a reverent passage from Bacon's famous essay "Of Atheism."[6]

Old School Presbyterians joined with a will in the general beatification of Bacon. No fewer than five conservative writers found occasion to quote ceremonially from the essay "Of Atheism" or from similar passages in Bacon's works.[7] In 1821 the *Evangelical and Literary Magazine* reprinted a small devotional piece from Bacon under the title "Lord Bacon's Confession of Faith," in order to prove that Bacon was not a Unitarian. Palmer quoted at length from the same document in an important essay in 1847; and Nathan L. Rice reproduced a portion of it in one of the 1850 *Lectures on the Evidences of Christianity* organized by William H. Ruffner at the University of Virginia. So compelling had Bacon's moral power become by 1851 that William S. Plumer could illustrate the probity of Socrates by a quotation from Bacon on the excellence of virtue.[8]

Meantime, if on a smaller scale, Newton was receiving like treatment. Since his record was free from overt scandal, it proved less difficult to associate him with evangelical orthodoxy. The introductory essay in the inaugural issue of the *Evangelical and Literary Magazine* styled Newton outright as "an humble disciple of a crucified Saviour," moral and devout. This required a cavalier ignorance of the historical record, as did Samuel Miller's indignant denial in 1821 that Newton was a Unitarian.[9]

But Presbyterians felt too keenly the necessity of associating natural science with religious and moral purity to delve too openly into biographical details. For them, as for American thinkers generally, it was needful to prove and display the pious rectitude of Bacon and Newton precisely because of an overriding interest in harmonizing science with religious perspective. In elaborating this harmony, no instrument could prove more effective than the argument that Bacon—or Newton—"commenced his career as a philosopher with the Bible in his hand."[10] The assumption is clearly of high significance for the student of nineteenth-century religious ideas. It suggests that Presbyterian thinkers interested in science were aligning themselves with a movement they understood to be profoundly hospitable to Calvinist religion. Their actual concern was to elaborate and sustain a version of natural science that blended felicitously with the biblical and confessional affirmations which for them defined the shape and sense of human endeavor.

Doxological Science in Evangelical America

Historians of science, whose view of the discipline has been shaped by a twentieth-century secular world, at times have had difficulty grasping the richer scope of scientific enterprise in earlier epochs. If, as is generally acknowledged, science is to be understood as a culturally rooted activity, reflecting the values characteristic of its social community, how are we to approach the study of science in a period when Protestant revivalism was "the one clearly given truth" of American culture?[11] Investigating natural science as it was viewed both by practicing scientists and by theologians interested in science during this evangelical era, one will find the distinction between the "scientific" and the "religious" not as sharply etched as in today's world. Whereas the twentieth century finds in science an ideal of dispassion, evangelical America tended to perceive it as understanding and doxology and the scientist as an admiring priest of the beautiful Creation.

Actually, throughout the epoch, divergent ideals of science were in real and often acrid competition for the allegiance of scientists and laity alike. One widely diffused ideal represented science as "the knowledge of subduing matter to the use of man."[12] Numerous historians have noted the prevalence during the first decades of the nineteenth century of "an exceedingly pragmatic view" that found little value in science apart from its practical applications. Proponents claimed that the leading aim of Bacon's scientific program was material progress, and they seized upon the prominent utilitarian note in his writings: "Knowledge is power."[13] Pragmatic views could and often did coexist with an emphasis on the religious content of science, but the focus on material benefit easily tended toward indifference or hostility toward religious considerations. The scientific writings of William Maclure and Thomas Cooper, for instance, noted figures in early nineteenth-century geology and chemistry, reveal a predominant intention to clear the field of nature for purely secular induction oriented toward technological control and the increase of material "happiness." Both men regarded "the use of man" as the definitive issue of research; science must facilitate the manipulation of nature for

the benefit of civilization. Such views were well and broadly represented throughout the antebellum period.[14]

As if Protestants were not troubled enough by the utilitarian
reduction of science to use, they found themselves challenged on
another front by an explicitly scientific atheism. For the natural sciences also played a major role in the resurgence of "free thought,"
which Albert Post has identified as an important feature of American intellectual life from about 1825 into the 1850s. Free thought
was a movement of militant hostility toward organized religion.
Employing the typical devices of the age for propaganda and
action—voluntary societies, newspapers, tracts, lectures—it reju-
venated the basic tactic of the radical Enlightenment by projecting
scientific perspective as an exclusive and overpowering *alternative*
to religious belief. Leaders of the movement, among whom Gilbert
Vale, Frances Wright, and Robert Dale Owen were prominent,
unanimously regarded the scientific "observation of nature" as a
liberating corrective to religious illusion. Of particular interest
was the association of a number of well-known scientists under
the leadership of William Maclure with Robert Dale Owen's free-
thinking New Harmony community during the 1820s.[15]

There can be no doubt that narrowly utilitarian and occasionally atheistic interpretations of the meaning of the scientific
movement were widespread. Yet any careful cross-sectional investigation of the antebellum writings of both scientists and popularizers of science will disclose the massive presence of a contrasting
factor. The literature clearly shows that free thought was a minor
note of limited influence. The attempt to range science against
religion simply was not convincing to a great majority of articulate
American (and British) scientists and other thinkers. And the
utilitarian theme, which did mesh easily with other current values
and contributed perhaps the shrillest note in the widespread chorus
of enthusiasm for science, was nevertheless powerfully rivaled by a
view that found the highest value of science not in technological
progress but in the intellectual and religious elevation of the human
mind.

The view of science espoused by Cooper, Maclure, and the
freethinkers was a relic of the Enlightenment. Forces were indeed

at work within American and British civilization that provided a continual flow of support for secular conceptions of knowledge. A culture gradually but surely consolidating its commitment to material and technological "progress" never completely lost touch with the Enlightenment. In the latter part of the century, under the influence of Darwinism and a strong positivist movement, science increasingly asserted itself as an autonomous secular force indifferent or antagonistic to traditional religion. But during the antebellum era the initiative lay with evangelicalism. A much older conception of science, forged in the seventeenth century, was strongly reasserted and heavily conditioned the way in which many thinkers envisioned the ongoing scientific movement.

Richard Westfall and John Dillenberger have effectively portrayed "the convergence of science and theology in seventeenth century England."[16] Research has shown clearly that the scientists who formed and elaborated the founding concepts of modern science were pious thinkers who not only saw no incongruity between science and religion but carefully integrated science into a theological framework. Thus was forged what Basil Willey has dubbed "that peculiarly English phenomenon, the holy alliance between science and religion."[17] The relationship was weakened somewhat during the following century, reflecting widespread hostility to the traditional values of organized religion, but scientists like Harvard's John Winthrop continued to proclaim that "the consideration of a DEITY is not peculiar to *Divinity*, but belongs also to natural *Philosophy*."[18] The undeniable popularity and importance of natural theology during the century also attests to the continuing strength of the alliance.[19] Near the turn of the century, pious science received fresh encouragement from the rise of strong evangelical movements in the Anglo-American world. Throughout the period from about 1800 to 1860, at least a majority of scientists—and of the host of nonscientists who contributed to its interpretation and popularization—were evangelical Christians who showed themselves eager to demonstrate the harmony between their scientific work and their religious belief.[20]

In 1815, a prominent local jurist and amateur naturalist, John Davis, assured the Boston Linnaean Society that "there is a moral use in this fair creation, which . . . tends to . . . contribute to that beauty and harmony, by which the spirit of man is refreshed, soothed, and elevated, and beholds a present Deity, while he surveys . . . the rich and varied scenery of nature. . . . The marks of supreme wisdom and the consciousness of paternal goodness, sooth and tranquilize the heart of the naturalist as he surveys the rich domain [of nature]."[21] This passage reveals most of the key elements of the "doxological" conception of science that was to become increasingly significant in succeeding decades. For Davis's emphasis falls not upon the material benefits of scientific investigation, but upon the subjective, elevating, religious transaction between the investigator and nature. Here is an effective exegesis of science as an elevating closure with truth. The quotation presents a near-riot of subjective indulgence. Two elements are particularly conspicuous. First, the observer experiences a fulfilling, "moral" sense of pleasure, uplift, and integration.[22] Second, the effect is heightened by the invocation of religious themes. The "sense of present Deity" and its surrounding cluster of comforting and ennobling emotions seem justification enough for scientific activity.

In diverse forms and combinations, these elements were to supply the substance of many thousands of interpretive statements about science in the national period. Thus the *North American Review* could hail the study of geology in 1821 as a source of pure "amusement and delight" and again in 1836 as a stimulant of "the most sublime emotions"; in 1834 it could celebrate the "grand and overpowering conceptions, which the study of astronomy crowds upon the mind."[23] A contributor to the *American Journal of Science* in 1829 pictured physical science as "a high exercise of our intellectual powers; a source of the purest enjoyment to philosophical minds."[24] More often, religious values were stated explicitly. Edward Everett, as usual, captured the full essence of current conceptions: "The great end of all knowledge is to enlarge and purify the soul, to fill the mind with noble contemplations, to furnish a refined pleasure, and to lead our feeble reason from the works of nature up to its great Author." Everett considered this "as the ultimate aim of science."[25]

Scientists were no less ready than reviewers and popularizers to advertise the hallowing virtues of their work. "In the first part of the century," Howard Mumford Jones has observed correctly, "the professors of 'natural philosophy' . . . thought of the scientist as one who thinks God's thoughts after him." George H. Daniels's recent and detailed study of *American Science in the Age of Jackson* has stressed the prominence of religious invocations in scientific writings between 1830 and 1845.[26] The most significant developments in doxological science came in the period from about 1830 to 1860, as a generation of scientists directly affected by the spreading waves of evangelical influence was moving to the fore. Numerous commentators observed the increasing "sanctification" of natural science during these years. James Dwight Dana, a follower of Agassiz who during the 1850s climbed into the front ranks of American science as coeditor and later editor of the *American Journal of Science*, noted contentedly in 1856 that "almost all works on science in our language, endeavor to uphold the Sacred Word."[27]

Benjamin Silliman, converted in a Yale revival of 1802 and recruited by Timothy Dwight to supply a corrective to French scientific infidelity, became the earliest exponent of science as spiritual enrichment. Through decades of influential teaching at Yale College, numerous lecture sorties throughout the country, and editorship of the *American Journal of Science*, Silliman established himself as the "patriarch of science in America." It is therefore of great significance that this figure considered himself "the honored interpreter of a portion of . . . [God's] works" and consistently stressed the "beauty," "wisdom," and "benevolence" displayed in nature and their transforming, purifying impact upon the researcher.[28] The coming of exuberant and devout Louis Agassiz to the United States in the late 1840s further augmented the theological cast of much scientific thought. Agassiz, a zoologist and geologist who "saw his task as the discovery of the manner in which the individual life form attempted to approximate . . . [the] history and development stamped by the Deity upon the universe," quickly rose to a position of scientific eminence in America rivaled only by Joseph Henry of the Smithsonian Institution.[29]

Mediated by the pious zeal of such men as Silliman and Agassiz, theological motifs increasingly came to condition the manner in which American scientists understood their professional task.[30] Geology and "organic science" seemed the fields most amenable to religious interpretation. Henry D. Rogers, professor of geology at the University of Pennsylvania, informed the Association of American Geologists and Naturalists in 1844 that their profession conferred a unique and rich understanding of "the creative spirit that broods over nature and has clothed matter in the garb of time." Edward Hitchcock, prize pupil of Silliman and an eminent geologist in his own right, explained to his readers in 1853 that the aim of scientific study was "to learn from thence the great plan of the universe as it lay originally in the divine mind. . . . The [scientist] counts it the best use he can make of science to render it tributary to revelation and to the cultivation of his own piety."[31] James Dwight Dana told the American Association for the Advancement of Science in 1856 that "we but study the method in which Boundless wisdom has chosen to act in creation. . . . far profounder is [the investigator's] apprehension of truth when he realizes, in all its significance, that an Infinite Spirit . . . speaks through nature to man's heart as well as mind."[32] And Joseph LeConte, an Old School Presbyterian and future president of the American Association for the Advancement of Science who also began his work in the 1850s, gave perhaps the most clarion expression to the ramifying pattern of doxological science as he insisted that "the chief end of science" is "studying the thoughts of God." LeConte found that the study of organic beings especially "ennobles, elevates and purifies the mind." He began a series of important "Lectures on Coal" at the Smithsonian Institution in 1857 with the words: "Nature is a book in which are revealed the divine character and mind. Science is the human interpreter of this divine book, human attempts to understand the thoughts and plans of the Deity."[33]

Evidence thus abounds to demonstrate the centrality of religious components in antebellum conceptions of natural science. In geology, natural history, and related areas, at least, religion and science were firmly married. And it would be misleading to represent religious interests of scientists as finding expression in a "natural theology," as if that were a category peripheral to science itself. The views cited above indicate distinctly that doxology often was conceived as an integral function of the scientific enterprise, as a central dimension of experience that lent special focus and aim to all research in nature.[34] Science in its very nature was subjective, postured toward the infinite.[35] For obvious reasons, some understanding of this background is an indispensable precondition for any attempt to probe the meaning science possessed for religious leaders within the same period.

The Presbyterian View: Design, Care, and Order

Thus when nineteenth-century Calvinist theologians venerated a *godly* Bacon and spoke of natural science as a handmaid of religious perspective and devotion, they were not creating a sectarian conception indifferent or hostile to the actual science of their day. Finding a religious account of the natural world strongly represented within the scientific community itself, they added the full strength of their intelligence to the maintenance of the doxological cause against materialistic, secular, and utilitarian concepts of American science. Lewis W. Green, minister and college president, greeted in 1842 "the altered tone of science" which now seemed to be breaking decisively away from its polluting associations with French infidelity and from crass forms of utilitarianism: "The whole spirit of physical investigation has been revolutionized in the present century; and . . . the stupid Atheistic Materialism of the last century, has almost totally disappeared."[36] He might have added that Presbyterians had done much and were to do more to help bring about the salutary change. John Holt Rice's *Evangelical and Literary Magazine*, for example, had dedicated itself from its beginning in 1818 to the restoration of Christian confidence in science. If the ruining French connection was to be overcome, the journal repeatedly argued, and if science was to be kept congruent with religion, "it is entirely important, that the objects of sense should be associated with ideas, pure and lofty in their character." It reminded its readers that when the biblical authors advert to the works of nature, "they connect with them the perfections of the divine Architect in such a way, that one who contemplates this subject, . . . will associate with the heavens and the earth, the delightful feelings of true devotion." Ashbel Green's *Christian Advocate* likewise urged upon Americans the idea that "one important use of genuine science, is to enable us to perceive the immediate operations of Divine power, in all the changes presented to our view in the material universe."[37]

Such expressions conformed to the standard pattern of doxology. Their focus was upon science as an enriching mental event. This meant inevitably a resistance to the dominant bias upon applied science, which had little reason for concern with the emotional correlates of research. Presbyterians were not in the main hostile to the Industrial Revolution or to the growth of technology, but they were sure that the meaning of science could not be compressed into the spiritually meager formula of "utility." Accordingly, they joined forces with the doxological protest against reducing the Creation to mere usefulness and insisted that nature enriched mankind in a much fuller sense, ministering to a desire for emotional fulfillment and intelligible understanding.[38] Palmer and many others had nothing but contempt for "that despicable utilitarian spirit, which, like a huckster in the shambles, is always haggling with truth about her price."[39] Complaint against the utilitarian abasement of science is a frequent note in Presbyterian literature. The *Princeton Review* in the early 1850s printed an almost mawkish essay on "the sights and sounds of the creation . . . [as] beauties and melodies," whose author so belittled "utility" that science seemed solely a pursuit of emotion.[40] But more often the protest was a balanced note, not deprecating applications but calling for the rights of intellect and heart as well.

In Old School definitions of the meaning of science, three elements were conspicuous: design, benevolence, and order. The teleology of "final causes" had been a dominant element in Anglo-American science since the seventeenth century; it also had been energetically propounded in the writings of Reid and Stewart.[41] Scientific workers in that age generally assumed that each structure in nature was providentially "designed" with reference to a particular function and end. Thus the eye was "intended" for seeing and the clouds for watery nourishment of the earth.[42] Partly in response to new interests in organic science that began to emerge shortly after 1800, the teleological stress was especially marked in the later antebellum decades. "I do not believe that there is a single specimen of fossil or living fish," wrote Louis Agassiz in 1845, "that has not been created with reference to a special intention and definite aim."[43]

Conservative Presbyterians recognized the perception of design in nature as a potent ally of doxological science. They found everywhere in the Creation a display of intricate providential design. A writer in the *Evangelical and Literary Magazine* saw "every insect, and every blade of grass" as "a magnificent temple, which displays the design of an omniscient mind."[44] That every natural structure had its given place and function, its "appropriate office," was a reigning feature of the cosmos to which Presbyterian churchmen subscribed. From North Carolina, clergyman and scientist E. F. Rockwell provided a singularly clear statement of "design" as he elaborated on "the skill of the bee in making her cell with mathematical precision, having the angles and sides invariably the same." Such consummate and unvarying capacity in an unintelligent creature bespoke the operation of an overarching Deity imposing His purposes and patterns upon the natural world. The tiny motions of the bee were ordered by "a hand guided by infinite wisdom."[45] Even the oceans had their place and purpose. It seemed not the least incongruous to the *Southern Presbyterian Review* that the Atlantic Ocean had been made wide to serve as a buffer zone between Europe and America and yet liquid and passable to facilitate commercial intercourse between them.[46]

The Old School was equally certain that the leading aim for which the Creation in all its parts had been designed and adapted was the care of man. In a phrase from Paley, "continuing care" was a natural corollary of design.[47] The theme lent itself well to popular treatment. A widely used botanical school text of the 1830s could direct its readers to "remember to give praise to Him whose infinite mind directs and watches over . . . the most humble plant."[48] Presbyterians liked to reason from the Divine attention given to the subhuman portions of nature to the obviously greater care a benevolent Creator would lavish upon mankind. Lewis W. Green, president of Hampden-Sydney College, warmed a largely Old School audience at the University of Virginia with the thought that God "hath not disdained to lavish *all* the resources of his infinite wisdom, his boundless benevolence, and Almighty power, in moulding the minutest portion of the minutest member of one of those invisible animalculae, whose teeming myriads live and revel and die *unseen* . . . and will he not care for you, oh ye of little faith?"[49] Such doctrine made the universe seem comfortable and congruent with man. A world brimming with care—this was viewed by Presbyterians as a major contribution of doxological science to Christian assurance.

A third and equally salient feat of doxological science, in Presbyterian perspective, was its disclosure of order in nature. Order was, of course, a basic feature of the Newtonian world. Newton had left a small number of astronomical "irregularities" unaccounted for, but these were harmonized a century later by Pierre Laplace's explanation of them as normal effects of gravitational interaction.[50] As the *American Quarterly Review* explained in 1830, "it was left for Laplace to show, that . . . supreme wisdom . . . [has] rendered all disorder or confusion impossible."[51] Thus Presbyterians were now confronted with a world in which any trace of incoherence seemed conceptually impossible. A "deep sense of cosmic order" had always been a basic feature of Calvinistic thought, and Presbyterians who were able to read benevolent design in the patterns of the natural world had little difficulty affirming the universality of order being elaborated by current science.[52] The single web of order extending to every nook of the Creation merely deepened the wonder of providential design in individual structures. John C. Young told the seniors at Centre College in 1831, "We ordinarily look upon the works of God in detached portions, but how much greater is our delight, when, amidst all the complexity of the myriads of objects that compose our system, we can discover the uniformity and simplicity of those great principles, by which its Maker . . . brings order out of its apparent chaos."[53]

This meant that any definition of natural science must focus upon intelligibility. Science studies order; by the inference of general truths through the surveillance of particulars, it reduces the world to simplified intellectual unity. In the 1830s Presbyterians welcomed the publication of Alexander von Humboldt's *Kosmos*, a massive attempt to exhibit the interconnection of all phenomena within a single and providential "cosmic" scheme. Old School reviewers greeted it as an ultimate demonstration of "phenomenal harmony."[54] Thus nature had the power to impress upon the scientist a profound sense of oneness, of the interrelatedness of all singular effects. All the more reason, then, to find merely utilitarian conceptions wanting. If a primary goal of science was the understanding and enjoyment of an intellectually tractable universe, a narrow focus upon material benefits could only impoverish scientific vision. Thornwell pointed out that every contribution to the pattern of intelligible order in nature, however "useless" it might appear at the moment, "is necessary to the harmony and connection of the whole. There are many . . . facts in chemistry which of themselves have no useful applications but they are essential to the unity and completion of those sciences."[55]

Design, care, and order—according to conservative Presbyterians, without these perceptions, scientific endeavor could mean only the colorless assay of scattered material. But for a science properly construed, they were the ground of doxology. The nearness, graciousness, and rationality of the God exhibited in nature simply stunned the mind, leaving it no recourse but to praise. The evidence of harmony and universal kindness turned up by the geologist's pick "will produce upon the minds of men the profound and abiding conviction of *His existence* and *His presence*, of the awful majesty that overshadows us, the omniscient eye that rests upon us, the infinite holiness that encompasses us on every side."[56] Thornwell, to whose acute pronouncements his southern colleagues generally deferred with something akin to awe, provided his usual succinct summary of going ideas: "Science, when it has conducted us to God, ceases to speculate and begins to adore. . . . the climax of its inquiries is a sublime doxology."[57]

The conception of science as doxology possessed, in addition, a distinctive congruence with inductive methodology. If the over-riding aim of research is subjective, defined by the rarefying, transforming impact of truth articulated in patterns of care and order, then the appropriate corresponding mode of response is spontaneous receptivity. The pure and direct apprehension of truth was to be the proper object of the mind seeking the principles of nature. "Here is something addressed to our minds," wrote E. F. Rockwell, "courting our investigation, and admiration."[58] *Admiration*, an elevated state of the understanding in which it could only receive and affirm, was the climax of inquiry. The attitude required of the researcher was thus precisely the ingenuous recep-tivity demanded by the Baconian Philosophy. Here was a point at which Baconianism and doxology obligingly interconnected. The highest type of mental and emotional response to nature was a satisfied tranquillity. There could be no thought in the moment of praise for hypotheses that disengaged the mind from the nutrient facts being funneled through the senses. For it was the facts themselves, ordered into the panorama of system and wisdom called nature, that imparted completion and closure to the intelli-gence. This and this alone brought "repose to the understanding" and terminated all disputation about the meaning of the scientific enterprise.[59]

Secularism, Materialism, and Heresy: The Other Face of Science

Doxology, then, keynoted the version of natural science which the Old School was willing not only to embrace, but to defend. Thus construed, science offered substantial gains to religious life, enlist-ing nature in the cause of devotion, enhancing the Christian's awareness of Divine presence and activity, and establishing a happy accord between the inward and outward realms of religious experi-ence. In addition, it firmed the resistance of science itself to the encroaching utilitarian mood that often was indifferent or even antagonistic to spiritual values.

But it was not enough merely to affirm science as a handmaiden of devotion. If science had a sublime potential as an ally of belief, it also possessed possibilities of a more menacing sort. Improperly guided, it could spring out of its doxological traces, trample faith, and demoralize the inquiring spirit of man with a vision of an amoral, aimless cosmos. Presbyterians were keenly aware of the prospect that science, falsely conceived, could become a snaring noose of unbelief. To begin with, bloated with a growing sense of its own procedural and institutional autonomy, science easily could be transformed into a merely secular enterprise. Further, the Newtonian view of nature rested upon a frankly materialistic atomism which seemed ever capable of dissolving the teleological and therefore meaningful perspectives proffered by religion. And these pressures, secularism and materialism, when not governed by a taut framework of religious perception, were constantly finding release in "heretical" formulations manifestly incompatible with important biblical principles. At no time did orthodoxy manage to expunge the fear that science was tensely ready to break clear of the snug alliance with religion cherished by defenders of a theological world-view.

Historian Merle Curti has found the period from about 1830 to 1860 marked by an "increasing secularization of life."[60] Despite its widespread doxological affiliations, American science did not remain unaffected by the general cultural trend. Alert churchmen frequently detected symptoms of a secularizing spirit in the increasing flow of fresh scientific disclosures. An early alarm had been given unwittingly in 1816 when William Tudor, founding editor of the *North American Review*, attempted to squelch fears of conflict between the Genesis account of Creation and recent geological researches by explaining that "there was nothing irreverent in these investigations . . . [and that] men of science, who should be the last to interfere with any thing religious, conducted their inquiries without any reference to that sacred relation. They reasoned precisely, as if no such account existed."[61] This may have been an indication of Unitarian sophistication in determining correlations between religious doctrine and scientific progress, but Presbyterians could see in it but a foolhardy slashing of the ties that joined research to admiration and praise. By 1827, the *Christian Advocate* was lamenting that "philosophical inquirers have generally discovered a disposition to exclude God from the government of the world."[62] The fact was clear that increasing numbers of scientists were assuming, in the words of a speaker at Virginia's Bethany College in 1842, "mental independence . . . and fearless thought." In 1846, Alexander T. McGill, later of the Western Theological Seminary in Pennsylvania, warned that "science is full of dangers . . . her pastime is death to all but earnest men." McGill particularly had in mind the tendency, to which Laplace's work had administered a generous boost, to regard the spectacle of universal order in nature as a sign not of intelligent providential government but of the implacable regularity of mathematical laws referable to no higher force. This kind of science, which made "grandeur in the scheme" to argue the Maker's indifference to his own Creation, was "replete with lessons of revolt against God."[63] The ultimate and appalling issue of such "fearless thought" in natural science could be nothing other than the complete secularization of world-view championed by Auguste Comte, whose announcement that "the devotional spirit already languishes in scientific minds" was recorded with a tremor of anxiety by the *Princeton Review* in 1858. Cincinnatian Nathan L. Rice found it painful to think of the result. Pious science would then have to contend with "the irreligious astronomer, who inquires into the laws by which . . . [the heavenly bodies] are controled [*sic*], without beholding and adoring, the power, the wisdom, and the goodness of the mighty Architect."[64] Architecture without an architect! This was the arrant issue of reasoning "as if no [biblical] account existed."

Presbyterians were sure that the brash autonomy practiced by the Tudors of science must lead ultimately to a vision of reality in which life and spiritual values would cease to be significant. John C. Greene has discerned that the tradition of doxological science as developed in the seventeenth and eighteenth centuries represented a rickety compromise between two contrary views of the natural world. Newton had believed that all bodies in nature were composites of "divided but contiguous" particles, whose principal qualities were extension, hardness, impenetrability, and moveability. "The whole of natural philosophy," on this model, was to be a description of the mobile interaction of corpuscular bodies.[65] This was the menacing order-of-things presupposed in Newtonian physics, a world "hard, cold, colourless, silent, and dead; a world of mathematically computable motions in mechanical regularity."[66] Doxological science actually developed as an attempt to meliorate the unbearable chill and deadness of the atomic metaphysics to which Newton had committed natural science.[67] By camouflaging atomism with a subjective image of the world as a scene of providential purpose and wise design, pious scientists and cooperative theologians had made the universe seem spiritually habitable after all. As long as atoms could be arrayed and controlled under the Divine purpose, assurance could be given to a hard-pressed mankind that, somehow, the universe bore meaning. Yet having accepted the Newtonian physics as essentially true, Christians found it necessary to twist and turn dexterously to avoid giving assent to its final ramifications.

The trouble with this coalition of atoms with purpose, from the standpoint of nineteenth-century Presbyterians, was that it lacked the ease of comfortable permanence. A poignant sense of "lurking anxiety" about its ultimate cogency and stability had been present even among its seventeenth-century architects and had found characteristic expression throughout the following century in a vocal abhorrence of Epicurus and the Epicurean cosmogony presented in Lucretius's well-known poem "On the Nature of Things."[68] In the nineteenth century, the stock figure of Epicurus, the archetypical atomist, was still virile. Along with the British deists, Voltaire, and Hume, Epicurus occupied a prominent place in the Old School gallery of villains. Constantly associated with the "fortuitous concourse of atoms," a formulaic phrase that occurs hundreds of times in Presbyterian literature, Epicurus evoked an image of the formation of the world and of life through the random interplay of "atoms dancing in a wild and fortuitous confusion."[69] The Epicureans, Benjamin Morgan Palmer scoffingly told his giant New Orleans congregation in 1858, "supposed the matter of which the universe is composed to have existed as the minutest atoms—and that in the lapse of ages, these atoms came together and hooking to each other, formed the earth."[70] This was intolerable. It stood athwart all conceptions of providential presence and government. It replaced the kindly, regulating hand of the Almighty with the unrule of "chance," which not only emptied human life of significance but rendered the seamless order and symmetry of nature inexplicable, "as if chance, which never built a house, nor composed a book, could produce a world."[71] Churchmen needed desperately to believe, with Ashbel Green, that "there is no such thing under the divine government, or providence, as real *chance* or accident," that the orderly system of nature owed its symmetry to something greater than random agglomerations of material. Yet the cruel image of an amoral, purposeless universe would not exorcise. It was constantly infused with new vitality by scientific theories that gave the initiative to material forces, rather than acknowledging the common rootedness of all phenomena in "a *first great cause*."[72]

The period from 1800 to 1860 appeared to Presbyterians especially prolific in materialistic explanations in natural science. The menace of a "cold and irrational materialism" surfaced again and again, especially in chemistry and physiology. Presbyterian commentators made constant and anxious reference, especially during the later years, to "the powerful tendency of science towards an atheistic materialism," which tendered explanations of natural phenomena purely in terms of mechanical or chemical agencies. "Our Gods are now gravitation, electricity, chemical affinity," complained Old School scientist Joseph LeConte in 1858; men seemed ever more ready to find the grinding of dead mechanistic operations more appealing than a chant of praise.[73]

Perhaps the greatest single threat posed by materialist science was to the uniqueness and free agency of mind. The sharp dichotomy between "matter" and "mind" which underlay Newtonian conceptions functioned partly to protect the intellect from materialistic reduction. Presbyterians lived uneasily with this inheritance. A tiresomely common refrain in their literature is the rehearsal of the totally "incompatible" and "antithetical" character of the two entities. The most frequent tactic was to delineate the properties of each and to conclude that their essential contrariness precludes any suggestion that mind may be a derivative from, or even directly dependent upon, material organization. Presbyterians like Cortlandt Van Rensselaer were taught in the denominational colleges that matter is "wholly passive, [has] no active qualities, but merely moves."[74] All were agreed that matter is "passive," "sluggish," "dead," and "inert"; that it "cannot think, nor will"; and that its only capacity was mechanical response to force externally exerted.[75] This formulation, which clearly reflects the passive version of causation espoused by the Scottish Philosophy, carefully purged matter from all power to act of its own accord. Thus the way was cleared for an interpretation of all power, motion, and change in comfortably human terms: "Either matter, that sluggish, passive thing, reasons, desires, exercises spontaneous motion, and so on; or something immaterial acts upon matter. . . . One of these must be true."[76] And on these terms, mind alone was adequate to account for natural effects.

Presbyterians never tired of rehearsing the mastery of mind over material. "We know from experience," indicated Henry Ruffner, "that by a spiritual power within ourselves, we can put matter in motion."[77] And by the same measure the Creation and ordering of the world must be ascribed to the spiritual agency of God. "There must be a continual exercise of divine power," wrote Ashbel Green in his popular Lectures on the Catechism, "in order to those movements and operations which constantly take place in the material world. Matter is of itself inert." This meant, as John Matthews later explained, that "inanimate matter, in all its combinations and forms . . . is completely subject to the controlling hand of Omnipotence."[78]

Obviously, mind could impose its designs upon the material world and thereby vindicate its independence from matter only as long as the distinction between them remained absolute and unbridgeable. Yet Presbyterians found workers in the chemical and physiological sciences constantly expounding theories that threatened to dissipate the precious distance between matter and intellect. Memory of Enlightenment materialism, which Miller had scored in the Brief Retrospective, had been kept active in the new century by prominent thinkers like Thomas Jefferson and Thomas Cooper, both of whom maintained that the mind was "an action of a particular organization of matter."[79] And fresh support for materialism seemed continually forthcoming from the scientific community. The *Evangelical and Literary Magazine* reviewed the situation in 1822: "We scarcely ever meet with a dissertation on . . . an *anatomy of the brain*, without encountering some new fangled notions respecting sensation, volition, thought. . . . It has been asserted . . . that *there can be no thought without a brain*."[80] If the tendency of research through the remainder of the period to 1860 was to explain more and more of mental activity in organic and chemical terms, Presbyterians could but rue it. Lyman Atwater was shocked to find Auguste Comte, reflecting the newest brain research, dissolving mind into material laws in the mid-1850s; but what were the orthodox to think when pious Edward Hitchcock, a full ten years earlier, acknowledged the contraction of mind before the onslaught of physiological research by engaging in this outright double-talk? "Every movement on earth . . . which is either mechanical or chemical, is equally dependent upon mathematical laws. . . . I do not assert that life and intellect are governed by mathematical laws; but their operations have all the precision of mathematics, and I doubt not, could be predicted by angelic minds, certainly by the Deity, with as much certainty as the astronomer foretells an eclipse."[81] Such expressions illustrate clearly an increase of materialist pressures upon intellectual formulations of the period. Shortly before the outbreak of war in 1861, Old School stalwart Joseph H. Jones could be heard denying that mind was a function of the brain but affirming at length the growing evidence of their chemical and "electrical" interconnections—without realizing the discrepancy![82]

A second area of trouble for orthodox churchmen was phrenology. Developed around the turn of the century by Franz Josef Gall, a German physician, and popularized in Great Britain by his pupil J. G. Spurzheim and a Scottish convert named George Combe, phrenology crossed the Atlantic during the 1820s. It quickly won an enthusiastic American following, eliciting substantial attention in the quarterly reviews and other journals, and produced a large literature of its own.[83] Phrenological teaching attempted to establish direct connections between gross brain construction and mental phenomena. Human psychology was explained in terms of physiological "aptitudes" or "organs" of which, it was held, the brain is composed. The development of these organs was said to affect the external shape of the skull in such a way that a man's character could be "read" by an examination of cranial contours. Becoming a substantial popular vogue, phrenology was propagated widely in many parts of the country— including the West—by traveling lecturers who excited "no little wonderment by examining the heads and describing the characters of all who presented themselves."[84] The dangers presented by phrenology to Christian doctrine could not be overlooked. This "impudent empiricism" equated mental and even spiritual characteristics with cranial form and function and did not hesitate, according to Alexander McGill, "to predicate endowments of immortality from nimble . . . manipulations of the skull."[85] Here too was a challenge that required incisive rebuttal if Christianity was to retain its hold upon the American mind.

A third area of controversy came to light during the later 1840s and early 1850s. "Polygenism" was becoming a popular term associated with the doctrine of a small group of scientists who represented the white and black races of man as springing from distinct geographical origins and thereby constituting separate species. Especially after their ranks were joined early in the 1850s by the eminent Louis Agassiz, whose scientific achievement was revered by enlightened churchmen friendly to science, polygenism came to be widely perceived as an influential and deadly insurgency against the central Christian tenet of the "unity of mankind."[86] Moreover, by relying almost entirely upon external evidence—body type, cranial measurements, geographical distribution, and the like—its advocates generally ignored the broader field of "spiritual" considerations touching the meaning of humanity, and thereupon they threatened to transform man into a creature solely of flesh, bone, and animal habit. What bearing could the unified scriptural history of spiritual adventure have upon the state of a pluralism of human types defined in material terms and no longer rooted in common Adamic heritage?[87] Albert Dod of Princeton College articulated the fears of Old School

Presbyterians generally that "some truths of natural science are so distinctly asserted, and so interwoven with the moral system therein revealed, that they must stand or fall together. Such . . . [is] the descent of all mankind from one original pair."[88]

A distinction cognate to that between mind and matter and maintained just as fiercely by Old School thinkers was that between life and matter. The struggle between vitalists and antivitalists was one of the classic debates in the history of science in the eighteenth and nineteenth centuries, and it was also being pressed to a climax in the antebellum decades by the steady march of research in chemistry and physiology and the emergence of organic chemistry as a distinctive field of study. Crucial events were the publication in 1842 of an American edition of Justus Liebig's *Animal Chemistry* and of John W. Draper's *Treatise on the Forces Which Produce the Organization of Plants* a year later.[89] Each of these works marked a significant defection from the standard vitalist belief in a unique vital principle which, like mind, was not reducible to material principles.[90]

Like the equation of mind with physiology, the suggestion that "that dread and glorious mystery—LIFE" was merely a chemical reaction threatened further to corrode the spiritual sensibilities upon which both religious faith and doxological science rested.[91] The Old School unanimously held out for a vital principle so "subtle" and "elusive" that it "escapes the knife of the anatomist, the tests of the chemist and the skill of the physiologist."[92] Assaying Draper's *Treatise*, the *Princeton Review* complained vigorously of his "explicit and repeated denial, of what the physiologists call 'the vital force.' He contends that all the phenomena of organization and of life, are explicable by the agency of known chemical and mechanical forces." There was reason to fear that, in the case of organic chemistry, the alliance between science and religion was decaying into outright antipathy. How could a theologian come to terms with a science that taught that a "dead cause" can produce "vital results"?[93] Christian theology could survive no such rendezvous with Epicurus. Joseph LeConte echoed the thoughts of many as he suggested in 1858 that the chemical and physiological sciences were so pervaded with materialism that only geology and the life sciences could be regarded as safe fields for the reverent observation of life.[94]

A shocking blow to the alliance between science and religion in the Anglo-American scene came in 1844 with the publication of an anonymous treatise entitled *Vestiges of the Natural History of Creation*. This work "provoked a pitch of popular excitement seldom paralleled in the annals of scientific discovery," for it set forth in frighteningly persuasive form a "developmental" version of earth and life history. While acknowledging the deists' "primitive almighty will" at the root of nature's process, the work explained the formation of the earth in terms of the popular "nebular hypothesis," an account of the condensation and congelation of gaseous formations in space. More startlingly, life-forms were presented as the natural issue of a long process of formation from a primitive "globule."[95] As an American geologist described the author's theory: "Animated existences were all introduced as mere points of vitality . . . from which by a natural process of development, without the interposition of creative agency, they advance through continuous, regular grades, to the highest state of perfection and complexity."[96] By extolling the power of law-governed matter to organize a world of living beings, the *Vestiges* aimed a piercing thrust at the vitals of the holy alliance; it thrust rudely aside the crucial doctrines of Creation, providence, and the unique status in creation of life and intellect. Matthew Boyd Hope found in the work a new Epicureanism, "destitute of all moral purposes and aims," in which man is but a "wheel in the machine"; Stuart Robinson commented that if the *Vestiges* account were true, Bacon and Newton themselves must forthwith be regarded as spawn of primitive wriggly animalcules.[97] This was a challenge that had to be met decisively.

Geology, too, was a continual storm center of controversy throughout the antebellum era. The half-century was marked by significant and controversial advances in geological science, and one may observe in Presbyterian literature a crescendoing concern about its unstable and dangerously shifting state. A chief worry of churchmen was the drastic modification being effected in traditional ideas of "the age of the earth." The conventional view allowed a span of only six thousand years from the miraculous Creation to the present, punctuated by supernatural interventions such as the Deluge. Now many geologists gradually were piecing together a new conception, which focused upon natural rather than miraculous causes of geological events and which required a much lengthened and more complex understanding of earth history. The new views and the threat they represented to traditional certainties were a major topic of discussion in the educated Anglo-American world throughout the antebellum era. Squaring "Genesis and geology" proved a treacherous and difficult task, particularly in view of the constant flux and advance in geological research.[98] Old School leaders kept in constant touch with the more significant geological literature, much of which was reviewed in the *Princeton Review*, the *Southern Presbyterian Review*, and other Presbyterian periodicals. Reflecting the diversity of scientific and theological opinions on the major issues, Presbyterians advocated a disparate variety of approaches to the coordination of Scripture and the better-established features of geological theory. Most hewed in some form to the position taken by George Howe of the Theological Seminary in Columbia that "whatever is written in the Scripture must be consistent with truth, and consistent with science itself. . . . There has never yet been discovered in the whole compass of the Bible, a single statement irreconcilable with true science."[99] But all were agreed that geology confronted the church with challenges that could not be neglected.

Going on the Defensive: The Right of Review

Natural science, then, was contemplated by Old School Presbyterians not only as an engine of praise but also as a cornucopia of troubles. They could never be certain that materialism and heresy were—or could be—overcome. "Infidelity has opened the campaign in a new field," lamented a Mississippi pastor in 1859, "she comes arrayed in all the attractions of natural science."[100] Throughout the decades of our period, pressure mounted on several fronts: geology, organic chemistry, phrenology and kindred movements, the *Vestiges*, and finally polygenism. Polemical activity, always intensive, reached a height about 1850 and stimulated Presbyterians to a near-frenzy of defensive maneuver during the remaining decade of civil peace. Matthew Boyd Hope expressed a fear always widespread in Presbyterian ranks but soaring to a climax in the 1850s as he remarked that "an impression lurks in thousands of young bosoms, that there is a conflict between science and religion, a want of harmony between nature and the Bible; and that the former rest upon a vastly more tangible basis than the latter."[101] The allegiance of large numbers of scientists, especially geologists and workers in the organic sciences, to a doxological view of nature could not quell the naturalistic commotions in many key areas of research. But Presbyterians were determined not to permit any science to surge into open and permanent infidelity.

Already bound to an affirmative view of nature and science, they were convinced on other grounds of the folly of adopting an adversary posture toward the tide of research. "Shall we attempt to stop the march of science?" asked the *Southern Presbyterian Review*. "As well think to dam the Nile with bulrushes." As early as 1818 the *North American Review* was recording a "universal intellectual excitement" engendered by recent discoveries. Every decade saw the scientific movement thrusting toward startling new thresholds. Especially the 1850s churned with scientific activity. "It is an age of scientific opulence," William Blackwood told an audience at Princeton Seminary. "The sciences are all teeming with . . . fresh discoveries."[102] The review columns of every major journal, religious or nonreligious, revealed that the book market was glutted with volumes on scientific subjects. Moreover, Americans never before had demonstrated such a general interest in scientific themes. Early in the century, Amos Eaton had found ready audiences in New England and New York for his pioneering lectures in geology and chemistry. In the 1830s and beyond, science provided the main focus of interest in the growing passion for the "diffusion of knowledge" and in the Lyceum movement; a reviewer for the *American Journal of Science* in 1840 was elated at "the rapidly increasing favor" science was finding with the public.[103] In cities from Boston to New Orleans scientists like Benjamin Silliman and Louis Agassiz lectured to overflowing and transfixed crowds eager for an introduction to the new worlds of understanding being opened up by geology, chemistry, and other studies.[104] By the early 1850s, the *Southern Presbyterian Review* found it difficult to find an "intelligent man" not familiar with the "facts and theories" of recent geology; Palmer observed in 1852 that scientific knowledge had become virtually "common property" of all literate sectors of the populace. Science had become simply an inexorable popular force, a fundamental value in the mind of educated society. It was, said Mississippian Richard S. Gladney, "emphatically the age of Natural science." The natural sciences constituted "the great oracles of the age."[105] Against such allure and influence, no church, no institution, no influence whatever could possibly stand as a blockading force.

The challenge of scientific naturalism and heresy therefore must be arrested with a positive strategy that discriminated between science and its occasional perversions. Church leaders never doubted that the only feasible way to cope with the growing menace of an expanding, secular, and materialistic science was to meet it, as much as possible, on its own terms. Their aim was not to oppose but to monitor the scientific movement. If a new and suspicious theory should arise, exclaimed Nathan L. Rice, Christians should "admit none of its claims, until they have subjected them to the closest scrutiny." True to his heritage, however, Rice had no intention of parting theology from the evidences of sense and reason. Any review of the "claims" of science must be conducted "on strictly scientific principles."[106]

In addition to ferreting out error, the "strictly scientific" approach furnished churchmen with a reply to sensitive researchers apt to charge "interference." The *Southern Presbyterian Review* rebutted protests against clerical meddling in polygenist debates with the reminder that educated clergymen versed in the basic principles of scientific method were in a good position fairly to review published research. The charges of meddling and bigotry would not stick unless the learning and acuteness they might display in the discussion were manifestly deficient.[107] Matthew Boyd Hope, an able Presbyterian polemicist and holder of a medical degree, gave an example of learned monitoring. Undertaking a discussion of the antiquity of the earth, he proposed "to give a full and candid hearing to all that can be said on both sides . . . by those who are best qualified to discuss them, and then adopt whatever theory we conceive to be best established by evidence and reasoning." There followed a careful review of the current scientific literature on the subject, concluding with a caveat that available evidence did not yet admit confident and final conclusions.[108]

In a majority of instances, Presbyterians did not intend that the right to monitor the results of investigation should be construed or employed as an abridgment of free inquiry. T. V. Moore felt that "the watchful and hostile jealousy with which science has sometimes been regarded by good men, as something fraught with possible danger to the truth of revelation, is as impolitic as it is unreasonable."[109] James A. Lyon cautioned his colleagues against "dogmatism and intolerance" by brandishing an unanswerable quote from Lord Bacon on "the ignorance of divines" who fear "that too deep an inquiry into nature may penetrate beyond the proper bounds of decorum." Nevertheless, freedom of inquiry could not feasibly be construed as unlimited license. Both the generally accepted canons of scientific methodology and appropriate deference to Scripture forbade, according to A. A. Porter, any promiscuous ranging "at will through the wilds of speculation, unchecked and unchastised." Charles Hodge, who long since had committed the *Princeton Review* to a policy of permitting "scientific men . . . [to pursue] their investigations, according to their own methods," yet explicitly restricted their license to limits befitting the painstaking "decorum" of induction. Inductive research, constantly refining and reconstructing its generalizations, was a self-correcting system and could be let alone as long as it did not presume to assault religious belief. But when science "transcends those limits," explained the *Princeton Review* in 1851, and pits "crude and hasty generalizations" against fundamental facts of Scripture, then "the friends of religion may wisely rebuke its intrusion."[110]

The "friends of religion," then, in the best interests of religion and science alike, could exercise a controlled right of review over the procedures and results of scientific research. But they had more than a prerogative; they had an infallible touchstone against which to measure those procedures and results. At this point, the Baconian Philosophy, to which the scientific community itself did almost ritual homage, was to provide the Old School with a reputable device for testing performance against profession and for safeguarding crucial tenets of Calvinist evangelicalism against the numbing incursions of renegade currents in science.

5.

Saving Doxological Science: Baconian Strategies for the Defense

Is it not "wonderful," asked Mrs. John Ware through the pages of the *North American Review* in 1851, that since human reason has "so vast a field to expatiate in . . . it now and then wanders beyond the limits of induction, and strives to establish theories before it is in possession of facts on which to build them?"[1] Those words, "the limits of induction," concentrated the faith of an intellectual establishment which, under the aegis of Bacon, was mainly dedicated to the mistrust and restraint of pure reason. The adamant empiricism of the inductive philosophy was to provide the Old School a major strategic resource with which to meet the foe of infidel science. If antebellum America knew no more potent precept—other than the sublime—than the philosophy of Bacon, conservative churchmen were prepared to demonstrate that its adeptness in discovery was fully matched by its capacity for the adroit defense and vindication of the harmony of all truth.[2] In 1854 the *Southern Presbyterian Review*, watchdog of orthodoxy in the South, buoyantly assured its readers, who increasingly were agitated by "infidel" scientific theories, that "the heaviest blow infidelity has ever received, was inflicted by the philosophy of Bacon."[3]

By enlisting the Baconian Philosophy in the defense of religion, orthodox thinkers were not retreating into an obscurantist posture at odds with generally received intellectual criteria. In fact they managed to do little more than reflect current ideology. The mistrust of conjecture, the esteem for facts, the faith in objective knowledge, and the confidence that stringent induction was the sole proper tool of scientific discovery—all had been from the early 1800s conspicuous elements of the intellectual "spirit of the age." Many scholars have remarked upon the widespread hostility in early nineteenth-century America toward "theories," "hypotheses," and "metaphysics."[4] A majority of scientific productions of the early republic are marked with a frank detestation of abstraction. Scientists and popularizers of science seized every opportunity to score the "speculation and conjecture," the "visionary" wanderings, the "dreams" of those errant researchers who imagined that speculative reason was the implement of scientific truth.[5] Underlying this animosity toward abstraction was not only a fear of the unchecked rationalism that had seemed to lead to the holocaust in France, but also a profound dissatisfaction among scientists with the results of the copious theorizing that had marked several areas of eighteenth-century science. This was particularly true in medicine and geology.[6] In 1824 the *North American Review* outlined the standard and contemptuous meaning assigned by this empiricist age to "metaphysics" and kindred errors: "Metaphysics is that which ascribes imaginary and plausible causes to existing appearances. . . . We would distinguish it from Philosophy, inasmuch as philosophy *ascertains* the causes of phenomena, and learns from *experience* the properties of things."[7]

Presbyterian utterances from the period reveal a total complicity in these attitudes. Samuel Miller noted in the *Brief Retrospect* that "the word metaphysics is seldom pronounced but with contempt, as signifying something useless, unintelligible, or absurd."[8] Contributing to the denomination's abhorrence of the abstract thinking embodied in metaphysics was John Witherspoon's initial experience with Berkeleyism at Princeton. The need for a strong empirical antidote to the influence of what Witherspoon's pupil and the future president of the college Samuel Stanhope Smith called "a philosophic delirium of hypothesis" helps to explain the eagerness with which Princeton had then turned into the paths of the Scottish Philosophy.[9] Throughout the acrid battles over scientific issues that were to fill subsequent decades, the options of metaphysics were mercilessly foreclosed. In a light moment in 1852, Stuart Robinson rose in the General Assembly to supply the cumulative and definitive response of the Old School to abstract speculation. Robinson related "a Western man's notions of metaphysics. He was asked to explain it, and pointing to some holes which the swallows were making in the river bank, he answered that it was the abstract notion of these holes after the bank had caved in."[10]

Throughout the antebellum years, conservative churchmen adapted the antihypothetical thrust of the inductive philosophy to a range of ambitious uses. They would show that the controls it placed upon reason and imagination were capable of eliminating any apparent discord between scientific and religious views of the world. Their procedure was fourfold. First, they would remind scientists of their strict obligation to *facts*. Second, they would underscore the derivative and provisional status of hypothesis and the corresponding necessity that the researcher be equipped with "humility." Third, they would demonstrate that the inclusive sweep of the inductive philosophy required the incorporation of biblical data into scientific explanation. And fourth, they would show how the painstaking thoroughness required in Baconian procedure undermined the claims of finality with which hasty infidel constructions often were garbed.

Natural "Fact" versus "Reasoning" in Science

The inductivist lines of defense within Presbyterianism were marked out long before the frenzied 1850s. Samuel Stanhope Smith's notable *Essay* on the causes of human racial variety had undertaken to show that the theory of multiple origins of the human race was contrary to "the evidence of facts, and to conclusions resulting from these facts." Smith also attacked the hasty "results" of geological research which were manifestly inconsistent with Genesis as "wild conjectures" brazenly exceeding the range of Newton's "just philosophy."[11] Miller's *Brief Retrospect* measured the "visionary" spirit guiding changing geological appraisals of the age of the earth against "Lord BACON's plan of . . . induction" and found it hostile to all the lights of natural philosophy. By the 1820s, Ashbel Green was finding Baconianism a well-forged weapon for the continuing battle against a wayward geology. He expressed shock at the implicit contempt for Baconian caveats revealed in the "bold and unphilosophical conclusions" and "vain speculations" characteristic of the work of many geologists. They would rather indulge an easy fancy than induce sober conclusions from "the actual situation and structure of the rocks composing the strata of the earth's surface." The *Evangelical and Literary Magazine* similarly reproached insensitive and "unphilosophical" efforts to reduce mind to brain physiology, which "rush to their conclusions without sufficient induction."[12]

Throughout the following decades the pattern was endlessly elaborated and occasionally refined. Growing numbers of leading Presbyterians pointed to a lengthening list of infringements against the Baconian way.[13] Prior to the late 1840s such protestations were but skirmishes; the truly heavy engagements came in the ensuing decade when Presbyterians unbuckled their heaviest armaments, spurred on by the recent appearance of the *Vestiges*, the mounting dangers in geology and organic chemistry, and the renewal of interest in polygenism. In this critical time, a cascade of calls was issued for a renewed and more vigilant adherence to "the true principles of conducting our quest after knowledge."[14]

A major resource thoughtful clergy found in the inductive philosophy was its incisive distinction between "fact" and "reasoning" and the clear priority it assigned to the former. This was a bonanza for the defense, for it suggested an easy strategy of neutralizing impious error by identifying it with the contingent and dubious realm of theory or hypothesis. Accordingly, the *Southern Presbyterian Review* professed certainty that "no *fact* in any department of human knowledge has yet been discovered even in appearance contradictory of any of the statements of the Bible. It is the *reasoning* of men on facts which conflicts with it."[15] Always, when critically perused, a scientific claim that clashed with religious values could be found vaulting beyond the supports of factual evidence. The *Princeton Review*, which when aroused on a scientific issue always went for the jugular of theory, thus located the flaw in pluralist approaches to human origin in their irresponsible defection from a close adherence to facts. The direct solicitations of fact by the senses were "the only data from which sound reason can draw her conclusions." The *Review* found the basis of facts to which polygenists appealed a flimsy structure indeed. The sovereignty of fact was perhaps the most frequent and distinctive theme in the deluge of Baconian critiques that poured from Presbyterian pulpits and pens during the frantic 1850s. Presbyterians North and South forgot sectional differences and joined voices in a chorale of acknowledgment that "the first great injunction of the Inductive philosophy is faith in well-authenticated facts." In settling the matter of the earth's antiquity, for instance, Matthew Boyd Hope served notice on the scientific community that "the only thing which weighs with us is the exhibition of facts."[16]

Hence the palpable prerogatives of "fact" were contrasted endlessly with the comparatively feeble and moot operations of "hypothesis," "speculation," and "theory." "There is of course a vast difference between facts and theories," wrote Hodge. "The former, and not the latter are authoritative." It was a time to capitalize upon the long-standing distrust of abstraction, which was now driven to a pinnacle of detestation. The Scottish Enlightenment was far away, but the influence of Reid's hypercautious approach to abstract reasoning in science had never been stronger. Orthodoxy exerted itself to the utmost to curtail the privileges of metaphysics by stiffening the line of demarcation between fact and theory. The disparity between observed phenomena and conjectures upon them, contended the *Princeton Review*, is "as palpable as that between light and darkness."[17]

As Presbyterians understood the matter, then, the core of inductive discipline was the demand that the powers of inference be regulated unconditionally by the observation of phenomena. It was seldom difficult for churchmen well-read in current scientific literature to discern some point of asymmetry between facts and the explanatory capacity of theologically dangerous conclusions founded upon them. Nathan L. Rice found phrenology especially vulnerable to the test. No one could object to an examination of brain structure and an attempt to trace relationships between shape and function, as long as these might be revealed unequivocally in behavior. But when the pretending physiologist exceeded these legitimate points of inquiry and hazarded "rash speculations in reference to the nature and modes of action of the mind, because he has ascertained the peculiar formation of the human brain, and upon this . . . grounds the assumption that there is no such entity as mind . . . he at once throws off the reserve and modesty which ever characterizes true science and surrenders himself up to all the vagaries of a reckless *a priori* fallacy."[18] In every case the blame for ignoring the boundaries of actual evidence was thrust upon a weak liability to "rash speculations." Presbyterian disputants learned to comb through scientific literature for facts at odds with a hated theory. Critics of phrenology like Rice pounced upon the results of dissections and other experiments showing that the brain "is not a congeries of separate organs, but a single organ, the whole of which is necessary to the full functions of any one of our mental faculties."[19] Again, the discovery of highly organized forms in the earliest strata of fossils was brought forward in confutation of the "mad conjectures" developed in the *Vestiges of Creation*.[20]

Although during the decade of stormiest engagement, Old School thinkers were led to focus so heavily upon direct contact with the natural order that the role of "abstraction" seemed reduced to a nullity, they did not, as a rule, thereby intend to disqualify altogether explanatory hypotheses in science. As we have seen, many churchmen did acknowledge a subtle process of generalization by which the mind moved beyond mere categorization of data to seize upon their underlying laws. To disqualify hypothesis outright would have eviscerated this master procedure. As a rule, therefore, the stigma was not applied to hypothesis considered as a cautious inference from observational and experimental data. Nor was it applied to the sage "guess" designed to spur and guide further research. Albert Dod, Princeton professor and intimate of Hodge, was perfectly assured that "without an hypothesis, by which the philosopher supposes some explanation of an observed fact by which it may be related to other facts, he could only make his experiments at hazard, instead of putting to nature the 'prudens quaestio' of Bacon." John B. Adger, professor in the Theological Seminary at Columbia, and Thornwell both agreed. Adger quoted Bacon to prove by highest authority that "we must guide our steps by a clue," and his colleague supplemented the thought by invoking the mighty Newton. In forming his doctrine of universal gravitation, Sir Isaac likely "had formed a sort of . . . hypothesis on the subject, before he commenced the examination of nature, and only confirmed or rectified his previous conjectures by a cautious and accurate induction." It was indeed questionable, thought Thornwell, "whether induction, without the aid of hypothesis . . . could ever lead to the discovery of a new truth."[21]

Presbyterians claimed to take umbrage, not at hypotheses rigidly coordinated with factual evidence and held with befitting tentativeness, but at purported explanatory propositions not immediately deduced from phenomena. The right distinction had been made by Dugald Stewart, who carefully sifted "theory obtained by induction" away from "hypothetical theory," which was not.[22] For the aim of investigation should be not to reconcile facts with a hypothesis but to adjust, repair, and even abandon the hypothesis as the flow of evidence required. Matthew Boyd Hope reviewed a recent suggestion that the "earth" mentioned in Genesis 1 referred only to a local area in Mesopotamia as a transparently desperate maneuver designed to support a greatly extended earth chronology. Hope found this idea "purely hypothetical, and not an inference from geological facts."[23] Similarly, the ingenious nebular hypothesis, upon which the author of the *Vestiges* had relied to explain the initial stages of terrestrial formation, was scarcely capable of bearing the colossal weight of the theory erected upon it. The "primitive constitution of the nebulous mass" could never be firmed into the palpable shape of fact because it was obviously and forever beyond the reach of observation.[24] Such examples of hasty and careless surmise were not taken as an outright invalidation of theoretical guidance, but they revealed the need for scrupulous circumspection in its use. While the ambitious researcher, ever extending his generalizations, might employ "the most recondite abstractions, *yet will he ever keep in view the facts upon which his whole train of reasoning depends*."[25] These Presbyterians would be the last to arraign theory as such, but they would insist upon meticulous adherence to the restraints embodied in the rules of induction.

Induction and the "Data" of Scripture

Another absolutely trustworthy means of detecting theoretical humbug was to check scientific results directly against commonly received scriptural doctrine. The conviction was general that since truth in every domain of experience was designed in the peerless unity of the Divine mind, it must everywhere be consistent. There was therefore no possibility of an actual discrepancy between the facts of Scripture and of nature. Presbyterians would countenance no thought of "conflict between the truth of God's word and any other truth in the universe."[26] That disciplined observation of actual data could disclose such a conflict was simply unthinkable. Thornwell was convinced that "nothing in the *facts* of the earth's history could be found in contradiction to the Sacred Records. . . . None dare assert *the facts themselves* were contravened by the Bible." Also for this reason, any attempt to degrade the biblically affirmed spiritual dignity of life into mere chemistry could be identified as reckless abstraction. S. J. Cassels, Old School pastor in Savannah, passed wearily in review the excesses of theory by which workers in organic chemistry had sought to account for "the singular phenomenon of vitality." Displaying a dangerous bent toward unchecked reasoning, chemists had "promulged [naturalistic] theories . . . contrary to the dictates of . . . Divine revelation." In this case, the perception that a scientific construction was at variance with biblical dictates was felt to be sufficient cause for the charge of speculation. Likewise, Nathan L. Rice argued that since the Bible teaches "that all the human race sprang from one pair," Christians cannot "allow the devotees of science to shake . . . their faith in this truth by mere *inferences* from the facts" of anatomy.[27]

Here was a lesson which churchmen tried again and again to impress upon scientists and laymen interested in science. Propositions that did not mirror the firm accord between revealed and natural truth required surgery, not publicity. Thereby even non-scientists lacking a detailed grasp of the relevant research situation possessed a right of review over purported "findings" that did not square with the biblical record. Christians have a license to require of scientists, wrote Hodge, "that they shall be cautious in announcing . . . results even apparently hostile to the generally received sense of Scripture." These should be withheld until "the evidence admits of no contradiction or doubt." In the meantime, the suspect result should be rechecked patiently against the whole assemblage of pertinent data.[28] Facts, and straight conclusions from facts alone, with the reliable access to nature they represented, offered the only harbor of safety in the darkening storm of secular theorizing.

To be reliable, an induction must be a mirror of facts. But it must also, Presbyterians agreed, represent as nearly as possible *all* the facts. If, as Reid and Stewart had taught, a scientific law was the individual fact writ large, the scientist could not be allowed to rest confident in his work until satisfied that he had taken "a full view of *all* facts connected with the subject."[29] This was also of strategic value because it was often easy to locate important evidence not fairly represented in the formation of an induction at odds with Scripture. Some Presbyterians argued, for instance, that the range of evidence upon which polygenists had drawn was far too narrowly conceived. The pluralist hypothesis had been built primarily upon anthropometrical data—skull measurements and the like. For Hodge, this was a frivolous constriction of the evidence which only confirmed again the perversion of method and vision inherent in infidel science. If the subject of ethnology was *man* and the point at issue was the existence of fundamentally differing types of men, then a narrow focus upon bodily conformation could hardly hope to yield adequate results. "Would that [the polygenists] could lift their eyes above the dissecting table, and believe that there is more in man than the knife can reveal."[30] Hodge and many others wanted to show that polygenism was a blatant case of materialism which dissipated the biblical perception of man as spirit. The question of species, involving a basic determination of the nature of men, clearly must embrace their inward as well as outward nature, and must therefore be determined by a much more wide-ranging and complex series of factual considerations than most polygenists were accustomed to acknowledge.

Several writers pointed, for example, to philological evidence that suggested that existing languages could be referred to a common origin.[31] The "moral character and condition" of men were also relevant and must be determined by investigation of the historical and contemporary moral performance of the various races.[36] Finally, elusive psychological factors must be contemplated. T.V. Moore advanced "the psychological argument for the unity of the human race," which he interpreted in terms of the evident universality of sin among mankind. Hodge and Thornwell both pointed to the acutely felt "spiritual relationship of men," which must lead every honest observer to recognize in the Negro "the same humanity in which we glory."[33] Scientists who failed to entertain these essential data had not appreciated the factual breadth indicated in the Baconian version of generalization.

From the assumption of the consistency of all truth and the necessity of inclusive induction, it was but one step to the thought that biblical "data" themselves, their factual authenticity underwritten by the Old School doctrine of plenary inspiration, must be included in the range of scientific investigation. Nothing could more adequately assure that science remain doxological. Benjamin M. Palmer argued in "Baconianism and the Bible" that the smooth concurrence of science with religion demonstrated in the holy alliance precluded any sharp distinction between the two realms. Would Bacon have excluded Scripture from induction on the grounds that it was meant to teach religion and not science? "No! The very genius of the inductive philosophy forbids the exclusion of a single pertinent fact from its generalizations. . . . The philosophy . . . which will ignore the Bible . . . has apostatized from the fundamental articles of the Baconian creed." This was additional proof that theories clashing with biblical doctrine must be a spurious compound consisting more of spongy conjecture than of solid induction. Science that pokes carefully amid fossils but ignores Genesis is as much a conjectural geology as the earlier cosmogonies, which had given scant heed to fossils but generously unleashed the imagination. Hodge had kindred advice for polygenists. He declared it "unphilosophical" for the man of science to ignore scriptural "facts." The study of man was common to theology and ethnology; the data yielded by each was complementary. How, then, could any legitimate science of man disregard the treasures of observation accumulated in the biblical writings? Hodge was convinced that Agassiz, who in the early 1850s had lent the weighty prestige of his name to the polygenist school, would not have become mired in such error "if he had appreciated the immense a priori probability against that theory arising from the teachings of the Bible."[34]

Induction and the Psychology of Humility

But the precautionary requirements of the inductive philosophy could not be fully satisfied with a mere listing of procedural caveats. Recognizing that the tutoring of reason in deference to natural and scriptural facts was partly an attitudinal problem, some Old School Calvinists sought to delineate the proper emotional correlate of research. They found it necessary to inculcate the mood, the cast of mind appropriate to the restraining tug of facts. If the restive reason and imagination were amply to be "chained down" to the deliverances of empirical data, if, as Thornwell put it, effectual "*limits*" were to be impressed upon the sweep of scientific curiosity, then the auxiliary power of disposition and habitude must be pressed into the service of induction.[35] Presbyterians located a helpful extra measure of restraint in the psychology of Christian "humility."

Much of the polemic carried on by churchmen on behalf of the inductive method may be understood as an effort to attune the emotions to the humbly creeping pace of true research. Calvinists attentive to the inscrutable and overwhelmingly powerful operation of Divine grace were in a good position to recognize the values of humility. Ashbel Green, patriarch of the Old School, instilled in a generation of youngsters at Princeton College the merits of "that profound humility which is so characteristic a feature of evangelical religion." William S. Plumer thought that "true religion" consisted *"first*, of humility; *secondly*, of humility; *thirdly*, of humility."[36] This doctrine, originally designed to bring the believer quaking to his knees before the throne of grace, was to be equally useful in the fight against flagrant theorizing in science.

Conservative Presbyterians did not hesitate to elevate humility into a psychological platform for induction. They liked to think of Newton, Bacon's most powerful exponent and the most acute intellect of modern times, as a paragon of self-abasement. This had been the Newton presented in the works of Reid and Stewart, a man whose "great genius" was strenuously controlled by an equally potent "modesty."[37] From early in the nineteenth century, the "glory" of Newton's achievements had been coupled with the unassuming deference with which, it was said, he had submitted to the teachings of nature and of the Christian gospel.[38] Thus in the later period of crisis, it was comforting to remember and embellish the aura of humility that had surrounded the researches of the preeminent practitioner of induction. Joseph H. Jones, faithful Calvinist and biographer of Ashbel Green, resurrected the idea, first offered by one of Newton's earliest British popularizers, that Newton had learned scientific method not only from Bacon but also from Christ. The "Saviour's example" of modesty and self-sacrifice had purged him of the pride of pompous theorizing and instructed him in humble receptivity to facts.[39]

What was right for Newton assuredly was right for lesser fry. Since the scientist was the servile interpreter and not the fabricator of nature, his work must be marked throughout by "patience, diligence, and caution."[40] These states of mind were applauded universally by the orthodox. They corresponded to the agonizingly slow pace by which data must be recorded, sifted, examined, generalized, and tested. They lent vital inward authority to the crucial and painful teaching of the Baconian Philosophy that inquiring reason is most effective when most teachable and conscious of its weakness. Recognition that "the greatest minds have been the humblest, and the most extensive knowledge has been the result of the most docile and patient research" was simply the beginning of scientific wisdom and a solid emotional barricade against the buccaneering spirit of conjecture which would run roughshod over the plain indications of fact.[41]

Induction and the Incompleteness of Science

The constituent strategies of the overall Baconian defense show clearly that its controlling aim was *restraint*: the establishment of rigid and delaying empirical controls over scientific "theory." "Principles," in the words of James W. Alexander, now could be "nothing more than generalized facts."[42] The empirical accent that soared into the 1850s was designed to make it difficult for prideful scientists to embellish their unfinished edifices of theory with the pomp and certitude of law. Pondering the difficulties involved in achieving a safe eventual correspondence between fact and theory, the orthodox defenders of godly doctrine were conducted to a weighty stress upon the incomplete, impermanent, and fluxing in science.

Old Schoolers were markedly impressed by the rapid metamorphosis of recent scientific explanation. Astronomy, the "perfect" science, seemed a whole and flawless structure. But the greatest expenditure of scientific energy to date in the nineteenth century had been in the raw and fluxing areas of chemistry, organic science, and geology; these were also the prolific sources of naturalism and heresy. To Presbyterian eyes, research in these fields presented an almost comic spectacle of inconsistency. Yesterday's vaunted theory lay despised upon today's scrap heap. Textbooks regarded as definitive in 1800 were relics by mid-century. Again, the Baconian lesson was evident. The history of geology since 1800 was enough, thought Matthew Boyd Hope, to inspire meticulous caution in the announcement of research findings.[43] If surveyed in historical perspective, material explanations of mind, cosmogonies that ignored the Creation, and polygenism—these and all unsavory scientific doctrines—were flayed of the smugness in which they often appeared. Eventually they would take their place in the gallery of "exploded theories." The more one examined the history of science the more he must be impressed with the harrowing difficulties of accurate and full induction. If there be any instruction in the scientific past, felt a South Carolina pastor, "it is that we should distrust the conclusions of its students, and beware how we rashly accept their hasty, confident and dogmatic assertions."[44]

Stress upon the mutability of scientific explanation permitted churchmen to retain a measure of flexibility and calm in the face of successive shocks. They were comforted to know that the heresy of the moment was probably but the symptom of a confused and obnoxious adolescent stage in the growth of a science toward maturity. Presbyterians disturbed by the abusive contentions of infidel geology or ethnology avoided disillusion with science itself with a reminder that both were "beardless," suffering the normal throes of "infancy."[45] Speaking at Davidson College about 1850, Benjamin M. Palmer gave a tongue-lashing to impertinent scientists swift to claim that the latest theory had undone religion. They were irresponsibly "mistaking the first generalizations of science for its ultimate conclusions." Hypotheses framed only for the purpose of investigation were being assumed as fixed facts and then arrayed in deadly conflict with the teachings of revelation. When would the infidels learn that current generalizations were only momentary rounds in the ascending ladder of induction? The confidence attending the final determination of a law must await the day when a theory had at last and with toilsome patience been adjusted and contoured to fit the complex indications of the total class of pertinent data.[46] In the interim, science must acknowledge its beardless state, keeping in mind that there was scarcely an extant theory "which would not be overthrown, and the whole science revolutionized, by the discovery of a single new and extraordinary fact."[47]

Viewed in hindsight, the formidable requirements thus imposed by Presbyterians upon scientific work seem difficult to reconcile with the real appreciation of progressive generalization and of deduction simultaneously being given expression by several of their number. Convinced that irreverent developments in science had jeopardized crucial theological interests, and thoroughly committed to a philosophical perspective in which empiricism was by far the uppermost note, the orthodox found themselves falling back upon positions in which it was difficult sincerely to endorse any theoretical dimensions in science. Although more acute members of the Presbyterian front constructively appraised hypothetical and deductive procedures, they were at the same time forced to acknowledge that the theoretical element appeared more often to operate as a floodgate of theological errors than as a source of insight into nature. To the extent that they dealt specifically with scientific issues, especially during the 1850s, they therefore found far more occasion to blame theory than to praise it. A broad exposure to the relevant sources of Presbyterian reaction leaves the reader with the predominant impression of a concept of scientific methodology nearly strained of abstraction and consisting of a direct closure with facts operating through the channels of sense.

6.

Positive Strategies in Doxological Science

The hard, empirical fortifications within which Presbyterian thinkers had sought to shelter the comforting assumptions of doxological science apparently were able to provide a tolerable sense of security. With their flanks thus covered, some churchmen were nerved to go on the offensive. Sustained by the traditional Calvinist confidence in the ultimate consensus of all forms of truth, they ventured upon two additional constructive projects in Christian Baconianism. Both the millennium and the Protestant Reformation were now to do service in the "holy alliance." In each case, the aim was to knit science even more stably to doxology. Bacon and the Bible were to be meshed in so inextricable a conceptual embrace as to banish once and for all the ghastly prospect of a triumphant scientific secularism forcing religion to make its way against the evidences of accepted knowledge.

The Concord of Truth

Presbyterians were not to be daunted even by the most quarterless assaults of unbelieving science. They traced a standard pattern of development in every field of investigation as it broadened and deepened its inductions in search of final formulations. Each science in its youth appeared prone to generate odious theories destructive of religious belief, but as it slowly firmed its grasp upon truth, its infidel grimace was transformed into a smiling countenance of faith. "Each science is seized at its birth and declared to be a champion of scepticism; but as soon as it can speak, . . . it proclaims itself a true knight, and a defender of the faith."[1]

Despite the disconcerting blows dealt to belief by irreligious science, Presbyterians never really had lost confidence in the final feasibility of the holy alliance. Up to 1860, few voices had faltered. "Gentlemen," urged a Princeton orator in 1852, "we hope that your faith is too well founded to fear any of the sciences"; he then regaled his auditors with a quote from Bacon on the harmony of nature and Scripture.[2] Although one may sense rumblings of anxiety beneath the surface poise, everywhere the uppermost note was positive. Again and again the insidious suggestion that "Scripture is a foe to science" was thrust aside as the work of alarmists. Especially in a period when natural science was "the great oracle of the age" it could not be permitted to plunge out of the restraining halter of religious perspective. Illiterate revivalists would do little good in winning the heart of the nation if a belligerent naturalism was laying waste its intellect. Orthodox spokesmen were uniformly appalled by the appearance in the early 1850s of Comte's *Positive Philosophy*, with its contemptuous claim that scientific advance was "elevating" mankind into a postreligious phase of knowledge.[3] Benjamin M. Palmer found the prospect that science might "build up its glory upon the ruins of revelation . . . most appalling." No, the thought could not be countenanced. Churchmen would continue to be controlled by their long-standing conviction that nature and Scripture were intimately consistent forms of one truth. On all hands they reaffirmed their persuasion that science itself was intensely religious: "It is only where its instructions have been garbled, . . . that its trumpet has ever given an uncertain sound."[4]

From early in the century, the chorus of orthodox reaction to scientific issues had rung innumerable changes on the refrain of truth's unity. Ashbel Green had schooled more than one generation of young Presbyterians to believe the works of Deity flawlessly concordant: "That all truth is really consistent with itself, or that every truth is perfectly reconcilable with every other truth, no one who knows what truth is, can for a moment doubt."[5] Expressions in this vein reached a peak of frequency about mid-century. Bacon and Newton, now convincingly transfigured into evangelical believers, were cited repeatedly to demonstrate that profound science and a fervent trust in Scripture might coexist happily in the same mind.[6] A barrage of testimony was given to the "delightful harmony" existing between the "book of nature" and the biblical volumes.[7] There was general agreement that the one fatal, ruining concession would be "to imagine that, in the heavens above, or in the earth beneath, or in the waters under the earth, in the domain of nature, explored to its uttermost recesses, something may possibly be found *true* which shall render faith in the Bible unreasonable."[8]

So tenacious — perhaps even desperate — was the belief in truth's unity that a number of churchmen suggested that a firmly established induction which conflicted with a point of received doctrine might fairly be taken as a challenge to theological reinterpretation. Ashbel Green had already admitted that "facts, when ascertained to be such, must be admitted, let the consequences follow as they may."[9] It is revealing that five prominent Old Schoolers, including three professors of theology, were now willing to suggest that if an "indisputable" result of thorough induction manifestly contradicted an existing doctrine of the church, "the theologian *must reconsider* his interpretation of God's word, and see if he has not misunderstood it."[10] In view of the firm biblical literalism as well as the unbending confessionalism to which the Old School was committed, this was a substantial concession.

But the need for such "reinterpretation" was not in fact expected to arise. The general anticipation was that continued research would issue in a straightforward accord with basic Christian teaching as generally understood. Thus if students of the Bible and of nature would explore their own departments without jealous or untrusting reference to the other, the results would be agreeable to both. "We are perfectly sure of ultimate agreement between the inductions of true science and the truths of revelation," announced the *Princeton Review* in a statement of policy, and "we are content to let [*sic*] the devotees of the former, to prosecute their researches and correct their deductions till this agreement is reached."[11] The best interim strategy for the church, suggested Palmer, was to await the "larger inductions" which would blend apparent discrepancies into a single pattern.[12] Whether or not readjustment of current interpretations was required, the end toward which all such expressions directed attention was an ultimate union of ideas, religious and scientific, in which the discords of the past were covered and forgotten. Lewis W. Green summarized hundreds of pages of Presbyterian polemic with an invocation of "a sympathy deep, intense, all-pervading—a harmony profound, stupendous, universal, between the revelations of the Bible and the discoveries of modern science."[13] This would be the sublime and epochal result of unwavering confidence in the concord of truth.

Avowal of such dazzling hopes was evidence that conservative churchmen were straining their apologetic resources. They appeared able to translate every gloomy forecast into an augur of sunshine. Even yet, however, their strategy was far from exhausted. The pressures of mid-century acted as a mother of two final and conclusive apologetic inventions. Presbyterians were not satisfied that the alliance of Baconian science with religion was conceptually complete until an even more ambitious marriage of ideas had been effected. They would now enlist on its behalf the tremendous ratifying power of two of the mightiest ideas in nineteenth-century America: the millennium and the Reformation.

Catastrophism and the Millennium

In the 1850s, with the breastworks of Baconian defense virtually complete and with confidence in truth's accord being proclaimed on every hand, some churchmen were ready to move to the offensive. Having secured a measure of safety for devout science, they now sought to assure that the future as well would belong to God's praise. The logic of Green's "harmony profound" linking science with Protestant religion was now to find uncommon issue in a dramatic merger with millennialism, the hope for a wondrous thousand-year reign of Christ upon earth. Many scholars have commented recently on the force of millennial ideas in antebellum America. Especially illuminating is the discovery that the millennial beliefs of the period were largely "postmillennial," that is, focused upon a gradual, inner-historical realization of Christ's kingdom-upon-the-earth. The millennium, in this view, was not to be imposed from without history suddenly and supernaturally, but was to emerge slowly out of possibilities existing within the historical process.[14] An intriguing and heretofore unnoticed "scientific" example of this innerworldly spirit was an effort by two conservative Presbyterians to merge hopes for a "Millennial Day" with epochalist geology in a vision of cosmological fulfillment. In this pattern, apocalyptic hopes were integrated with a conception of the providentially phased Christianization of earth.

Both within and without Presbyterianism an association of millennialism with the march of scientific progress had been well established by the 1850s.[15] But now for the first time, the broad acceptance which the pious "catastrophism" of James Parkinson and Georges Cuvier had won among American geologists created a foundation for more remarkable formulations. Catastrophism was one of the grander syntheses in nineteenth-century science. Writing in the first two decades of the century, Parkinson and Cuvier were initial architects of a sweeping vision of earth and life history in which "epochs" of geological time succeeded one another in ascending progression. In each instance, the existing scheme of geological environment and life forms was destroyed by providentially engineered catastrophe and a new complex of flora and fauna were miraculously introduced. The movement from epoch to epoch was progressive, with the gradual creation of conditions suitable for mankind being the purpose of the whole. Agassiz, who studied closely with Cuvier for a time before the latter's death, appropriated the essentials of the scheme and served thereafter as its most influential advocate.[16] This cogent mix of science and theology proved readily palatable to numerous American scientists, and there is evidence of its widespread adoption in America during the half-century before the Civil War, accelerated by Agassiz's arrival shortly before 1850.[17]

The vivid coordination of religious and scientific insights

achieved by the catastrophists proved convincing to a significant number of leading Presbyterians.[18] Although vitiated in its early stages by menacing and naturalistic "speculations," by mid-century geology could be counted as a solid doxological ally of faith, "one of its noblest champions." The force of confidence with which many Presbyterians greeted this soothing rapprochement can be seen in a brief passage from a sermon preached by Thornwell in 1857: "The appearances of our globe are said [by catastrophists] to be utterly inexplicable upon any hypothesis which does not recognize the fact that the plan of creation was so formed from the beginning, as to include at successive periods, the direct agency of the Deity. . . . The geologist begins with miracles. . . . Geology and the Bible must kiss and embrace each other, and this youngest daughter of science will be found . . . bringing her votive offerings to the Prince of Peace."[19]

But it remained for Lewis W. Green and E. F. Rockwell, both prominent in the denomination, to blend the epochalist imagery of "successive periods" into a pattern of millennial hope. Both men were recognized leaders in the Presbyterian front against infidel science, and they liked to appeal to "repeated, sober, and indubitable observation" as the basis of scientific inference.[20] Working without apparent mutual influence, they both traced the operations of *"one vast and comprehensive plan"* directing the universe through a course of ascending arrangements to a natural and glorious cosmic fulfillment.[21] Green's "The Harmony of Revelation, and Natural Science; With Especial Reference to Geology," first delivered as a lecture at the University of Virginia in 1850 and later published in the *Southern Presbyterian Review*, set forth an enthusiastic account of the "ascending series" of miraculously initiated stages of earth history. If previous stages had been temporary, intended in the counsels of providence to "prepare" the world for human habitation, so the present also was filled with indications of instability and impermanence. In an earlier essay, Green had detected "a vague consciousness of changes, about to come upon the earth; a universal hope." He also had identified "the [doxologically] altered tone of science" as a major sign pointing toward a nearing millennium. Now he was ready to picture the vast coming change as the last and consummating epoch in the geological-cosmic plan of providence. This awful and final step in the ascending series was already in the making. Recent geological researches, for instance, seemed to indicate "a progressive increase of heat in the unobserved depths of the earth," implying an explosive accumulation of volcanic power. Celestial events, such as the accelerating play of "sudden, tremendous and evanescent forces" associated with sunspots, also were portentous. This and other evidence, assayed in accord with "inductive philosophy," pointed toward "AN INEVITABLE CATASTROPHE," a millennial transformation produced not from without by supernatural means but from within by titanic and distorting natural energies. The ultimate issue of the impending catastrophe was, of course, not to be universal destruction, but the "new day" forecast in Scripture. Radically purged of its present corruptions, the earth then could be refitted as "the theatre of a glorious moral manifestation, the blissful abode of holy, happy beings." Whether this was to be the traditional "millennium," the thousand-year reign of Christ prior to the resurrection and final judgment, or the state of heaven itself, is unclear.[22]

Three years later, the Reverend E. F. Rockwell of Davidson College found the new geology similarly suggestive of millennial themes. The integration of geology and Divine purpose represented by catastrophism also led Rockwell to set the mighty eschatological events forecast in Scripture in a geological perspective. Edward Hitchcock, a reverent American catastrophist whose work often was cited by Presbyterians, recently had distinguished six progressive stages of earth history. Of these, five were preparatory to the sixth and culminating "Age of Man" called for by catastrophist logic. As he pondered this outline, there suddenly dawned upon Rockwell a connection with the "perfect" scriptural number seven. Since the present epoch manifestly did not represent completion of the Divine plan, why not view it as itself a preparation for a seventh, "a final, a perfect stage?" So compelling a thought warranted publication, and Rockwell elaborated it in an article on "The Final Destiny of Our Globe" published in the *Southern Presbyterian Review* in mid-1853. Passing in review recent astronomical evidence of the fiery "appearance and disappearance of stars" in deep space, he argued by analogy for an ultimate conflagration of the earth. This conclusion, however, in the light of Hitchcock's developmental sketch, did not imply that the destiny of the globe was flaming ruin, for that would nullify the epochalist inference that providence is always preparing this world for a better state of things. The earth, therefore, was to be transfigured, not wrecked, by its forthcoming ordeal, "and not only continue on its course, but in a state of splendour and perfection far surpassing the present." Rockwell left his readers with no doubt that this seventh and triumphant age was not itself a prelude to further transformations, but was the "perfect, permanent, immovable" state of heaven itself.[23]

The millennial speculations of Green and Rockwell represent an extraordinary projection of Presbyterian confidence in the final coherence of science and religion. Rockwell spoke for both as he elatedly concluded that the "two great lines of truth, that from physical science, and that from inspiration," had been fitly joined in his vision of the earth's geological transformation. Although both proclaimed alignment with the inductive philosophy and attempted to weave their conclusions from a profusion of facts, the ties joining fact and inference in each case reflected perhaps less of Baconianism than of religious ardor. If their results had been less palatable to Presbyterian belief, they might have suffered some rough handling from their stern inductivist colleagues. But it was hard to fault an endeavor that had offered lip service to the rules of induction to show that "the teachings of science exactly fall in with and confirm inspiration," and this, in terms of current ideas, was indeed the significance of their effort.[24] Here was post-millennialism with a vengeance! The millennium now could be construed as the unfolding of a natural plan providentially wrought into the geological constitution of the globe. Thus it was more evident than ever that the role of properly directed scientific understanding was to corroborate the Scriptures and to deepen the faith of Christian believers. If, however, the logic of geology as an expositor of the millennium guaranteed that the future belonged to doxology, so the "deep, intense, all-pervading harmony" of

Protestant religion and Baconian science dictated a tactic for seizure of the past as well. Churchmen now undertook to prove that the formative stage of inductive science was moored in the biblical piety of the Reformation.

Bacon and the Reformation

The idea was long embedded in British and American Protestantism and much accentuated in the eighteenth century that the Catholic Middle Ages was a period of culture and intellectual gloom. The intelligence, initiative, and progress characteristic of Protestant countries was held to be in good measure an outgrowth of the Reformation doctrine of private judgment. At no time had this neat pairing of ideas been more habitually invoked than during the decades of reaction against the French Enlightenment. Every historian acquainted with the primary sources knows how readily Reformation vigor was then contrasted with Catholic torpor and superstition.[25] This was, of course, a vital part of the Protestant answer to the French thesis that religion was an enemy of enlightenment. But it was to prove of equal utility to those eager to demonstrate an essential rootage of the modern scientific revolution in the biblical orientation of Protestantism.

Presbyterians had shared fully in the conventional appraisal of the medieval period as a "long, dark, starless night" of intellectual bondage.[26] They looked too to the Reformation as the fountainhead of Protestant energies. Suddenly into Catholic darkness had beamed a light, a sun, "the Sun of the Reformation."[27] But most important, the focus of such remarks fell usually not upon the renascence of right doctrine, but upon the arousal of the "slumbering" human intellect: "the monk of Erfurth . . . unchains the Bible. . . . a flood of light pours in. . . . The world's intellect is resuscitated."[28] Drawing upon the ambitious intellectuality characteristic of Calvinist theology, Old School thinkers clearly and repeatedly underscored the mentally energizing effects of the contact between Scripture and the "mind" instituted in the Reformation. "What power broke the spell?" asked Nathan L. Rice, "and let the human mind go free? . . . We maintain that the *Scriptures* were the power."[29]

The Reformation, then, was the time when "the mind of the world awoke." It left "the mind of man expanding in all directions."[30] And far from being limited to a rejuvenation of personal faith, the effects of this awakening radiated to all areas of culture. The Old School wished to identify in the Reformation nothing less than the foundations of modern learning and enterprise. While Catholic centers were left stagnating amid "miracle-mongering and lying wonders" and in the mental stupor of "implicit faith," Protestants were registering the powerful impulses which the Bible gave to the human mind on "every subject."[31] No area of thought or enterprise escaped the vivifying touch of Reformation energy. Literature, commerce, polity, "all the arts of life, and all the ranges of science" were goaded into new life and progress.[32] Against this background of assumptions, churchmen saw nothing incongruous in the ambitious claim that modern natural science had taken its birth and essential intellectual nourishment from the Protestant Christianity of the sixteenth century.

"The intellect of the world, struck free from its shackles, and quickened and intensified by the Reformation, was thrown, with intense ardour, upon the observation and study of nature."[33] This was the remarkable conclusion toward which Old School thinkers carefully nursed the traditional inclinations of Protestant thought about the Reformation. The apparent coincidence of Protestantism and natural science in the United States, Britain, and western Europe was often remarked upon and the obvious inferences drawn.[34] As, in the 1840s and 1850s, the wish intensified to incorporate science safely within a controlling matrix of Protestant conceptions, it became evident to a number of church leaders that in order to explain the zeal with which Protestants had undertaken the exploration of nature, pointing to the biblical sources of mental activism was not enough. Activity must be focused, directed toward congruent objects, and supplied with the techniques of knowledge. Only through the complementary assumption of an intimate correlation between the inductive spirit of Baconian science and the biblical genius of Protestantism could the historical evidence fully be accounted for. Thus Presbyterians busily set to work elaborating a catalogue of special congruences between them.

Evidences were advanced that the Bible itself reflected significant scientific curiosity and achievement. The *Southern Presbyterian Review* claimed that the Pentateuch was filled with scientific knowledge "so varied, so profound, and so accurate, that the noblest results of modern scientific research are only an approximation to a recovery, in our times, of scientific knowledge perfectly familiar to Moses."[35] Solomon, according to the *Princeton Review*, was "the greatest physical philosopher of his day" and had strewn his Psalms with accurate observations in natural history.[36] R. B. McMullen of Tennessee assured an audience of alumni at the University of Alabama that Scripture "everywhere abounds with the principles of scientific truth." Galileo, for instance, had discovered that the atmosphere had weight, yet "Job had written more than 3000 years previous to that time that 'God maketh weight for the wind!' " Lewis W. Green, speaking at the University of Virginia, thrilled his audience with the claim that the apostle Peter "has furnished us with a broad outline of modern science." In a passage from 2d Peter 3, Green was confident that he had discovered a detailed forecast of the epochalist geology to which he subscribed.[37]

Scripture, then, was scientific through and through. Small wonder that the most diligent assaults of infidel science upon the sacred text had failed to strike their mark. So flawless had been the operation of God's spirit in guiding the scriptural authors that the polemical needs of nineteenth-century exegesis already had been taken into account! The language of inspiration not only was consistent with the march of knowledge but also the later discoveries of inductive science often were variously and wonderfully foreseen. Robert J. Breckinridge beamed with assurance that "the results of all knowledge, in every department of our researches into the state of the universe, are assumed as already clear and known, thousands of years before our researches commenced."[38] Some Presbyterian writers, including Breckinridge, cautioned that it would be naive to assume that the Spirit had in every case supplied the biblical writers with a precise scientific comprehension of natural phenomena. They may have been directed in the use of conceptions whose technical features in measure exceeded their understanding.[39] But the important fact was that the images of nature that pervade Scripture had been "discreetly framed" into accurate congruence with the Newtonian view of the world.

What better way to demonstrate this congruence than with a detailed scientific exegesis of a scriptural text? The impeccably orthodox minister and scientist E. F. Rockwell tried to do just this in a fascinating article published in the *Southern Presbyterian Review* for 1852. Rockwell attempted an account of the "phenomena of freezing water" as recorded in Job 37:9, 10 and 38:29, 30:

Out of the north (cometh) cold; By the breath of God frost is given, and the breadth of the waters is straitened.

Out of whose womb came the ice? and the hoary frost of heaven, who had gendered it? The waters are hid as with a stone, and the face of the deep is frozen; . . .

These passages, describing "the process by which ice is formed upon streams of water," were found perfectly conformable to the strictest scientific account: "The surface of water in lakes and rivers cools by exposure to the air, or by the passage over it of the wind, here called poetically the breath of God. That film of water that is on the surface . . . becomes contracted. . . . [Filaments of ice develop, and,] interlacing in all directions, cross one another regularly at angles of sixty and one hundred and twenty degrees. . . . the sharp pointed crystals continue to advance and the ice to grow outward from the banks, . . . till the two edges meet in the middle: then they shoot their filaments across and join their work in one solid bridge, from shore to shore, . . . The mobile fluid is congealed." Thus "scientific" exegesis, according to Rockwell, inevitably would demonstrate "perfect agreement" between the biblical and the Baconian reports of natural effects.[40]

The detailing of harmonies between the religious and the scientific views of nature helped to explain why the human mind, once vitalized by the Reformation, had been "thrown" upon the study of the natural world. The reformers had put into the hands of men a book laden with knowledge of nature, authored partly by persons of scientific genius. Its preparation had been overseen by the same God who had designed the Creation. Little wonder if it had whetted an appetite for further and direct exploration of nature. But more analysis was required to clarify the full relationship between science and the Reformation. For according to Old School thinkers, the key to the history of science was not zeal for the analysis of nature, but the development of the inductive philosophy by which that zeal must be coached and ordered. They must therefore show that the Bible had supplied the initial inspiration for the methodological genius of Bacon.

An important and interesting development within the history of nineteenth-century American ideas was the effort undertaken in the 1850s by Benjamin Morgan Palmer and Nathan L. Rice to demonstrate that *the only philosophy which has given to the world a true physical . . . science, is itself the product of Protestant Christianity.*[41] This was, indeed, a natural and easy extension of existing assumptions. In his famous essay on "Lord Bacon," Thomas B. Macaulay had suggested that "it is chiefly to the great reformation of religion that we owe the great reformation of philosophy." Macaulay, however, had pictured the connection chiefly in negative terms. Martin Luther and his reforming colleagues had facilitated the rise of the inductive philosophy by demolishing the Aristotelian monopoly on ideas. By assaulting the "deductive" methods of scholasticism, they had cleared the way for Bacon's inductive reformulation.[42] A more important step had been taken by Samuel Tyler's *Discourse of the Baconian Philosophy*, for Tyler attempted to trace an explicit correlation between historical Protestantism and inductive science. The Baconian Philosophy, he argued, not only "accords with Christianity," but is actually "assumed in it." Protestant biblicism assumes that Divine revelation is not disclosed a priori to the naked reason, but is "contained" in the Scriptures. From thence it is to be appropriated by the believer, just as the facts of nature are gathered and analyzed by the scientist. In each case, the basic appeal is to data bearing an unconditional claim. The formative experience of Protestantism, therefore, provides a kind of direct training and "preparation" for science. Tyler was able to conclude that "Protestant christianity and the Baconian philosophy originate in the same fountain."[43]

Following the course of thought suggested by Tyler, Rice and Palmer were prepared to spell out in more detail the manner in which Protestantism had flowered in the Baconian Philosophy. Rice first presented in an address in 1845 the thesis that "the key of sound philosophy, the clue to correct philosophical investigation, is found in the Scriptures, and was thence obtained by Bacon and Newton."[44] But full development of the position awaited his addresses on "The Moral Effects of Christianity" (1850) and "The Influence of Christianity on the Progress of Science" (1851). Palmer's case was presented in full in an address first delivered at Davidson College and published in the *Southern Presbyterian Review* in 1852 under the title of "Baconianism and the Bible."

Rice's argument for Baconianism as an offspring of Protestantism differs in some details from that of Palmer, but the framework of basic conceptions is the same. Each concentrated on Bacon. The task was to explain how the biblical thrust of Protestantism had conditioned the creative impulses of this legislator of science. With an already beatified Bacon at their disposal, both could assume that he "commenced his career as a philosopher with the Bible in his hand." In fact, while poring over his Bible, Bacon imbibed "the first great truths of philosophy."[45] Rice stressed that classical and medieval thinkers had squandered the bulk of their intellectual energy in futile speculations about the origin and nature of matter and mind. By providing cogent and definitive solutions to these elemental problems, the Scriptures directed the inquiring mind into more fruitful explorations.[46] Biblical "truth," moreover, being of "sublime" and invigorating scope and richness, enlivened the mental powers and readied the mind for vigorous efforts in all areas of inquiry.[47] Yet the pivot of Rice's argument was the doctrine of Creation. By teaching that matter was Divinely created and therefore good, the Bible subverted the ancient contempt for the realm of material, thereby eliminating a primary obstacle to scientific study.[48] But, even more important, the idea of Creation sponsored by Scripture implies a total disqualification of speculative approaches to nature. Creation means that reality is already "given" and complete in itself. The purpose of science, on this premise, can only be the sheer passive discovery upon which the inductive philosophy was to center; hypothetical constructions not deduced directly from phenomena are solidly ruled out.[49] "The *inductive philosophy*," concluded Rice, "is the legitimate offspring of this sublime truth. . . . To the Reformation, then, which was the work of the Scriptures, we are indebted for a sound philosophy."[50]

Palmer had an equally compelling table of correlations to offer. Openly relying upon both Tyler and Rice, he proposed to locate the "genesis" of Baconianism in the biblicist core of early Protestantism. He pounced upon Tyler's suggestion that the believer's unquestioning acceptance of scriptural "facts" had created a humility of temper appropriate to inductive investigations in science. "In both alike, man is but an interpreter." He followed Rice's analysis of the liberating significance of proper basic teaching about mind and matter and of the bracing effects of biblical truths upon mental effort.[51] But the center of his argument was an enthusiastic treatment of the "absolutely reigning" biblical idea of "LAW." The realm of nature, like the realm of human society, was presented by the biblical authors as a direct effect of the ordering will of the Almighty. This conception of law, like Rice's notion of Creation, stressed the literal givenness of things and by clear implication confined the work of science to the straight empirical reading of the laws governing the universe. And this, in turn, "is the germ of all true science."[52] These trains of thought could have but one issue. As Palmer most eloquently stated it, "There never could have been a Bacon without the Bible. . . . Francis Bacon was the offspring of the Reformation."[53] Here was a highly significant nexus in American ideas: Baconianism and the Bible, neatly intersected within the frame of Anglo-American Protestant civilization. Now it was possible for inductive science both to share in the general prestige accorded the Reformation and to be tamed by it into tighter compliance with Protestant religious ideals. Francis Bacon not only had begun his career with the Bible in hand; he had extracted from that Bible the vital themes he then integrated into the formula of induction. It was, in fact, difficult to conceive how science could survive without the immense intellectual subsidy represented by the Protestant fixation upon Scripture. A virtual assimilation of science to orthodox Protestantism had been a-chieved. Rice and Green agreed that the two must stand or fall together and that neither could prosper without enriching the other. This thought, informed by the rapid progress of science, opened the vast prospect of a worldwide expansion of Protestant civilization. Catholicism, Hinduism, Islam—any and all false religions eventually would "vanish" before the light of Protestant natural science. The Reformation, having set science in motion, would with its help achieve at last its original goal of universal Christianization on a biblical platform. "Hence," concluded Green, "Knowledge, Science and Religion, march *hand in hand* around the earth." The end of Protestant endeavor was to be a sublime global consummation of the holy alliance of Baconianism and biblical Christianity.[54]

But this thrilling chain of inferences also pointed toward a new dispensation in American theology. Not only had science been rendered Protestant to the core, but the Bible had been transformed into the *Volksbuch* of Protestant Baconianism. After Rice and Palmer had performed their magnificent correlation, a loyal Presbyterian like James Read Eckard could announce in the *Princeton Review* that the Bible was the supreme existing textbook in inductive method, for its message was framed throughout on a Baconian agenda. It was through a direct display of cogent inductive reasoning that the Bible had inspired Bacon to reform science. We may even "reduce to a strictly inductive form the scriptural arguments which terminate in the conclusion that Jesus of Nazareth is the Christ, the Son of God."[55] This was indicative of a key commotion in hermeneutical ideas. To be understood fully, the linkage of Bacon with Protestantism must be considered in relation to an additional ferment in Presbyterian thinking. For the necessity to come to terms with science that had weighed so heavily upon the orthodox also was leading them to divine positive prospects for the theological application of induction. If the Bible was an inductive book, the Christian exegete himself must become an expert inductivist. The last and perhaps most fascinating chapter in the relations between Baconian science and Presbyterian religion was an effort to render biblical interpretation itself a function of the Baconian Philosophy.

7.

Baconianism and the Bible: Hermeneutics for an Age of Science

If Methodists, Baptists, and similar groups in antebellum America tended to deprecate learning and to sponsor popular anti-intellectualism, Presbyterians considered themselves missionaries to the American intellect. Scholars have not readily noted that the huge Presbyterian literature from the period presents an unrelenting resistance to the spreading vogue of hostility toward intellectual acuteness and achievement. Leading churchmen persistently voiced their opposition to the "levity and superficialness" that marked current thought. They scorned a growing "distaste for severer intellectual toil" and singled out for particular assault the sentimental adulation of folkish wisdom which informed the Jacksonian movement and the narrow psychology of the "heart" expounded by many revivalists.[1]

Presbyterian intellectualism reflected both the church's identification with the educated classes and a sense of obligation continually to provide an up-to-date intellectual account of the Christian message that would appeal to those classes. Ministerial candidates must be thoroughly schooled in the liberal arts and sciences, as well as in theology, because men out of touch with ongoing intellectual culture could not articulate the contemporary relevance of Christianity for "men of liberal minds and pursuits" and "youth of aspiring views." The message expounded by Presbyterian ministers, according to Nicholas Murray, must always be fitted "to obtain for the gospel the attention and the respect of the thoughtful."[2]

To a church accustomed to framing its message in intellectual terms, the separation of church and state in America had a special meaning. The replacement of coercion with opinion as an arbiter of religious belief meant, in the Presbyterian view, that the nation had become a battleground of ideas. William S. Plumer thought that "polemical theology" was of unique importance in the republic because "in our country, who will may preach, and what he will, who will may publish and what he will, who will and can may found a sect in religion." Under such circumstances, it was evident that ministers and theologians would be called upon to furnish frequent, fast, and convincing accounts of orthodox belief. "It is manifest," added Plumer, "that many a hard battle for the truth must here be fought."[3]

The need to carry on an open and competitive battle for the American mind was complicated for antebellum churchmen by the rapid diffusion of knowledge on all subjects, and especially science. For to argue the case for religion cogently before a literate and well-informed congregation obviously presupposed a timely acquaintance with the major issues now agitating thoughtful men and women everywhere. And with the diffusion of scientific knowledge proceeding apace from the 1830s Presbyterian leaders knew, as we have seen, that any attempt to remain intellectually abreast of the age entailed an articulate, positive, and wide-ranging response to natural science. With science becoming a matter of salient and permanent interest for the educated citizenry, it was not enough to baptize research with evangelical and Baconian unction, or even to provide generally acceptable defenses against the various challenges of infidelity. For to allow the whole focus of Baconian effort to rest upon scientific affairs inevitably would draw attention away from the weightier matters of sin, salvation, and churchmanship. Recognizing this danger, Presbyterian churchmen coupled their attention to doxological science with an urging that the devices of Christian theology itself be reshaped in part to accord with scientific modes of thinking. This was the way to win the religious allegiance of a public becoming fascinated with science; it was also an ingenious counterthrust against anti-intellectual trends within the broader evangelical movement. Theology henceforth must be able to "present itself . . . before the scientific world" with a convincing claim for its attention.[4] Presbyterians thus engaged in an extensive exercise in theological "relevance" attuned to the first great age of American popular science. Perhaps the most significant documentation of the marriage of religion and science within the framework of the Old School was the widespread appeal of an effort to adapt Lord Bacon's method of induction directly to the uses of biblical exegesis.

Christian Theology and the Critique of Pure Reason

During the period of our study, conservative churchmen inveighed no less heavily against metaphysics and speculations in theology than in natural science. As malicious a crowd of irresponsible theorizers seemed bent upon thinking away the solid foundations of Westminster doctrine as ever had lured geology into the misty paths of cosmogony. Hence admonitions poured from Presbyterian pens against those who "substitute the conjectural deductions of human reasoning . . . for the truths of the Bible."[5] "Christianity," exhorted the *Evangelical and Literary Magazine* in 1822, "is not a religion of speculation."[6]

In giving initial shape and force to the orthodox war against abstractions in theology, nothing was more important than the conflict with Unitarianism. Most intense in the first three decades of the century, the confrontation between orthodox Calvinism and the new liberalism of William Ellery Channing and Andrews Norton had not ceased by the Civil War to arouse Presbyterian hostility. As conservative Presbyterians perceived the matter, the key issue raised by the liberals was the role of reason in religion. More specifically, what were the prerogatives of human reason in biblical interpretation? Until the later 1830s, a decisive majority of orthodox statements regarding the theological function of reason emerged directly from debate over this question.

Then, during the 1830s, a fresh sense of intellectual emergency was created within Old School ranks by the emergence of an emphatically non-Baconian philosophical movement. Quickly replacing Unitarianism as the leading challenge to traditional belief was the new Transcendentalism, which troubled conservatives associated with J. G. Fichte, G. W. F. Hegel, Friedrich Schleiermacher, Samuel Taylor Coleridge, Ralph Waldo Emerson, J. D. Morell, and other figures. Presbyterian literature from the late 1830s teems with anxious and scathing references, book reviews, and full-scale attacks against what was called variously "Pantheism," "Rationalism," and "Transcendentalism." All writers concurred that the root error of the new movement was its stress upon the intuitive, "speculative" power of reason exceeding the limiting perspectives of sense.[7] Again at stake was the determination of reason's province in matters of religion. The polemic against overconfidence in the capacities of the human mind, which took form during the Unitarian engagements, was carried on and kept at a grueling intensity in the equally heated battle against "the new infidelity" of romantic idealism.

Spurred on by what Old Schooler John Bocock called "the love of intellectual triumph engendered by the past achievements of science," antebellum Americans engaged in a feverish campaign of praise for "mind."[8] Celebration of "the march of mind" was but one facet of a larger movement of adulation. Literature of the day is filled with paeans to the reach and might of the human mind, some relatively restrained, others passing into the language of utter extravagance. The *Southern Literary Messenger* offered a typical rhapsody in 1840 to "the mind—the immortal mind! . . . When we approach a subject so intricate and so spiritual, the recollection should force itself upon the mind, which rested with such awful solemnity upon the mind of the Patriarch as he gazed upon 'the burning bush,' that the place whereon we stand is holy ground."[9] Unitarianism may be understood in part as an immodest theological appropriation of this adulating spirit. Certainly no one could outpace Channing in extolling "mind, thought . . . [as] the sovereign of the world." He would have no hesitation to "call God a mind. . . . God is another name for human intelligence, raised above all error and imperfection, and extended to all possible truth."[10]

For the spiritual heirs of John Calvin, this was heady and explosive doctrine. Alexander McGill and his colleagues found "no people on earth . . . so much entranced as we . . . with . . . apotheosis of the human mind."[11] And they did not fail to mark Channing's repeated and cutting broadsides against those backward and "gloomy" Genevans whose somber notion of sin "insults" the "Godlike faculty" of intellect.[12] Nevertheless, the conservative Presbyterian reaction to Unitarianism was no simple matter of touching up the traditional stress on the sinful corruption of human faculties. In the first place, Presbyterians themselves were willing to concede much to the merits of "mind." In the second, they intended to work out a solution to the theological problem of reason in accordance with the Baconian Philosophy.

In view of their remarkable performance as educators and missionaries to the American intellect, Presbyterian leaders understandably were prone to scoff at Unitarian charges of mental backwardness. Though they did not paint in such glaring hues, they were as convinced as Channing that God was a "Supreme Reason" and the human mind a glint of Divine intelligence.[13] "Thought is sublime," offered a contributor to Van Rensselaer's *The Home, The School, and the Church* in 1859; "the power of thinking is a grand approximation towards the nature of God."[14] Joining the fashionable enthusiasm for "progress," orthodox thinkers also readily assented that "the mind is susceptible of indefinite expansion and invigoration" and found its continuing triumphs in science and technology "almost too dazzling to be looked upon."[15] Taking the thought a significant step further, they argued that the mind, being an emanation from Divine reason, is itself immortal. Geared into progressive development in this life, it continues to expand into infinity. Many prominent Presbyterians thus conceived heaven as a field for the unimpeded advance of intellection, of "inquiry without fatigue, and knowledge free of doubt."[16] Thornwell once marveled, "Ah, what is man!" as he imagined the "inconceivable grandeur" of Newton's mind unfolding in unceasing progression throughout eternity.[17]

For these reasons, Presbyterians faced a ticklish problem in forging a suitable and consistent response to Unitarianism and sustaining it in the face of the later Transcendentalist challenge. Lacking any intention of "insulting" the dignity of the human mind, yet they must protest against its exaltation into a self-justifying principle capable of independent speculation over against the contents of Scripture. At this point, it was easy to see a parallel with the problem of conjecture in natural science. And here also the answer appeared to lie in recourse to the severe Baconian stress upon "facts."

The modest adulation of mind in which the Old School indulged was not inconsistent with their emphatic censure of speculation in theology. For speculation, in its normal pejorative sense, was construed as an unfounded use of the mental powers. Presbyterian criticism of "metaphysical reasoning" within the church partook directly of the broader animosity against unchecked theorizing in natural science. In each case, the adversary was a conception of the human mind which imputed sovereign prerogatives to reason. Channing might believe that men could attain an adequate knowledge of God and human destiny by conforming the contents of Scripture to "rational" criteria; with Coleridge, American Transcendentalists might uphold the power of reason immediately to apprehend religious truth; but Presbyterians, anchored in the sobering perspectives of both Calvinism and the Baconian Philosophy, looked aghast upon such views. It was in combat against both forms of "rationalism" that they fashioned the wide-ranging critique of "the propensity to form [theological] theories" and the marked stress upon biblical "facts" so characteristic of Presbyterian writings of the day.[18]

"The moment we commence *speculating* on spiritual things," remonstrated Breckinridge's *Baltimore Literary and Religious Magazine* in 1840, "we abandon those safe principles of philosophizing that have conducted to such astonishing results,—the boast of modern science." Many Presbyterians hoped that the Channings and Emersons alike might be brought to heel with a pointed reminder of the fruitful restraints of the inductive philosophy. The objectionable feature of Unitarian doctrine, for instance, was its principle of "receiving nothing as true but what . . . reason approves," hence its rejection of the "unreasonable" notions of atonement and the Trinity. To the Old School, this procedure was directly equivalent to the elevation of hypothesis over fact in science. It subordinated scriptural truth to an antecedent and man-made norm. "Is it not," queried Samuel Miller, "as Lord Bacon long ago observed, treating God just as we should treat a SUSPECTED WITNESS?"[19] The Christian and theologian had to come to terms with the unconditionally given data of the biblical account. The function of mind confronted with revelation must be quiet and reverent cognition, never a presumptive forging of "conditions." Only a philosophical "smatterer" would have the temerity to determine ahead of time and upon independent grounds "what revelations it becomes infinite wisdom to make."[20] Here, as in science, the only safety lay in *facts*.

Biblical "Fact" versus "Reasoning" in Theology

Thehtwentieth-century expositor of eighteenth- and early nineteenth-century thought will quickly observe that the age made no clear distinction between natural, social, and psychological phenomena. Perhaps the most impressive achievement of the eighteenth century had been the extension of scientific analysis to man and society, and it was broadly assumed that "moral" structures and events were as palpable and orderly as the movement of the planets in their orbits.[21] Nineteenth-century thinkers, including orthodox churchmen, demonstrated that the wide catholicity of scientific method was still accepted by applying the category, "truth," without discrimination to "knowledge" both in natural science and in religion.[22] Hence there was no incongruity in the application of the term "fact," with the precise empirical implications it had acquired in the natural sciences, to matters which a succeeding age would consider much less amenable to empirical analysis. This is essential background for understanding the readiness with which the Old School, in complete accord with existing assumptions, could adapt both "fact" and "induction" to the uses of biblical interpretation. "Christianity regards religion as a matter of fact," announced Stuart Robinson, and "its doctrines, as revealed facts."[23] And just as the role of reason in natural science was to be closely delimited by rigorous attention to natural facts, so the theologian must humbly adjust his own reason to the specific "factual" teachings of Scripture. "Christianity," wrote William B. Sprague, "founds *her* claims upon palpable facts. She does indeed . . . appeal to Reason; . . . but the office which she prescribes to her is that of considering and estimating facts, rather than framing theories."[24]

Both the concept of theological fact and the corresponding estimate of the role of reason in religion had been nurtured since the early 1700s in the now nearly forgotten tradition of the Evidences of Christianity. Formulated in Britain by theologians dramatically impressed with the initial successes of Newtonian empiricism, and elaborated in succeeding decades as the chief orthodox defense against both deism and "enthusiasm," the Evidences quickly became a mainstay of orthodox Protestantism in both Britain and America.[25] Antebellum Presbyterians composed several treatises on the Evidences; shorter expositions in sermons, addresses, and essays number in the hundreds.[26] Briefly put, the Evidences of Christianity were an affirmative theological response to the demand for sensible evidence advanced by Newtonian science. The basic premise was that items of biblical revelation, like propositions in science, could and must be verified empirically. This enabled orthodox Christians to provide theological reason with an impressive function commensurate with its eighteenth-century dignity, yet to skirt rationalist excesses by binding it to factual evidence.

In a time when the increasingly dominant Methodists and Baptists were championing religious emotion, Old School Presbyterians held out staunchly for a more balanced psychology. Fully appreciative of the power of "Experimental religion," they insisted that the biblical message is designed to grasp with integral force the feelings and the understanding.[27] Despite their devotion to a fixed confessional standpoint, they refused to identify dogmatism with the whole of Christian assurance. Before one could attain to the complex state of faith, intellectual work must be done. Christianity does not come with a naked appeal to passion; it "comes, surrounded with evidence . . . ; it challenges investigation; and boldly relies, on the irrefrageable proofs which support its claims." This demand for open and external "evidence" as a ground of belief was a central and guiding tenet of conservative Presbyterian theology during the antebellum years. Revelation was not self-evidencing. Virtually all churchmen agreed with Archibald Alexander that "unless the Christian religion is attended with sufficient evidence, we cannot believe in it, even if we would."[28]

What were the principal "evidences" to which the rational believer might look? The answer had been standardized for over a century in the legion of treatises on the Evidences produced by British—and a few American—Protestants. The evidences were chiefly two: miracles and prophecies.[29] Since historical "facts" did not differ essentially from the physical facts of the natural world, miracles and prophecies could meet admirably the need of the moment, as voiced by Thornwell, for "an external, objective, palpable test."[30] Hence the biblical revelation accorded fully with the empirical baseline of inductive science. The Christ presented in the New Testament summoned his hearers responsibly to appraise the miraculous, *factual* evidences with which his teaching was attested. Did the apostles have misgivings about the reality of the risen Christ? "His personal presence, *manifesting to their senses* the print of the nails and the spear, dispelled every doubt."[31] Trust in the senses was as much a keynote of biblical as of scientific proof. "We must hold that our senses give infallible evidence of what they perceive," explained Henry Ruffner, and the direct sensory experience of the apostolic witnesses recorded in convincing detail in the biblical report could be no less cogent, for example, than the journal of observations and results kept by an experimental chemist. Hence "with such evidence as these twelve men alleged for the death and resurrection of Christ,—the evidence of their senses fortified by the evidence of many others,—who could doubt or who could be mistaken?"[32] The recorded instances of prophecy fulfilled that crowded the pages of Scripture were likewise objective evidences which Christians might marshal to confirm their faith.[33] The whole weight of the Evidences thus rested upon an empirical conception of biblical events and doctrines as *facts* directed to the senses, as "*Knowledge*—like any other complete and positive knowledge, capable of a purely *Objective* treatment."[34] Thus theology, like natural science, dealt in the hard currency of substantial, reliable, verifiable fact.

Consequently, biblical authority did not rest upon the simple fiat either of its authors or of the Spirit by whom they were guided. Protestant Christianity, Presbyterians never tired of saying, was not an ignorant faith that believed on trust unsupported by reasons. Contrary to Unitarian insinuation, it did not oppose but championed free inquiry. The submissive "implicit faith" of Catholics who trusted blindly in ecclesiastical authority was held in high contempt, as befitting a closed, totalitarian system of religion.[35] Presbyterians were good republicans because they compelled the citizenry to the labor of personal inquiry and rational decision. But at the same time, they avoided assigning exorbitant privileges to the human mind by identifying rational inquiry with the disciplined assessment of palpable evidence. By this token, such speculative notions as Jonathan Edwards's "Being-in-general" must be excised from theological discourse, for there was nothing explicit in either nature or Scripture to which it could be said to correspond.[36] This also was the criterion consistently applied by Presbyterians to the presumptive freedom from the direct and literal sense of Scripture to which Unitarians and Christian Transcendentalists laid claim. "A book comes to us purporting to be a revelation from God. Examine the proofs which it brings to substantiate this claim. If they are incontrovertible, believe the book. . . . If they are insufficient, burn the volume." This passage, by James W. Alexander, mirrors concisely the major Presbyterian conception of what Alexander's father had called "the right use of reason in religion."[37] Both their heavy interest in Baconian science and their unquestioning devotion to the tradition of the Evidences had taught the orthodox that the intellectual commitments that Scripture demands of believers "depend upon and are controlled by evidence."[38] The reason that a man consents to the truth of Scripture, in the words of William S. Plumer, is that "he sees the force of the evidence." God had made it obligatory upon the minds of men to pursue evidence alone. If in the first instance Scripture was but a claim to revelatory truth, it had not rested its claim upon humanly discernible criteria of reasonableness or intuition, but had surrounded itself with "a blaze of evidence." Thornwell referred the whole duty of man in regard to the right use of reason in religion "to the single comprehensive principle that evidence is the measure of assent."[39]

The main point was that facts in Scripture, as facts in nature, were irreproachable: "The relation in which we stand to the supernatural disclosures of an authentic revelation is analogous to that which, according to . . . Bacon, we sustain to nature. As the phenomena of the material world are not to be *judged*, but *seen*, so the mysteries of heaven are not to be *judged*, but apprehended."[40] This was Thornwell's authoritative summary of the general orthodox position. Reason had no more right to criticize given phenomena than to ignore them. The analogy between nature and Scripture was sweeping. John H. Rice's early *Christian Monitor* had concluded that Newton was the best-equipped exegete of all time because he brought to the Bible "a mind tutored by the philosophy of facts. . . . He saw that the religion of the Gospel is a religion of facts." Reason was restricted to operating upon data which in themselves were already inviolably whole, fully invested with the overwhelming prerogatives assigned to empirical data in the inductive philosophy. Lewis W. Green fairly shouted, "*The Gospel is a Religion of Facts*."[41] The atonement, the Trinity, the sinfulness of man, the resurrection of Christ—all the great doctrines of biblical Protestantism were facts, as solid and unimpeachable as the upheaving of geological masses in the earth's crust.[42] The Unitarian presumption that would subject the atonement to the test of reasonableness was therefore of a piece with the perverse theorizing spirit that would "frame plausible objections to the structure of the universe."[43] Facts were simply facts, by nature incontrovertible. And if evidence was the measure of assent, then reason, once satisfied of the evidences buttressing any doctrine, culminated itself in the role of obeisant recipient. Reason, finally, was to faith like the telescope to the eye of the astronomer; it could only gaze, receive, adore.[44] With that, the demolition of "rationalism" was stunningly complete. Unaccustomed to giving the slightest quarter in theological debate, however, the *Southern Presbyterian Review* proceeded to sever the final nerve of subjective pretension with a quote from pious Bacon: "We are to believe His word, though we find a reluctation in our reason."[45]

So it was, in the end, again a question for the Baconian Philosophy. James W. Alexander thought it "the doctrine of the Baconian philosophy, that theology is grounded only upon the word and oracle of God."[46] The empire of fact was thus as securely established in theology as ever in natural science. Yet the naturalization of Scripture was to bring forth still greater results. If the Bible was in effect now integrated into the manifold of natural truth, might it not be approached with the methods of science? And might Christian theology on these grounds not establish itself as a genuine "science" according to the canons of the day? From early in the century these thoughts often had obtruded themselves into key Presbyterian minds. The Evidences of Christianity were styled by one thinker as an "inductive philosophy of religion," in which "by an induction of facts we prove that the Bible comes from God." Presbyterians could find no fundamental difference between the proper function of the rational intellect in science and in theology. A Bible construed in terms of "phenomena" admits "the same rules of investigation that are applied to any department of knowledge." Thomas Smyth agreed that reason "has precisely the same office, and the same province, in regard to all truth."[47] Nothing could be more revealing of the orthodox mind than these unabashed admissions. They indicate a sweeping commitment to Enlightenment modes of thought and point to a fundamental antipathy with the newer romantic Transcendentalism and its radical distinction between the scientific "Understanding" and the nonempirical, nonratiocinative "reason" of poetry and religion. But more, they lay the conceptual groundwork for one of the most remarkable hermeneutical undertakings in the history of American Christianity.

Baconianism and the Bible: The New Organum of Christian Theology

"It has been an extended notion, since the prevalence of the Baconian method in scientific research, that just as the facts of nature lie before us in the universe, and have to be generalized and systematized by the process of induction, so also the facts of theology lying before us in the Bible, have simply to be moulded into a logical series, in order to create a Christian theology." These were the words, penned in contempt, of J. D. Morell, an articulate Transcendentalist and mediator of the theology of Schleiermacher to the Anglo-American world during the 1840s and 1850s. Transcendentalist disdain for the heavy empiricist strain in British and American theology peaked in Morell's repeated and snarling abuse of "the Baconian method" as a theological instrument.[48] Yet his commentary is a valuable register of the extent to which by mid-century the Baconian ideal had been appropriated by traditional theologians as a technique of biblical interpretation. It was indeed "an extended notion" that the method that had proved so capable of unraveling nature's secrets might achieve equally gratifying results when brought to bear upon the biblical materials. As the prestige of the Baconian Philosophy began to rise, the logic that had equated Scripture with natural fact led almost irresistibly to a program of Baconian theology. The height of this fascinating development was reached in 1860 when J. S. Lamar, a Georgia pastor and theologian affiliated with the Disciples of Christ, published his *The Organon of Scripture: Or, the Inductive Method of Biblical Interpretation*. This remarkable work, which deserves some attention from intellectual and church historians, submitted to the Christian public a plan to methodize Protestant theology on the basis of the inductive philosophy. Lamar's starting point was the naturalization of Scripture: *"The whole Bible is founded upon facts."* Relying heavily on Herschel's outline of induction, and with plentiful invocation of "Lord Bacon," he wished to show that "the Scriptures admit of being studied and expounded upon the principles of the inductive method; and that, when thus interpreted, they speak to us in a voice as certain and unmistakable as the language of nature heard in the experiments and observations of science." This procedure would render theology *"a science"* in the literal acceptation of the word. In thus plotting an inductive science of the Bible, Lamar understood himself to be presenting "radically and essentially" a new departure in Christian theology. Induction, he believed, had "never been presented and urged as the Method of Biblical Interpretation."[49] Nothing, however, could have been farther from the mark. The *Organon of Scripture* was as uninformed as it was intriguing. It was, in fact, the culmination of an effort in theological reconception that had been carried on and developed by British and American theologians for at least three decades before Lamar published. In this movement, conservative Presbyterians seem to have played a major role.

The idea of an inductive biblical theology was not born in the nineteenth century. A number of Puritan thinkers had maintained that the Bible should be approached exactly as was the natural world. Richard Baxter specifically "gave his approval . . . to the Baconian method of induction and experiment, recommending that it be used for ferreting out the truths of the Bible as well as nature."[50] But the suggestion produced little result. Puritans developed no natural science of Scripture, and the closest approximation of it in the following epoch was probably the Evidences. The rapid rise and the wide appeal of Baconianism in the early decades of the nineteenth century first created the conditions under which the effort might flourish. As indicated by Morell, the pattern of induction won "extended" recognition within current religious thought. It was by no means limited to American Presbyterians, although it does appear to have had particular appeal to the various Calvinist churches. J. S. Lamar, as mentioned, was a Disciple. A cardinal intention of the Congregationalist *Literary and Theological Review*, established in New York in 1834 by Leonard Woods, Jr., was to coordinate Bacon and the Bible. This was to be done through a literal and rigorous application of "the method of observation and induction" and was expected to produce as sound and complete a "system of knowledge" as any branch of natural science.[51] In 1835 the same journal published a significant article by an Episcopalian scholar entitled "Theology a

Strictly Inductive Science." B. B. Smith, the author, asserted that the key to a modern system of theology must be "the Baconian system" and predicted that the proper use of the inductive method would place the theologian upon a par of prestige and certainty with the scientist.[52] In the mid-1840s Laurens P. Hickok, a prominent New School Presbyterian thinker, presented an essay in the *American Biblical Repository* on "Christian Theology as a Science," which pleaded similarly for inductive reconstruction in theology.[53] Later in the decade a second Episcopalian, Silas Totten, added his quota to the growing Baconian consciousness. Let the exegete employ induction, and he may put biblical theology "in form like a treatise on Mathematics and Natural Philosophy."[54] Immediately after Totten wrote, the great Scottish Presbyterian Thomas Chalmers picked up the theme in his *Institutes of Theology*. Theological construction approached from the standpoint of "Lord Bacon's Philosophy" could make the doctrine of atonement, for example, "as little a thing of invention and as much a thing of discovery, as the doctrine of gravitation in nature."[55] The *New Englander* and the *Bibliotheca Sacra*, prominent Congregationalist periodicals, shortly presented reviews of the *Institutes*, giving particular and highly affirmative attention to "the application of the Baconian principles of philosophizing to theology." Here at last was a procedure that could vindicate to theology "the name of *science*."[56] That at least one writer attempted to carry out the inductive project in a specific treatise was indicated in the mid-1850s by William Lindsay Alexander's *Christ and Christianity*. Alexander, a Scottish Presbyterian whose work was published in an American edition, explained that "my aim has been, by a process of strictly inductive reasoning, to place the claims of Christianity upon a solid philosophical basis."[57]

Though far from exhaustive, this sketch of available evidence makes it amply clear that Morell was right. The Baconian ideal exerted a highly significant impact upon religious thought in the period of our study. Presbyterian contributions to an inductive norm of theology must be understood against a much larger background of activity. A more detailed investigation of theological Baconianism in the context of the Old School will shed valuable light upon the shape and meaning of this little-studied configuration in American religious thought. It will also suggest that the conservative Presbyterian contribution to its development was vital.

The irresistible power of the inductive philosophy began to manifest itself early in nineteenth-century Presbyterian theology. It could be seen in rudimentary form in a frequent and emphatic appeal to "facts" in support of a given proposition. On the premises both of plenary inspiration and of the naturalization of Scripture, an assemblage of pertinent biblical data could serve as unbreachable heavy artillery in any theological debate. Thus in 1835 Samuel Miller could undertake to establish "infant Baptism Scriptural and Reasonable" by a simple gathering and display of the "evidence." So potent was the argument from facts that an epitome of "the direct evidence in favour of infant baptism" seemed "nothing short of a *demonstration*."[58] In the following year the editors of the *Baltimore Literary and Religious Magazine* proposed to prove "that there is a future and eternal state of rewards and punishments." Having collected the "direct Scripture proof," blocks of passages ordered under relevant headings, they considered the matter settled by proof "more firm than the enduring earth and glorious sky."[59] Simple recourse to the data was eminently common. It reached its ultimate expression in Hodge's huge *Systematic Theology*, where the word "fact," or its equivalent, "truth," occurs twenty-seven times in the first section of three pages![60]

An additional logical step toward a full Baconian theology was taken by a number of authors who appealed to fact under the specific rubric of induction. In his influential *Lectures on the Shorter Catechism*, published serially during the 1820s in the *Christian Advocate*, Ashbel Green marshaled "the whole force of inductive reasoning" on behalf of the social and moral utility of "temporal punishments." That the good of society was plainly served by the frequent visitation of misbehavior with punishing consequences was a principle easily induced from the data of social experience as any "philosophical induction from the visible universe."[61] A more vivid example of inductive procedure appeared in the *Evangelical and Literary Magazine* in 1824. Induction, asserted a contributor in a remarkable passage, is preeminently "the method of the Christian. . . . The conclusion that he is a child of God, and his hope of acceptance, rest on the evidence of induction from a number of particulars. Indeed this is as complete an exemplification of this method as can be found in the whole range of philosophy. His faith, his love, his repentance, his gratitude &c. are all examined. . . . his conclusion, and his hope . . . rest on the evidence . . . furnished by all of them combined."[62] All major theological doctrines seemed susceptible of inductive demonstration. The universality of sin, the "felt necessity" of a saving revelation, the fallibility of all men—including, to be sure, the Pope!—the connection between "trifling with the Truth" and "fearful retribution," the operation of grace upon the heart—all were open to "a rigid induction of particular facts."[63] Benjamin M. Palmer was even convinced that the event of the Fall could be inducted from the facts of sin and suffering just as geologists had inferred the Deluge from the "whole layers of rock thrown up transversely" on the earth's surface![64]

As revealing as such references are for the intellectual historian, they are but introductory to the fuller and more important pattern of Baconian theology that simultaneously was being worked out by key thinkers within the Old School. From its sixteenth-century beginnings, Calvinism had elaborated a highly systematic ideal of Christian theology. Calvin's own *Institutes of the Christian Religion* had established a pattern of rigorous systematic thinking which was carried to a height in the immensely ordered productions of seventeenth-century Reformed scholasticism.[65] Since its emergence early in the eighteenth century, conservative Presbyterianism in America had been doctrinally oriented to the great Reformed scholastics—Francis Turretine, Johannes Wollebius, and others—and particularly to the harmonious body of dogma produced by the Westminster Assembly of 1647.[66] One of the distinguishing characteristics of the Old School was its continued allegiance to the systematic orientation of traditional Calvinism, especially as represented by Turretine and the Westminster standards.[67]

Accordingly, Old School literature contains a persistent note of derision for the singular and "isolated" fact, for "fragments and atoms, floating hither and thither, without centre of attraction or bond of unity." No Presbyterian thinker would have disagreed with Robert J. Breckinridge that "Pervading order and coherence" were inexorable demands of the human intellect in its search for salvation.[68] There is also apparent a tendency to conceive the orderliness of Christian doctrine by analogy with the sweeping coherence of the Newtonian cosmos. Revelation, like nature, was "a mighty whole," whose parts interlocked in a program of law no less integrated than the principles that regulate the movements of astronomical bodies.[69]

In the early nineteenth century, however, Presbyterian devotion to theology as an interconnected system had come under heavy fire. For the detestation of speculation and hypothesis which so deeply affected intellectual life of the era often was accompanied by an equally fervent distrust of "systems" of thought.[70] Presbyterians abhorred the widespread tendency, epitomized by the "Christian" movement of the 1820s, "to do away with all human creeds and systematic treatises, and to study the Bible only."[71] Throughout the preceding century the systematic ideal of knowledge had played a sovereign part in the mainstream of ideas. Yet despite the heavy empiricism characteristic of the Enlightenment, system was conceived throughout primarily in deductive terms.[72] But owing to the mounting infatuation with facts and Baconian inductivism precipitated by the Scottish Philosophy, this older ideal suffered quick abridgment. In both America and Britain, the rise of Baconianism signaled a deep crisis in the realm of ideas. Now for a time an ascendant and intolerant empiricism was to thrust the long-standing deductive approach to the articulation of system into disrepute and to force reconception along the more consistently "factual" lines of the inductive philosophy. The Baconian theology, which in succeeding decades gradually moved toward the center of Presbyterian ideas, represents just such an inductive reconstruction of systematic theology.

The close analogy between Scripture and nature, the interest of abstraction, the use of induction in theological debate—all the elements that were to converge in a new Baconian program for theology—were present by the 1820s. Already in 1830 an anonymous Calvinist pamphleteer was presenting himself as "a Baconian Biblist."[73] Late in the same decade, these themes suddenly began to intersect in the solid conservative mind of Jacob Jones Janeway. Entering the professorship of theology in the new Western Theological Seminary in 1828, Janeway gave a nearly complete expression to the pattern which was heavily to condition Old School thought in the ensuing period. Janeway set out to answer recent critics who had attacked systematic theology as a "speculative" venture, as an unwarranted manipulation of the "natural" order of Scripture:

We conceive that, by classifying and arranging the doctrines and precepts of Holy Scripture, in a different and connected form, we do not reflect on the wisdom of . . . [God's] plan. . . . [The theologian] only does what has been done in every other branch of knowledge. The astronomer exhibits the results of his study of the heavenly bodies in a systematic form. . . . The natural philosopher makes his observations and experiments, and thus ascertains a number of facts. These facts he compares and studies, and thus learns certain general principles. These principles he arranges under particular heads, to which he refers the several facts that go to support them; and so form his branch of science into a regular system. In the same way acts the Botanist, the Mineralogist, the Chymist [sic] and all students of nature. . . . And why may not the student of Theology imitate philosophers in conducting his studies of the sacred Scriptures? Why may he not, as he reads his Bible, refer its various portions to particular heads? . . . I wish to know what the inspired writers have said of Jesus Christ. I collect their testimonies, scattered here and there in the Bible, under particular heads; such as his natures, his person, his humiliation, his exaltation, his offices and his benefits. Thus arranged, I compare them, and find my faith established in his divinity and mediatorial character; and I am convinced that there is salvation in him, . . . In a word, I find that, although the Bible has not been presented in a systematic form, yet it does contain a beautiful, harmonious and glorious system of divine truth.[74]

The Bible "not presented in a systematic form"!—here was the gnawing thought which seemed to put all theological systems to an impossible test. But the Baconian model of scientific construction was adequate to the emergency. Janeway, in short, had found the obvious way of restoring the intellectual prospects of "beautiful, harmonious" system in the new inductivist climate.

Since the sensed danger to systematic thought is clearly the precipitating factor in suggesting the analogy drawn between scientist and theologian, the analogy itself has not yet become the focus of interest. Yet the seed of future developments has been implanted securely; the claim has been put forward that theological method is a detailed imitation of natural science. No idea was to be more important in giving distinctive shape to later Old School concepts of the theological task.

Writing in 1832, James W. Alexander gave additional indication that Presbyterian determination to protect systematic theology was a primary force giving rise to the new scientific formula. Like Janeway, Alexander was agitated by claims that the "beautiful simplicity" with which scriptural truth was already arranged was perverted by "the artifice of systems." Repeatedly citing Bacon and Herschel, Alexander worked out a response which may be taken as an advance beyond Janeway to a full statement of theological Baconianism:

Let the Scriptures be considered as analogous to the visible universe; and its several propositions as holding the same place with regard to the interpreter, which the phenomena of the heavens do with regard to the astronomer. Let it be agreed that the method of arriving at truth is in both instances the same, that is, by careful examination of these data, from which result generalization, cautious induction, and the position of ultimate principles. . . . exegesis answers to experiment or observation in the natural world, and consequently . . . the theologian is to consider exegetical results as the basis of all his reasonings. . . . We avow our belief that the theologian should proceed in his investigation precisely as the chemist or the botanist proceeds. . . . [This] is the method which bears the name of Bacon.

With this passage, the chapter could well close. Although by the 1850s the Baconian formula was to become widely adopted by the intellectual leadership of the Old School church, no thinker added essential details to Alexander's conception. Whereas Janeway had been satisfied with an imprecise announcement that the exegete "does what has been done" in natural science, Alexander had pinpointed the functions of the theological scientist. Scripture, nature, facts, induction, and Bacon were now interwoven into an unprecedented construct of theological *science*. Janeway's principal purpose had been defense. His leading aim had been to show that systematic construction did not involve destruction of the natural integrity of Scripture. But Alexander was more distinctly interested in the positive, constructive possibilities of conforming exegesis to a scientific model. He was disposed to urge the virtues of Baconian technique as a means of ascertaining the plan and harmony of scriptural truth. Armed with the crucial premise that the "propositions" given to the theologian answer to the "phenomena" with which the scientist's work begins, he then was able quickly to render the Calvinist veneration for systematics consistent with the increasingly sovereign vogue of induction.[75]

In the course of his Baconian deliberations, however, Alexander came upon an arresting difficulty. The immediate appeal to singular facts with which the inductive theologian must begin left the status of *preexisting* systems and creeds dangerously in doubt. Induction might easily be seized upon as a pretense to scuttle the elaborate forms of orthodoxy and begin afresh with a direct examination of Scripture in the manner of the "Christians" and the Disciples of Christ. Whether Alexander actually knew of such efforts is not clear from his account, but in future years both Laurens P. Hickok and J. S. Lamar were to design their sketches of theological induction as an assault upon "the conflicting systems of doctoral divinity."[76] Alexander at any rate, and Leroy J. Halsey a decade later, took pains to eliminate the possibility of discrepancies between a Baconian theology and orthodox doctrine. The answer was as obvious as the objection. No competent researcher ever comes to nature void of a thorough knowledge of precedent scientific labors. The theologian, then, no less than the scientist, will make full use of the aid afforded by prior research. But this reply carried with it an interesting implication for the dogmatic concerns of conservative Presbyterians, for it distinctly subordinated the existing body of doctrine to present biblical research. The inductive analogy did not admit fresh interpretation to be merely a ratification of work already completed. Thus Alexander, than whom there was no more dedicated proponent of orthodoxy within the Old School, explicitly designated "a system of theology" as "a simple *hypothesis*, an approximation to the truth, and a directory for future inquiries." Halsey's response to the problem was similar. In this way, the logic of induction served to magnify the strength of biblicism over preexisting doctrinal authority.[77]

From about 1830, the Baconian adaptation of Christian theology suggested by Janeway and Alexander was quickly diffused into conservative sectors of American Presbyterianism. John H. Rice's fledgling Union Theological Seminary in Virginia had in 1828 explicitly styled its professorship of theology an inductive office. The incumbent's role was to be formed openly on the model of science.[78] In the following year Hodge's *Princeton Review* pronounced its approval of "exegetical induction" and followed up in 1831 with an expression of regret that "very few of the theological works most in vogue, appear like the productions of thoroughly inductive minds. And yet no department of knowledge needs to be more entirely under the guidance of the inductive mode of reasoning and exhibiting truth, than theology."[79] In later years this advice was taken seriously by an impressive number of important figures like Halsey, Thomas Smyth, George Howe, Benjamin M. Palmer, Nathan L. Rice, James Read Eckard, Benjamin Morgan Smith, and A. A. Hodge, all of whom invoked the solidifying image of the theological scientist, steeped in the Baconian Philosophy, patiently and inductively coaxing the chaotic raw materials of revelation into scientific order.[80] For Palmer, the fact that "the Theologian and the Inductive Philosopher proceed on similar principles" was an additional consideration marking the rootage of Baconianism in Protestant Christianity.[81]

When James H. Thornwell and Charles Hodge added their voices to the growing acclaim for a truly scientific theology, it could no longer be denied that the inductive philosophy had been established at the core of conservative Presbyterianism. For by common consent these were the two preeminent intellects of the Old School church during the last two decades before the Civil War.[82] Since both were intense admirers of the work of Samuel Tyler, it was undoubtedly of first significance that the latter's *Discourse of the Baconian Philosophy* had included an affirmative examination of the theological potential of induction, which he regarded as "the proper mode . . . of interpreting the Scriptures."[83] By 1847, at any rate, Thornwell had caught the vision of theology as inductive science. Writing the lead article in the first volume of the *Southern Presbyterian Review*, he added an impressive quota of proof that the Baconian hermeneutic was taking the South by storm:

Interpretation is to theology what observation and experiment are to philosophy. As it is the business of science . . . patiently to investigate the facts of nature . . . so it is the business of reason in regard to revelation . . . to interpret with humility and digest with reverence what God has chosen to communicate. . . . The facts of uniformity, constitute law, and these laws, arranged into system, constitute science. . . . The facts of revelation are its doctrines . . . and these reduced to method, according to their dependencies and connexions, constitute theology. . . . These seem to have been the views of Bacon.[84]

Although the specific application of induction was not spelled out in this passage, Thornwell's later "Inaugural Address" delivered at the Theological Seminary in Columbia did indicate that the data of revelation were not "reduced to method" until they had been inductively referred "to the laws, the philosophy if you please, which underlies them."[85]

In his published antebellum writings, Charles Hodge does not appear to have given direct attention to the Baconian formula, although there is a passing clue in 1850 that he too was falling in to the ranks of those giving homage to the idea of inductive exegesis. In one of his noisy broadsides against Edwards Amasa Park, he reminded his antagonist, who appeared to be fudging on biblical literalism, that "generalizations of the intellect . . . are summations of the manifold and diversified representations of Scripture."[86] Throughout the period, however, in his stimulating and immensely influential courses in theology at Princeton Seminary, Hodge's massive *Systematic Theology* was gradually taking form. And the final product, which was not published until 1873, gives evidence not only that Hodge had adopted the Baconian pattern but also that he saw in it a basic foundation of his systematic work. For here, in what is indisputably the most complete and definitive theological production of the Old School, the methodological statement is explicitly founded upon the scientific analogy. That theology is a "science" is illustrated with reference to the organization of knowledge in chemistry and "mechanical philosophy." Biblical propositions are compared with the "oceans, continents, islands, mountains and rivers" and "the distribution of land and water" studied by the geographer. Most important, the modes of analysis and generalization in science and theology are closely assimilated. God, thought Hodge,

does not teach men astronomy or chemistry, but He gives them the facts out of which those sciences are constructed. Neither does He teach us systematic theology, but He gives us in the Bible the truths which, properly understood and arranged, constitute the science of theology. As the facts of nature are all related and determined by physical laws, so the facts of the Bible are all related and determined by the nature of God and of his creatures. And as He wills that men should study his works and discover their wonderful organic relation and harmonious combination, so it is his will that we should study his Word, and learn that, like the stars, its truths are not isolated points, but systems, cycles, and epicycles, in unending harmony and grandeur.

The method of theology, Hodge added, is the "Inductive Method," so called because "it agrees in everything essential with the inductive method as applied to the natural sciences. . . . The Bible is to the theologian what nature is to the man of science. It is his storehouse of facts; and . . . [he] must be guided by the same rules in the collection of facts, as govern the man of science. . . . [The] collection must be made with diligence and care. . . . In theology as in natural science, principles are derived from facts. . . . [Just so will the theologian induct] his theory of virtue, of sin, of liberty, of obligation, from the facts of the Bible."[87] Hodge's is at once the most thoroughgoing and revealing statement of the identification of theological method with the inductive understanding of natural science to which the Old School had come to be devoted.

The project of a Baconian theology obviously was resonant to the zeal for science which loomed as a formative factor in antebellum American life. Arising among a group of churchmen who themselves were partaking enthusiastically of the diffusion of scientific interest, it reflected a conviction that positive confrontation with contemporary intellectual culture was a vital function of theology. How better to formulate a mission to the increasingly "scientific" intellect of educated America than to exhibit Christian theology as a royal example of the inductive philosophy? And how more appropriately to defend the dogmatic positions of orthodox Calvinism in the modern era than to present them as the inevitable issue of inductive research in the text of Scripture? Theologians, further, need no longer cringe before the common charge that creedal Calvinism was a "dead orthodoxy" out of tune with the times, or that it brought reproach upon the dignity of human reason. Doctrine rested upon no less extensive an application of the reasoning powers than the generalizations upon which the Newtonian view of nature was founded. A theology neatly yoked to Baconianism plausibly could claim to be attuned to the progressive state of learning demanded by the "thoughtful and argumentative race" to whom the Presbyterian message was principally addressed.[88]

For numerous additional reasons, inductive theology suited the theological needs of conservative Presbyterianism. In the first place, it provided a ready means in terms of currently popular ideas to foil the "speculative" pretensions of Unitarians and Transcendentalists. To identify high doctrines of reason with the fanciful "a priorism" and disregard for fact so odious to all good Baconians was a resourceful if obvious tactic. The implication was that opponents of strict Calvinism were not only enemies of the cautious spirit of modern science but also—incredibly!—disbelievers in the refulgent genius of Lord Bacon himself. Baconian theology thwarted alike the "reasonable" scruples of Unitarians and the inordinate prerogatives which Transcendentalists granted to intuitive reason by limiting the range of inquiry to the indubitable facts of Scripture. These alone were to form the basis of general formulations in religion. The inductive philosophy, as James W. Alexander explained, corresponded with the nature of biblical Christianity because it "is limited in all its speculations by the facts of revelation."[89] The scientific investigator "sees, or ascertains by observation, what are the laws which determine material phenomena," taught Hodge; "he does not invent those laws. His speculations on matters of science unless sustained by facts, are worthless. It is no less unscientific for the theologian to assume a theory . . . and then explain the facts of Scripture in accordance."[90] Hence the massive opprobrium which Baconians long had heaped upon abstraction now plausibly could be brought to bear upon the a priori tendencies with which conservative Presbyterians found much current religious thought adulterated.

Second, aside from specific polemical concerns, the inductive conception of theology underwrote with peculiar efficacy the stringent biblical literalism characteristic of the Old School.[91] Churchmen drilled to think of Scripture as an objective display of revelation understandably were pleased with the privileged treatment accorded "given" data in the Baconian Philosophy. The Old School was predictably charmed with the logic by which a text could be equated with a rose and a star in the broad field of nature. And further, if the inductive philosophy was a systematic method of enforcing "the great Baconian principle, that . . . we are . . . simply to take facts as we find them, as the ground of every inference," then the immediate authority of Scripture in its obvious meanings was delightfully enhanced.[92]

Third, and by the same token, orthodox dedication to a carefully systematic, ordered ideal of doctrine gained much in intellectual strength through the analogy with the physical universe. For Presbyterians, with educated Americans at large, were dazzled with *the order and harmony of nature* elaborated in Newtonian science.[93] This vision of a symmetrical and grandly interconnected Kosmos was now superimposed with thrilling effect upon the sprawling profusion of biblical thought, producing a heightened sense of doctrinal harmony and proportion. For Hodge and his colleagues, the "wonderful organic relation and harmonious combination" of things were as real in revelation as in nature. The proper harmony of scriptural thought, moreover, was not to be discerned within the deductive frameworks of the past. James W. Alexander damned the orderly but venturesome reasoning of Nathanael Emmons as "nothing else but a string of bold, unconnected assertions. . . . there is no [factual] proof of any one."[94] In the same manner, Hodge, reviewing Charles G. Finney's *Lectures on Theology*, appraised the work as a cleverly linked but specious performance which arbitrarily asserted postulates and traced them out to logical conclusions. The end result in each case was tidily systematic but not inductively anchored.[95] Thus the Baconian theology to which the Old School had granted allegiance by the latter antebellum years denoted a thoroughgoing disillusionment with the deductive force of "reason alone" as an instrument for ordering knowledge.

An interesting corollary of the inductive approach to Scripture was an implicit deprecation of its singular events and texts. "Facts" in any domain, however essential they were as the basis of authentic generalizations, were of themselves inarticulate, "isolated," "incoherent," even "hostile" until reduced to a system of order. Hence "if among the facts of science an isolated truth here and another there, seems to lift its frowning front in irreconcilable hostility, it is only because we have not yet descended to the solid base where all stand knit together."[96] This clearly expressed disdain for the singular is additional evidence for the continuing commitment of Old School orthodoxy to Enlightenment premises. Early in the century, the *Evangelical and Literary Magazine* had enjoined its readers against an uncritical equation of scriptural and natural facts, warning that "the facts recorded in the gospel, are of an extraordinary nature; that, in a certain sense, they are solitary . . . [and] *sui generis*."[97] But to this caveat the later inductivists gave little heed. The identification of Christian doctrine with scientific generalizations explicitly denigrated the realm of the particular and unique in biblical thought. The theological scientist was conversant indeed with facts, but facts only as they indicated universal "laws." In Scripture as in nature, "every fact is single," declared Thomas Smyth, but these must serve as fodder for the elaboration of "general truths and comprehensive systems of knowledge. Otherwise, the human mind would know *nothing* . . . *but particular facts*."[98] And this was unacceptable to a church dedicated to an orderly pattern of dogmatic teaching.

Finally, the identification of theological with scientific generalizations provided an additional line of defense for crucial doctrinal positions. Numerous churchmen found the concept of "inducted" doctrine a welcome aid in rendering orthodox principles invulnerable to assault. Thomas Smyth thus was able to rebut Unitarian detractors of the Trinity by adverting to the strictly scientific manner in which the doctrine could be derived. "First," said Smyth, "the facts or truths as they actually exist must be discovered and then they must be arranged, classified, and systematized, in order that from them may be deduced general truths." When this procedure was followed in reference to the truths about the divine nature strewn through Scripture, the inevitable result must be—the Trinity![99] This venerable doctrine was thus both guarded from muddled rationalist objections and enriched with the special certitude enjoyed by the established principles of natural philosophy.

In sum, these considerations make it evident that the Old School was in a unique position to appreciate the advantages of a Baconian model of theological interpretation. The combination of doctrinal traditionalism with the most recent scientific concepts was a striking indication of the intellectual versatility of a church determined to render the insights of the past functional in the present. The Baconian focus upon method made it possible to alter theological tactics without compromising the content of biblical teaching as traditionally understood. Underlying this adaptation was the common understanding that the apparatus of Baconianism was designed to explicate and *not to modify* an already given and completed order of things. With the help of this premise, the Old School finally found it possible to incorporate induction itself into the purview of the sacred and orthodox. Just as science was grounded in Protestant Christianity, so was induction, simply, the reverent and efficacious handmaid of the science of divinity.

8.

Summary and Concluding Reflections

The previous chapters of this study have sought to elaborate a progression of argument which may be summarized as follows:

1. Origins of the configuration "Baconianism" may be traced in the writings of the two principal Scottish Realists, Thomas Reid and Dugald Stewart. Of its defining characteristics, the two most important for the subsequent history of the Baconian Philosophy were zeal for "natural philosophy" and an acutely focused hostility toward abstraction in science. Francis Bacon, the originator of inductive method, was put forth as the father of modern science. "Induction" meant a direct generalization of fact that left little place for speculative ingenuity or for theoretic elements in scientific explanation.

2. Mediated by the tremendous popularity of the Scottish Philosophers, Baconianism became established in the early decades of the nineteenth century as a major pattern in the American mind.

3. In view both of its breadth of intellectual interests and of its intimate connection, through the lineage of John Witherspoon and Princeton, with the Scottish Philosophy, the antebellum Old School is a highly suitable candidate for an American case study in the Baconian ideal.

4. A thesis that found much influential support in the eighteenth and early nineteenth centuries depicted religion as a bigoted opponent of the searching spirit of inquiry presupposed in science. Old School churchmen countered this "infidel" perspective by

portraying Protestant Christianity as an energizer and friend of scientific inquiry. Since the natural world was a Divine construct, its investigation could only advance the cause of belief. The problem was to assure that inquiry did not stray from the immediate elevating "truth" of the Creation. This was achieved by associating truth with Realist empiricism and with the inductive philosophy fathered by Bacon.

5. Illustrative of the Presbyterian wish to secure a broad harmonization of science with religion was the "beatification of Bacon," a portrayal of the founder of science as a pious evangelical believer. This Protestant hallowing of Lord Bacon reflected a "doxological" view of natural science, which styled the scientist a worshipful elucidator of the Divine Creation. The conception of research as praise rested on a long tradition of scientific piety and concentrated on manifestations in nature of providential design, order, and care.

6. Churchmen, however, were aware that science, if divorced from religious controls, could elaborate a secular and heretical view of nature. This menacing prospect was kept before the American public by the publication of scientific theories which not only avoided attributing cause and order to Divine agency but also failed to exhibit the necessary harmony between the God of nature and of Scripture.

7. The Presbyterian reaction was not withdrawal from science, but an aggressive effort to monitor it. For this purpose, the inductive philosophy seemed a strategic godsend, suggesting at least five basic tactics: (a) identify objectionable findings with the dubious realm of "theory" and "hypothesis"; (b) emphasize that authoritative induction must embrace *all* relevant facts; (c) point out that biblical "facts" cannot logically be excluded from a scientific induction if pertinent; (d) present a self-effacing style of "humility" as the prerequisite attitude for inductive research; (e) underscore the incompleteness and mutability of scientific explanation.

8. Thus richly assured that scientific affronts to doxological science and to religious orthodoxy could be met with the Baconian fund of restraints, a number of prominent Old School churchmen turned their attention in the 1850s to additional constructive

projects in Christian Baconianism. Two major developments under this heading were: (a) a fusion of catastrophist geology with the biblically forecast millennium; (b) a proof that the Baconian Philosophy itself originated under the stimulus of the Protestant Reformation. Hence "there never could have been a Bacon without the Bible."

9. The linked train of Baconian and doxological associations reached its culmination in a widespread Presbyterian attempt to turn the inductive method directly to the service of biblical interpretation. Based on a concept of biblical content as fact verified in sensory experience, this would produce as pure a strain of literal truth as any of the Baconian natural sciences and equally uncorrupted by arrogant abstractions. The Baconian Philosophy, in the end, thus was tidily assimilated to the Bible-oriented Protestant Christianity which the Old School understood itself to represent.

Drawing upon the main points developed in the preceding chapters we may now venture some concluding reflections. That until the late nineteenth century Americans either inherited or imported most of their ideas is clear and has been noted by many scholars. The career of Bacon in America is but another example of this talent for borrowing, for it is readily established that the Baconian pattern had a definitive Scottish history. To understand fully the selective principles that guided the transplantation and accommodation of Baconianism to the new world would require a comparative examination of British and American sources beyond the range of this study. Yet it appears evident that the Presbyterian appropriation of the various themes referred to "Lord Bacon" was too enthusiastic and too specifically adjusted at some points to American needs to have been entirely derivative. The dominant notes of empiricism and restraint were well suited to the experiential, earthy, and conservative tone of mind native to nineteenth-century Americans. In Presbyterian orbit, at least, the Baconian Philosophy stimulated thought, encouraged a serious dealing with several intellectual issues of the day, provided a positive and comfortable perspective upon the natural sciences, offered a ready defense against the excesses and dangers of science, and suggested new strategies for the increase of religious influence in the national mind.

An effort has been made throughout the study to relate the Baconian pattern in the Old School mind to a broader environment of ideas. As the history of religious thought always demonstrates, the theologian is part of a larger culture whose patterns condition his outlook in innumerable ways. Antebellum Presbyterians were very much involved in the intellectual life of their own era, and their participation carried forward a long tradition of theological responsibility among Calvinists. It is surely erroneous to presume —with not a few historians of ideas—that nineteenth-century Calvinism was dominated by a tedious preoccupation with outdated dogmatic ideas and not truly worthy of serious study. The churchmen examined here have demonstrated through a direct and intelligent attempt to do justice to the deliverances and issues of then current science that they were in some respects in the forefront of intellectual debate in their own day. If contemporary relevance is one valid criterion by which the significance of historical patterns of thought may be evaluated, the Old School cannot be disregarded as a scholastic anachronism; and if the strict Calvinist insistence upon human depravity, predestination, and other traditional notions seemed daily more archaic in the optimistic and profoundly Pelagian milieu of antebellum America, Presbyterian involvement with natural science produced an important and modernizing counterpoint. To many, the denomination's allegiance to Turretine and the Westminster standards connoted an inflexible and impairing commitment to the past, but its avid reception of Lord Bacon as a patriarch of Protestantism functioned without doubt to reduce tensions between Calvinist doctrine and the modern beliefs and interests of Presbyterian communicants.

The harnessing of epistemology and science into Christian perspective also supplied a second element of counterpoint in antebellum religion. In an age swept and formed by cycle after cycle of revivalism, the controlling attribute of religious life popularly conceived was the personal inwardness of the "new birth." Timothy Smith and others have shown that the inward tides of evangelicalism often were channeled into a larger framework of social concern and reform,[1] but larger concern for the outward and public explorations of the mind was not native to the spirit that bred revivals. Conservative Presbyterianism, too, had by the early nineteenth century accepted initiation in the conventions of evangelical pietism, and the depth of this accommodation was shown by an aggressive emphasis upon the practice of an "eminent piety" of self-searching, prayer, and devotional contemplation which surfaced early in the century as a leading conservative theme.[2] The foregoing study of Presbyterian Baconianism distinctly reveals, however, that evangelical passion had no more claim than the aged structure of Reformed doctrine to be regarded as the last word in orthodox religion. However anchored in the marked caution expressed in the doctrine of facts, the Old School had remained open to the view strongly represented in traditional Calvinism that positive confrontation with the intellectual achievements of contemporary culture was an essential function of the church; few churchmen in this line had ever believed that Christian theology and life could thrive on piety alone or could be sustained apart from the evidences of reason, science, and learning. In the pattern of Old School thought, the configuration Baconianism pointed not only to a holy alliance between science and religion but also to an up-to-date correlation between the emotions sponsored by evangelicalism and the outward and public inquiry into nature organized in science. In time, these two domains were again emphatically to be disengaged, as they had been among the *philosophes*. The age following the Civil War found scientists increasingly indifferent to considerations of purpose and design in nature and more fully accepting of an ideal of impersonal objectivity which left no rationale for doxology. By 1900 the day was past, as William James aptly expressed it, "when it could be said that for Science herself the heavens declare the glory of God and the firmament showeth his handiwork."[3] But in the period before the rise of Darwinism and the decisive breakthrough of post-Newtonian physics, the ties which for nearly two hundred years had joined belief and nature, praise and research, were still very much intact. No picture of Calvinist thought in the period can suffice if it does not recognize the extent to which piety and dogma were interconnected with a serious and critical involvement with the scientific issues then engaging thinking Americans.

Far from corroborating the common view that American Protestantism after 1800 "turned against the ethos of the Enlightenment," the Presbyterian fusion of Bacon and Scripture reveals the continuing and significant hold of Enlightenment ideals upon a central Protestant tradition throughout the antebellum era. The additional notion that this "age of romanticism did not take science seriously" is predicated upon a virtual and unsound equation of "the American mind" with Transcendentalism. Engrossed by the charm and brilliance of much Transcendentalist literature, and gullible to the widely held premise that "evangelical" and "Calvinist" America produced nothing but incoherent emotion and illiberal dogma, too many scholars have been tempted into neglect of broad and representative strata of the day's intellectual remains. A fair and cross-sectional probe of the great mass of pamphlets, journals, and treatises which that age left behind will convince any investigator that what John C. Greene has called its "general presuppositions of thought" are neither devoid of interest nor shaped to the eccentric needs of Ralph Waldo Emerson.[4]

Presbyterians were not attuned to the Enlightenment in Gay's sense, of course, and they were more concerned than Unitarians to hold optimism and reasonableness under meaningful theological control, but they were distinctly receptive to a Christianized selection of themes from the eighteenth century. Science, empiricism, distrust of metaphysics, a love of generalization and systematic order—these all would have suited a Diderot or an Adam Smith as well as Samuel Miller or Charles Hodge. But their merger with a highly personal point of view in natural science, with doxology and a deeply humanized outlook upon nature, enabled Presbyterians to become champions of a later Christian Enlightenment, which, at least prior to mid-century, was much more expressive than Transcendentalism of the general intellectual scene in America. These additional elements, furthermore, were not creations of the moment but were drawn from a tradition older and more venerable among intellectual Christians than the Enlightenment. The holy alliance of Newtonian science and Protestant religion, nourished for more than two centuries by a steadily expanding literature of pious science and natural theology, was probably the strongest tradition in American science before the Civil War; in this respect "infidelity" was, as Presbyterians correctly suggested, a departure from the dominant tradition in Anglo-American scientific learning. Presbyterians who elaborated the Bacon-Bible pattern were in effect helping to bring this older heritage up to date in view of advances in ideas made in the Age of Reason.

If the philosophy of facts had not been available to Presbyterian and other apologetes, the disengagement of science from traditional piety in America might have occurred decades earlier than was actually the case. Yet the means by which the holy alliance was sheltered from infidel assault also served to incur a number of grave liabilities. The Baconian ideal of restraint and caution gave churchmen a becalming sense of their ability to squelch theological errors in science, but it was regrettable that the case upon which most of their defense rested was the abhorrence of theory concentred in the formula of induction. In spite of the homage done by many scientists to Lord Bacon and to the "philosophy of facts," the crusade against abstractions which formed the cornerstone of Baconian Philosophy was a selective and potentially subversive exaggeration of certain elements in the most advanced science since the time of Newton.

A major premise of Baconian inductivism that was to be proved wanting was its insistence that hypotheses must originate in immediate observation of data; another was its near-categorical exclusion of theoretic components in scientific explanation. Sir David Brewster, mid-century biographer of Newton and eminent scientist in his own right, attacked the former assumption in 1855 by pointing out that successful hypotheses in science may have any origin—"fancy" included—and may come into play at any stage of research, even prior to actual observation. To force the scientific reasoner into lockstep with observation is to suppress the fruitful impact that merely "suggestive" hypotheses may exert upon research. As for the validation of hypotheses, the important thing is not whether they originate in experience, but whether, once formulated, they can survive subsequent empirical check.[5] And William Whewell, mathematician and philosopher of science at Cambridge University, had presented to the world in 1840 the first edition of his *Philosophy of the Inductive Sciences,* in which orthodox Baconianism was depicted as a type of crude addition scarcely capable of producing the higher terms of scientific explanation. Whewell outlined with formidable brilliance the view that the senses alone open only partial perspectives upon the natural world; explanations in science involve an intuitive breakthrough representing far more than a generalization of fact in the Baconian sense.[6] These and related insights did not come to a focus in native American thought until given expression in the later 1860s by Harvard's Chauncey Wright. No longer satisfied with the iron restrictions of the inherited empiricism, Wright and many others were attaining a fresh appreciation of the intuitive and deductive side of scientific explanation. Understanding in the scientific sense was now seen as a creative, intuitive mental activity, enabling the mind to grasp relationships it could not experience directly. Wright reminded his readers that basic scientific concepts such as uniform motion and momentum cannot be referred directly to sensation.[7] These ideas, which seem almost self-evident to twentieth-century scientists, would have dismayed antebellum Baconians, for they sweep beyond the assumption that the lessons of nature can and must be read exclusively in an open language of fact. Baconianism, however useful it appeared in the moment, froze churchmen into a position which was to become less and less tenable from the standpoint of actual science and thereby less effective either as a control over scientific heresy or as an approach to further doxology as the century progressed.

From the Presbyterian standpoint, the startling turns taken by the scientific movement after the Civil War must have seemed to cast a shadow of deep irony over the theological enterprise. For in saving antebellum science for doxology, the Old School had unwittingly affixed a time bomb to their synthesis of faith and knowledge. The publication of Charles Darwin's *Origin of the Species* in 1859 triggered a series of explosions which was to work havoc with the intellectual life of conservative Calvinists through the remainder of the century and beyond. Wedded both to an identification of doxology with a doctrine of static design in nature and to an inflexible understanding of objectivity in science, most orthodox Presbyterians now were found clinging to an increasingly outmoded concept of nature and science and drifting gradually from vital contact with the scientific learning of their times. The inadequacy of Baconianism as a description of research was soon to be well illustrated in the attempt made during the 1860s and 1870s to nullify the heresy of "development" as a "visionary hypothesis" far in excess of observation.[8] Tensions became unbearably acute when the developmentalists heaped up "facts" at odds with those of the Baconians. Unable to comprehend how a view of the world directly inducted from the objective truth of nature could change fundamentally, or how science as a method of knowing might be distinguished from science as a content of knowledge, orthodox Presbyterians ceased by and large effectively to correlate the Christian message with going canons of knowledge. This was especially true in the South, where James Woodrow, Perkins Professor of Natural Science in Its Connection with Revealed Religion at Columbia Theological Seminary, was dismissed from his post in 1886 for acknowledging the weight of scientific evidence in favor of evolution; but the break was more clearly evidenced when Charles Hodge, the great leader of orthodox Presbyterianism after the death of Thornwell in 1862, published *What is Darwinism?* in 1874. For the conclusion of this essay on the new science was a judgment that evolution, which seemed to Hodge not only an extravagant hypothesis but also a scheme to purge design and higher purpose from nature, was "tantamount to atheism."[9]

Yet as the preceding chapters have shown, the emergence of the issue in this predominant form—science versus religion—was a new and uncoveted experience for orthodox apologists. They had regarded their previous skirmishes with impious science as passing collisions that did not endanger the central edifice of the holy alliance; a souring of relations with the community of science was what they long had hoped and labored to avoid. If conservative Presbyterians now largely joined in the general Protestant vilification of evolution, it is of utmost importance that their new role be viewed not as an exhibition of something inherently narrow or repressive or anti-intellectual within Calvinist theology itself. It must be seen rather as the outcome of ill-starred intellectual choices made by Presbyterians in previous periods of more constructive apologetic endeavor. The Presbyterian venture in Baconianism constitutes thereby an illuminating chapter of prehistory to the great "warfare of science with theology" which was to renew in many minds the radical Enlightenment conviction that religion is manacle upon inquiry.

Had circumstances been altered, had antebellum Old Schoolers not been driven into such dangerously intimate collusion with the narrow "philosophy of facts" and with static creationism, they and their theological descendants might have found themselves less threatened by developmentalism and thereby less alienated from the aims of Protestant liberalism in the age of Darwin. It may, indeed, not be stretching a point to suggest an element of preparation in Christian Baconianism for the newer liberal theologies. Newman Smyth's declaration that his version of postwar "Christocentric liberalism" began by "accepting loyally the results of scientific research. . . . We trust our senses," and Shailer Mathews's statement that "modernism . . . is the use of the methods of modern science to find, state and use the permanent and central values of inherited orthodoxy," would appear to be in some continuity with the pious Baconianism described in this study.[10] The Old School leadership's friendliness to scientific knowledge, their intensely held conviction that it would be theologically disastrous to conceive science and Christianity on separate premises, as well as their belief that "attitudes similar to those of the scientist are appropriate in religious inquiry," were far more akin to later liberal than to later conservative developments in American religion.[11] The contempt for science and learning that characterized much of the Fundamentalist movement represented a drastic break with the older Calvinist literalism, and the continuity to be noted below between the "Princeton Theology" and the intellectually lean theology of the "fundamentals" should not be allowed to obscure equally salient points of dissimilarity. Antebellum Old School orthodoxy, at any rate, represents a clear case of trying to have Calvin's cake and eat Bacon's too.

Nevertheless, in the period of this study, the limiting focus of

Baconian induction did enable churchmen to weather the series of shocks to orthodox faith administered by irreverent geologists, organic chemists, polygenists, and others without blurring the focus of literal biblical belief or destroying the concept of science as priesthood and praise. Measured by twentieth-century canons of scientific dispassion, doxological science may seem founded on a patent confusion of categories; but historically appraised it must be recognized as an ennobling enterprise which succeeded for a time in charging natural science with humanistic value. The wish to discern behind the motions of material in space a living and purposive framework of meaning was a primary theme in the diverse types of romantic Transcendentalism that during the antebellum years were becoming increasingly popular in some areas of the country. Transcendentalism, however, as a rule identified materialism so closely with Newtonian science that it could only preserve spiritual values by repudiating or ignoring the main development of scientific research. Doxological science, to the contrary, taught Americans how to affirm empirical science and the Newtonian picture of the universe without eclipsing the vital sense of "meaning." By affirming that spiritual dimensions of personality have a vital part to play in scientific investigation as well as in the lesser undertaking of "popular science," it preserved an instinct for human nobility and ultimate meaning in the face of naturalistic and mechanistic challenges that relied no less heavily upon metaphysical premises and were not always able to project a high and motivating sense of purpose into the scientific movement. This achievement may well be envied by a later age plagued by problems of relationship between science, morality, and ultimate value.

As was true on the broad front of science-and-religion, so within the stricter precincts of biblical theology the empiricist commitments of Christian Baconianism proved helpful for the moment but boded difficulty for the future. It has been indicated above that *sense* was the link bolting together Protestant faith and the beatified science of Lord Bacon. The role of sensory experience in Old School thought is central and striking. A direct implication of the Baconian hermeneutic developed by Old Schoolers was that Christian beliefs constitute knowledge in the scientific sense because they are verified in sense experience. This frank assimilation of biblical revelation to the natural domain of truth strongly conditioned Old School concepts of faith, for it meant that the "knowing" involved in religious conversion and edification was in vital measure like the knowing of science.

The assimilation was never complete, of course. Although, in the present study, the concern has been with the scientific rather than with the inspirational side of Presbyterian theology, it should not be forgotten that the two were not separated in the orthodox mind. Old Schoolers knew that Christian theology could not live by science alone. Religious knowledge finally must be ratified by the inner testimony of the Spirit; it must be enlivened by "internal evidence"; it must be *felt*. One of the most common refrains in orthodox literature was the primacy of "heart" over "head." Hodge, for example, repeatedly expressed his preference for internal over external "evidence," and once assured the readers of his journal that "where argument can no more produce the intimate persuasion of moral truth, than it can of beauty . . . As it depends upon taste, what things to us are beautiful, so it depends upon our religious feelings, what doctrines for us are true."[12]

But it was inevitable that theologians who saw no impropriety in the application of inductive method to Scripture should tend to conceive faith as a state of sensory gnosis, as a primarily cognitive relation to the objective content of Scripture. For religious belief, in this view, was not solely an affair for one's private soul; personal it was, but it could and must be verified by particulars of concrete experience open to public perception. Christian beliefs did constitute knowledge in a scientifically intelligible sense; they could be stated in precise propositional form. This emphasis was manifestly related to orthodox confessionalism; it could operate as well as a control both upon the undisciplined reveries sometimes associated with revivalism and upon the Transcendentalist's celebration of the powers of immediate intuition. The religion delineated in the Bible, as Gardiner Spring explained it, is not a religion of speculation, revery, or reason; it is "a religion founded in knowledge . . . the basis of it is the knowledge of the truth."[13]

But an important fruit of our inquiry must be the recognition that here, in the concept of biblical truth as a precise, "factual," unalterable objective order open to unbiased cognition, is a historical root of the dogmatic biblicism later to be arrayed under the banner of Fundamentalism. Ernest R. Sandeen, in a helpful recent study, has shown that the "strong, fully integrated theology of biblical authority" upon which Fundamentalists were to insist was not a simple inheritance from historic Protestantism. Fundamentalist biblicism was in many respects an innovation evolved under the pressure of circumstances peculiar to the late nineteenth and early twentieth centuries. It aimed chiefly to arrest the spread of "modernism," which from the later decades of the nineteenth century had subjected the scriptural text to relativizing historical analysis and often measured biblical ideas about world and cosmos against the latest scientific theories. Sandeen believes that the new and stricter doctrine of biblical inerrancy was the product of a "working agreement" between two major nineteenth-century traditions: dispensationalist millenarianism and the Princeton Theology of Archibald Alexander, Charles Hodge, and their successors at Princeton Theological Seminary. Upon the doctrine of the Bible, as another historian has put it, the Princeton theologians "became almost the official spokesmen . . . for a large sector of American Protestant conservatism."[14] In this way, the Baconian perspectives emanating from Princeton supplied major intellectual patronage to a wave of conservative biblicism which swept far beyond Presbyterianism.

A few words of clarification respecting Presbyterian history since 1860 may prove helpful. The Old School Presbyterian denomination split in 1861 over the issue of loyalty to the Union into separate southern and northern branches. The southern church has remained largely faithful to antebellum ideals until recent decades. H. Shelton Smith once noted that the theology of James Henley Thornwell "has dominated most of the history of southern Presbyterianism."[15] The southern sector of the Old School tradition may be accounted a solid, but provincial, historical entry in the ranks of conservative evangelicalism. Despite a gradual passage of denominational leadership into more liberal hands, the concepts of "factual" and inerrant biblicism inherited from Baconian days remain very much alive within the church. But there is little evidence of significant southern Presbyterian influence outside the denomination or region.[16]

The northern denomination, however, merged again with the northerly portion of New School Presbyterianism in 1869.[17] Within the new church, the conservative forces of Old School lineage, who continued to look to the seminary at Princeton for intellectual leadership, generally held sway until the decade of the 1920s.[18] Since thereafter the tune of northern Presbyterianism has increasingly been called by liberals critical of biblical inerrancy, it may be said that the Old School heritage has not prevailed denominationally either north or south in the recent period, however powerfully its effects may still be felt. It is therefore feasible to suggest that the most important contemporary echo of Baconian biblicism is not to be heard within Presbyterianism as such, but within the huge party of conservative evangelicalism which has adherents within every denomination and which today perpetuates in varying degrees the essential theological tenets of Fundamentalism, including biblical inerrancy. The Princeton Theology, then, with its historical pillars resting squarely upon the Baconian Philosophy of facts, is an important bridge across which influences continue to stream from antebellum to present-day American religion.

Two points remain to be made. First, recent historians of American religious history have explored the prevailing nineteenth-century concept of "A Christian America." They have shown that the nation's Protestant leadership tended to assimilate the gospel of Christianity to concepts of the nature of American civilization. It became, in fact, often difficult to discern any salient notes of discontinuity between gospel and culture.[19] The Protestant career of Baconianism affords additional documentation for this thesis.

With equal clarity, the association of Baconianism with millennialism and with the Reformation and the employment of induction as a tool of "scientific" exegesis testified to the confidence of many churchmen that the tenets of orthodox belief and of a culture increasingly devoted to science were mutually supportive. Baconianism may have facilitated an active response to live issues, but it also implied a degree of cultural accommodation that diluted the prerogatives of religion as a critic of culture. Having convinced themselves that Baconian science, in point alike of its fixation on facts and its doxological aim, was a creation and a dependent of Protestant belief, Presbyterian savants were less capable of making the distinctions necessary to preserve the distinctive affirmations of religion in confrontation with impending basic transitions in the scientific movement. They were too elated by the solid increase of appeal and cogency which a Christianized science could lend to the cause of religion and by the hope that Christian Baconianism —which seemed a secure Anglo-Saxon possession—would become the finally triumphant strategy of the church. It may be questioned whether religious leaders at any previous point in the nation's past had achieved a more unabashed union of gospel and culture than this. Doubtless if the Old School could have foreseen Darwin or the triumph of a physics of forces undermining the older empiricism they would not have been so eager either to canonize Bacon or to embrace scientific endeavor as a natural patron of belief.

Finally, no attempt can be made here to assess the impact of Christianized Baconianism upon the nation, but since in this evangelical era Calvinist churchmen as much as anyone supplied leadership in ideas to the God-fearing portion of the educated populace, their concerns must be recognized as in some sense formative. For the church leaders considered here were not limited in their influence, like their twentieth-century counterparts, to the weekly sermonization of Presbyterian congregations or the supervision of Christian education in the parish. The vastly overproportionate size, range, and interest of their written output as indicated in the citations suggest a sizable impact upon the public market of ideas, and when one remembers as well the remarkable Presbyterian leadership in higher education throughout this age of colleges, it is hard to avoid the conclusion that while Presbyterians may have been losing the battle of numbers waged so well by the less thoughtful churches, they were effective in extending the reach of religion on the frontier of American thought. Historians of science in particular should be interested in implications of the fact that many if not most of the men who in this time were rising to prominence in the American scientific community had received their basic orientation in concepts of the natural world and its scientific explication in the denominational colleges. In any case, the theological adaptation of themes in natural science undertaken by churchmen deserves to be regarded as a notable contribution to the larger process by which the hold of Protestant Christianity upon antebellum American culture was being broadened and consolidated.

Abbreviations in Notes and Bibliography

ABR	*American Biblical Repository*
AJS	*American Journal of Science*
AP	Thomas Reid, *Essays on the Active Powers of the Human Mind*
AQR	*American Quarterly Review*
BLRM	*Baltimore Literary and Religious Magazine*
BRPR	*Biblical Repertory and Princeton Review* (cited in text as *Princeton Review*)
BS	*Bibliotheca Sacra*
CA	*Christian Advocate*
CH	*Church History*
CWDS	Sir Thomas Hamilton, ed., *The Collected Works of Dugald Stewart*. 11 vols. Edinburgh: Thomas, Constable, 1854.
DRM	William Ellery Channing, *Discourses, Reviews and Miscellanies*. Boston: Carter & Hendee, 1830.
EPBM	Edwin A. Burtt, ed., *The English Philosophers from Bacon to Mill*. New York: The Modern Library, 1939.
ER	*Edinburgh Review*
FJ	*Franklin Journal*
FL	Firestone Library, Princeton University
HFP	Historical Foundation of the Presbyterian and Reformed Churches Library, Montreat, North Carolina
HSP	Historical Society of Pennsylvania
IP	Thomas Reid, *Essays on the Intellectual Powers of Man*
JHI	*Journal of the History of Ideas*
LEC	William H. Ruffner, ed., *Lectures on the Evidences of Christianity*
LTR	*Literary and Theological Review*

MVHR	*Mississippi Valley Historical Review*
NAR	*North American Review*
NE	*New Englander*
NEQ	*New England Quarterly*
OUSL	Alonzo Potter, ed., *Discourses on the Objects and Uses of Science and Literature*. New York: Harper & Bros., 1855.
PHS	Presbyterian Historical Society, Philadelphia
PM	*Presbyterian Magazine*
SCL	South Caroliniana Library
SL	Speer Library, Princeton Theological Seminary
SLM	*Southern Literary Messenger*
SPR	*Southern Presbyterian Review*
TRPW	Sir William Hamilton, ed., *Thomas Reid: Philosophical Works*. 8th ed. 2 vols. Edinburgh: Thomas Constable & Sons, 1895.
VELM	*Virginia Evangelical and Literary Magazine*

Notes

INTRODUCTION

1. See, e.g., William Warren Sweet, *The Story of Religion in America*; H. Shelton Smith, Robert T. Handy, and Lefferts Loetscher, *American Christianity*; Sidney E. Mead, *The Lively Experiment*; Winthrop S. Hudson, *Religion in America*; Edwin Scott Gaustad, *A Religious History of America*; Sydney E. Ahlstrom, *A Religious History of the American People*.

2. Mead, *Lively Experiment*, p. 127.

3. James Ward Smith, "Religion and Science in American Philosophy," p. 421.

4. A good example is Morton White, *Science and Sentiment in America*. With the exception of Ralph Waldo Emerson, White finds in the period of our study an array of thinkers so undistinguished as to be unworthy of treatment. However justified by his wish to focus upon the highlights of American thought, this exclusion results in a near-total neglect of the Baconian pattern which, in turn, seems peculiar in this history of the impact of science upon ideas (ibid., pp. 3, 71).

5. Ernest R. Sandeen, *The Roots of Fundamentalism*, pp. 103–31.

6. George H. Daniels has noted, for instance, that "publishing seriously intended works on the philosophy of science in theological reviews was not at all uncommon during that [Jacksonian] period" (*American Science in the Age of Jackson*, p. 247, n. 19).

CHAPTER 1

1. [Edward Everett], "Character of Lord Bacon," p. 300.

2. Richard Foster Jones, *Ancients and Moderns*, pp. viii, 170–71, 255–56, and passim; A. Rupert Hall, *From Galileo to Newton*, p. 104. Bacon occupied the place of honor beside King Charles II on the frontispiece of Thomas Sprat's *History of the Royal Society* of 1667.

3. This has been determined by a reading of the chief works in question together with a check of indexes in all available editions of the writings of each author. A characteristic reference appeared in Franklin's "Poor Richard" for 11 April 1749: Bacon was "justly esteemed the father of the modern experimental philosophy" (Benjamin Franklin, *The Papers of Benjamin Franklin*, 3:339); see also Hall, *From Galileo to Newton*, p. 103.

4. This excludes consideration of the "moral sense" theory, which although a principal tenet of Realism does not fall within the scope of this study.

5. Rudolf Metz, *A Hundred Years of British Philosophy*, p. 30.

6. First attention will be given to Reid, as the constructive mind of the movement.

Stewart will be noticed primarily as his work represents a clarifying development or illustration of themes first propounded by Reid.

7. Dugald Stewart, *Account of the Life and Writings of Thomas Reid*, p. 9. Referring to Bacon, Reid once observed: "I am very apt to measure a man's understanding by the opinion he entertains of that author" (ibid., p. 11).

8. Robert Blakey, *A History of the Philosophy of Mind*, 4:8. See also John Veitch, *Memoir of Dugald Stewart, with Selections from His Correspondence*, p. xii.

9. See Stewart, *Account*, p. 8. See I. Woodbridge Riley, *American Philosophy*, pp. 475– 566; Herbert W. Schneider, *A History of American Philosophy*, pp. 216–20; Torgny T. Segerstedt, *The Problem of Knowledge in Scottish Philosophy*; S. A. Graves, *The Scottish Philosophy of Common Sense*.

10. Reid's closest associates on the faculties at Aberdeen and Glasgow were mathematicians and scientists, and he corresponded warmly for many years with James Gregory, professor of natural philosophy at Edinburgh. He dedicated his major work, *Essays on the Intellectual Powers of Man*, to Gregory. Reid acquired real expertise in the Newtonian mathematics and in chemistry and conducted a number of experiments. His Aberdeen lectures in philosophy included instruction in statics, dynamics, astronomy, magnetism, electricity, hydrostatics, pneumatics, and optics. He lectured on Newton's *Mathematical Principles of Natural Philosophy* for twelve years at Glasgow, and for "relaxation" he collected natural history specimens. Full information may be found in Stewart's *Account*; James McCosh, *The Scottish Philosophy, Biographical, Expository, Critical, from Hutcheson to Hamilton*, pp. 192–226; A. Campbell Fraser, *Thomas Reid*, pp. 9–55; *Dictionary of National Biography*, s.v. "Reid, Thomas"; L. L. Laudan, "Thomas Reid and the Newtonian Turn of British Methodological Thought," pp. 106–7; TRPW, 1:39–92 and 2:736.

11. Veitch, *Memoir*, p. xi; McCosh, *Scottish Philosophy*, p. 278. On his visit to Edinburgh in 1805–6, the American scientist Benjamin Silliman noted Stewart's intimacy with prominent Scottish natural scientists (George P. Fisher, *The Life of Benjamin Silliman*, 1:178–80).

12. Veitch, *Memoir*, p. xxx. Stewart studied under Reid at Glasgow during the 1771–72 session, and the two formed an intellectual comradeship that lasted until Reid's death in 1796 (McCosh, *Scottish Philosophy*, p. 276). In 1785, Reid codedicated his *Essays on the Intellectual Powers* to Stewart; in 1792, Stewart reciprocated by dedicating to Reid his main production, the *Elements of the Philosophy of the Human Mind*.

13. Reid expressed interest in a project to establish a Scottish ancestry for Newton. Reid to James Gregory, 14 March 1784, in TRPW, 1:63; Reid to Professor [John] Robison, 12 April 1792, ibid., p. 91. L. L. Laudan has called Reid "the first major British philosopher to take Newton's opinions on induction, causality, and hypotheses seriously" ("Thomas Reid," p. 106).

14. IP, Essay 2, ch. 8, p. 145; Dugald Stewart, *Elements of the Philosophy of the Human Mind*, in CWDS, 2: Introduction, p. 84, and 3: pt. 2, ch. 4, sec. 1, p. 236; TRPW, 2:712: "Newton . . . had the rules of the *Novum Organum* constantly in his eye." This view had been promulgated earlier by Henry Pemberton, *A View of Sir Isaac Newton's Philosophy*, Introduction, and Colin Maclaurin, *An Account of Sir Isaac Newton's Philosophical Discoveries*, pp. 56, 59–62. John H. Randall, Jr.'s view that "Diderot it was who. . . created the myth . . . that [Bacon] had really founded scientific method" is not entirely accurate (*The Making of the Modern Mind*, p. 266).

15. IP, Essay 2, ch. 8, p. 145.

16. IP, Essay 6, ch. 8, p. 701. Reid wrote a critical analysis of Aristotle's logic, showing the "inutility" of the syllogism for scientific research (TRPW, 2:681–714).

17. See Gladys Bryson, *Man and Society*, pp. 17–26.

18. Reid to Hume, 18 March 1763, in TRPW, 1:91–92: "I shall always avow myself your disciple in metaphysics. . . . Your system . . . appears . . . justly deduced from

principles commonly received . . . ; principles which I never thought of calling in question, until the conclusions you draw from them in the Treatise . . . made me suspect them." Reid, of course, also regarded the work of Berkeley as a basic threat to scientific empiricism. See IP, Essay 2, chs. 10–11, pp. 167–87.

19. IP, Preface, pp. xxxiii–ix; ibid., Essay 2, ch. 8, p. 141.

20. IP, Essay 2, ch. 9, p. 162.

21. This is a summary of Reid's account of the Humean attack on "substance" and "causality." I am not concerned here with its accuracy. Reid did not, with some of his followers (notably James Beattie), indulge in denunciations of Hume, whom he regarded as "one of the most acute metaphysicians that this or any age hath produced" (Thomas Reid, *An Inquiry into the Human Mind*, ch. 2, sec. 6, p. 31).

22. IP, Essay 6, ch. 5, p. 642.

23. Reid, *Inquiry*, ch. 6, sec. 20, p. 206; CWDS, 2: *Elements*, ch. 1, sec. 3, p. 112. Scholars are not agreed upon whether Reid assumed a direct or mediate knowledge of objects "perceived." See Henry Laurie, *The Scottish Philosophy in Its National Development*, p. 143; Grave, *Scottish Philosophy*, pp. 126–29; Segerstedt, *Problem of Knowledge*, pp. 48, 59–65; A. D. Woozley, Introduction to Reid's *Essays on the Intellectual Powers of Man*, pp. xviii–xxv. R. L. Caldwell, in "Another Look at Thomas Reid," p. 548, sees Reid as claiming "an immediate apprehension of an object," and this appears to be Reid's most consistent assumption, although his various formulations are not always clear and consistent. See also IP, Essay 6, ch. 3, p. 573; Reid, *Inquiry*, ch. 6, sec. 21, pp. 214–15. Cf. IP, Essay 2, ch. 2, pp. 82–83, in which Reid outlines the "machinery" of perceptual intercourse between object and brain and even asserts that the sense "impressions" conveyed through the nerves to the brain "correspond exactly to the nature and conditions of the objects by which they were made; so our perceptions . . . correspond to those impressions."

24. IP, Essay 2, ch. 5, pp. 111–13, ibid., Essay 2, ch. 19, pp. 276–77; ibid., Essay 2, ch. 20, pp. 289–90. In ibid., Essay 2, ch. 20, p. 290, "belief" is compared with religious "faith." The cited texts indicate that Reid applied the same analysis to a series of "first principles" of knowledge, such as the existence of a perceiving "self" and an intact and regular universe. For Stewart's entire acceptance of Reid's formulations, see, e.g., CWDS, 3: *Elements*, pt. 2, ch. 1, sec. 2, p. 45. Important background was provided by Locke's discussion of the intuitive "ready assent of the mind to some truths" (John Locke, *An Essay Concerning the Human Understanding*, Bk. 1, ch. 2, secs. 11, 16–18; ibid., Bk. 4, ch. 17, sec. 14).

25. IP, Essay 2, ch. 5, p. 114. Reid also appealed to divine trustworthiness as a guarantee that the senses were reliable (*Inquiry*, ch. 6, sec. 20, p. 209); and see Olin McKendree Jones, *Empiricism and Intuitionism in Reid's Common Sense Philosophy*, pp. 25–27.

26. See, e.g., James Beattie, *The Works of James Beattie*, 4: pt. 1, ch. 2, sec. 2, p. 60: "All conclusions in natural philosophy . . . must finally be resolved into this principle, that things are as our senses represent them." Reid constantly emphasized that "there is no reasoning in perception," which depends upon a reflexive cooperation of sense and mind (*Inquiry*, ch. 6, sec. 20, p. 211; IP, Essay 2, ch. 5, pp. 114–17).

27. IP, Essay 2, ch. 20, p. 288. See also ibid., Essay 2, ch. 14, p. 220; Reid, *Inquiry*, ch. 6, sec. 21, p. 216: "[We have] no means of knowing how the body acts upon the mind, or the mind upon the body. . . . There is a deep and dark gulf between them, which our understanding cannot pass." For Stewart's similar formulation see CWDS, 2: *Elements*, pt. 1, ch. 1, sec. 3, pp. 111–13. Cf. with Locke, *Essay*, Bk. 2, ch. 22, sec. 14; ibid., Bk. 4, ch. 11, secs. 2, 3, and 8.

28. IP, Essay 2, ch. 20, p. 287; David Hume, *An Enquiry Concerning Human Understanding*, p. 603.

29. Moody E. Prior, "Bacon's Man of Science," pp. 349–51; Geoffrey Bullough, "Bacon and the Defence of Learning," pp. 14–16.

30. Francis Bacon, *Novum Organum*, Bk. 1, aphorism 67, p. 47. See also ibid., Bk. 1, aphorism 75, p. 52; and ibid., Preface, p. 24.

31. Ibid., Bk. 1, aphorism 92, p. 65; Francis Bacon, *The Great Instauration*, p. 11.

32. Bacon, *Novum Organum*, Bk. 1, aphorism 50, p. 38; Bacon, *Great Instauration*, p. 18.

33. Bacon, *Novum Organum*, Bk. 1, aphorisms 39–67.

34. IP, Essay 6, ch. 6, p. 655; see also CWDS, 2: *Elements*, pt. 1, ch. 1, sec. 2, pp. 97–98.

35. IP, Essay 2, ch. 17, p. 253; CWDS, 3: *Elements*, pt. 2, ch. 1, sec. 2, p. 45.

36. AP, Essay 1, ch. 6, pp. 43, 45–46. Much of Stewart's section on the "Logic of Induction" in the *Elements* is devoted to a proof of "our ignorance of *efficient causes*" (CWDS, 3: *Elements*, pt. 2, ch. 4, sec. 1, pp. 230–45). Again, the theme is clearly built upon Locke. See Locke, *Essay*, Bk. 4, ch. 3, secs. 24–29.

37. IP, Essay 1, ch. 3, p. 46.

38. CWDS, 2: *Elements*, pt. 1, ch. 1, sec. 3, p. 109. This too was an elaboration of a basic Lockean theme. See, e.g., Locke, *Essay*, Bk. 4, ch. 14, sec. 2. Reid once illustrated the confines of sensory contact with reference to a man "shut up in a dark room, so that he could see nothing but through one small hole in the shutter of a window" (IP, Essay 2, ch. 1, p. 77). Again, the image was derived from Locke, *Essay*, Bk. 2, ch. 11, sec. 17. Cf. with Bacon's image of a man groping his way through the dark, aided by the light from the "candle of induction" (*Novum Organum*, Bk. 1, aphorism 71, p. 57).

39. IP, Essay 1, ch. 3, p. 41; IP, Essay 2, ch. 8, p. 145.

40. AP, Essay 1, ch. 3, p. 46: "The grandest discovery ever made in natural philosophy, was that of the law of gravitation. . . . But . . . [Newton] was perfectly aware, that he discovered no real cause, but only the law or rule, according to which the unknown cause operates."

41. Reid to Kames, 16 Dec. 1780, in TRPW, 1:56–58.

42. CWDS, 2: *Elements*, pt. 1, ch. 1, sec. 3, p. 109. Bacon had banished "final," not "efficient," causes from science, and in a later passage Stewart acknowledged the difference (CWDS, 3: *Elements*, pt. 2, ch. 4, sec. 1, pp. 234–35).

43. Reid to James Gregory, n.d., in TRPW, 1:76.

44. This was in reference to Bacon (Alfred North Whitehead, *Science and the Modern World*, p. 96).

45. IP, Essay 1, ch. 3, p. 44.

46. CWDS, 2: 6–7; CWDS, 2: *Elements*, pt. 1, ch. 6, sec. 5, p. 398.

47. AP, Essay 1, ch. 6, p. 46.

48. IP, Essay 6, ch. 8, p. 701, emphasis mine; Bacon, *Great Instauration*, p. 16.

49. Reid, *Inquiry*, ch. 6, sec. 24, p. 248; CWDS, 3: *Elements*, pt. 2, ch. 4, sec. 2, p. 252. Laudan observes that Reid "sees no logical or epistemological difference between particular facts and general facts" ("Thomas Reid," p. 129).

50. IP, Essay 6, ch. 6, p. 655. See also IP, Essay 7, ch. 3, p. 737: "The evidence that . . . general rules have no exceptions . . . can never be demonstrative. . . . General rules may have exceptions or limitations which no men ever had occasion to observe." For Stewart's near-identical view, see CWDS, 3: *Elements*, pt. 2, ch. 4, sec. 4, p. 311.

51. See, e.g., IP, Essay 2, ch. 3, pp. 86–92, and Essay 2, ch. 8, p. 145. Laudan, "Thomas Reid," p. 102, n. 1, notes that many eighteenth-century British scientists had enthusiastically adopted Newton's call for a nonconjectural science. Often the admonition against conjectures was attributed to Bacon. See I. Bernard Cohen, *Franklin and Newton*, p. 67; Robert E. Schofield, *Mechanism and Materialism*, p. 3, n. 1.

52. See, e.g., IP, Essay 1, ch. 3, pp. 42–43, 46–47.

53. IP, Essay 1, ch. 3, pp. 45–46. Reid's contempt for hypothesis had been inspired in part by the views of Joseph Black, professor of chemistry at Glasgow, whom he venerated

as a master of science and whose lectures he frequently attended (Reid to Dr. David Skene, 20 Dec. 1765, in TRPW, 1:42). John Robison, eminent scientist and editor of Black's *Elements of Chemistry*, reported Black's "aversion to all hypothesis and conjecture in experimental science," which he branded as "a mere waste of time and ingenuity" (Introduction to Joseph Black, *Elements of Chemistry*, 1:xliv).

54. Mary B. Hesse, "Francis Bacon," p. 145; Paolo Rossi, *Francis Bacon, From Magic to Science*, pp. 138, 222.

55. Quoted in Rossi, *Francis Bacon*, p. 141.

56. Bacon, *Great Instauration*, p. 11; *Novum Organum*, p. 25.

57. Scholars have pointed out numerous salient differences between Bacon's and Newton's concepts of induction. Bacon's understanding of nature rested heavily upon medieval and Renaissance concepts; he employed induction not to discover the mechanistic "laws" of Newtonian physics but to discern "forms" such as "heat" or "whiteness." See Robert E. Larsen, "The Aristotelianism of Bacon's *Novum Organum*," pp. 435–50; Hesse, "Francis Bacon." Observing this divergence, a recent student has claimed that Reid's identification of Baconian with Newtonian induction is specious, that Reid must have been only "vaguely familiar" with the *Novum Organum* (Laudan, "Thomas Reid," p. 120). Without rejecting this judgment entirely, it should be pointed out that the great majority of explicit references to Bacon in Reid's works appear in the course of the recurrent assaults upon hypothesis that punctuate them. See, e.g., IP, Essay 2, ch. 3, pp. 87, 90; ibid, Essay 2, ch. 8, p. 145; ibid., Essay 6, ch. 8, p. 701. "Induction" meant for Reid, as it did for Bacon, primarily a systematic aversion to "fact," and he regarded Newton's famous disclaimer, "I do not feign hypotheses," as the essential prescription of natural science (IP, Essay 2, ch. 3, p. 87). As for Newton's more detailed "Rules of Philosophizing," Reid at the least was incautious when he insisted that they "were drawn from Bacon's rules," if by "rules" he meant the elaborate techniques for the investigation of "presence," "absence," and "degrees" expounded in the *Novum Organum*. But the tone and purpose, if not all the detail, of the two programs were in essential harmony; the culminating rule in Newton's list drew again the sharp contrast between true "induction" and the deceit of "hypothesis." Dugald Stewart, who chided those "more disposed to follow the letter of some detached sentences, than to imbibe the general spirit of Bacon's philosophy," explicitly identified the "method of induction" presented in the *Novum Organum* with the injunction to empirical search; he plainly regarded the specific procedures there propounded as secondary (CWDS, 3: *Elements*, pt. 2, ch. 4, sec. 4, p. 303; ibid., pt. 2, ch. 4, sec. 1, p. 246). Interesting to note, R. G. Collingwood also has maintained that "the rules of method which . . . [Newton] lays down . . . are drawn from Bacon" (*The Idea of Nature*, p. 107).

58. IP, Essay 4, ch. 4, p. 448. Cf. Bacon, *Novum Organum*, Bk. 1, aphorisms 45–48, 51, pp. 36–38.

59. Terence Martin, in his *Instructed Vision*, pp. 72–85, describes the Realist distrust of the imaginative "order of the possible" in reference to literature. This development went sharply counter to the gradual growth and widening of the concept of imagination in the latter portion of the eighteenth century and the following period of "romance."

60. IP, Essay 6, ch. 8, pp. 700–701, emphasis mine. Cf. Bacon, *Novum Organum*, Bk. 1, aphorisms 19–20, p. 31: "The mind longs to spring up to positions of higher generality. . . . [But my plan] derives axioms from the senses and particulars, so that it arrives at the most general axioms last of all."

61. Bacon, *Great Instauration*, p. 10; Bacon, *Novum Organum*, Bk. 1, aphorism 10, p. 29: "The subtlety of nature is greater many times over than the subtlety of the senses and understanding."

62. IP, Essay 2, ch. 3, p. 90. See also ibid., Essay 1, ch. 3, pp. 44–45: "Human worksmanship will never bear comparison with the Divine. Conjectures and hypotheses are the invention and the workmanship of man." See the brief discussion of "the illegitimacy of competing with Nature," in R. Hooykaas, *Religion and the Rise of Modern Science*, p. 56.

63. IP, Essay 1, ch. 3, p. 44. Thus also, by the "discovery" of the law of gravity, men "are made to behold some part of . . . this [natural] system, which before this discovery, eye had not seen, nor ear heard, nor had it entered into the heart of man to conceive" (IP, Essay 6, ch. 8, p. 696). Here again, Reid's view rests closely upon Bacon's. See Bacon, *Great Instauration*, p. 19.

64. IP, Essay 1, ch. 3, p. 46: "Let us accustom ourselves to try every opinion by the touchstone of fact and experience. What can be fairly deduced from facts duly observed, or sufficiently attested, is genuine and pure; it is the voice of God."

65. IP, Essay 1, ch. 3, p. 42; ibid., Essay 2, ch. 3, pp. 86–87.

66. Ibid., Essay 2, ch. 3, p. 91: "Let hypotheses . . . suggest experiments, or direct our inquiries; but let just induction alone govern our belief." See also Reid to Lord Kames, 16 Dec. 1780, TRPW, 1:56–57; CWDS, 3: *Elements*, pt. 2, ch. 4, sec. 4, pp. 309, 314, 403.

67. IP, Essay 2, ch. 3, pp. 85, 89; Reid, *Inquiry*, ch. 6, sec. 19, p. 200. Reid's exposition takes into account neither shifts of emphasis in Newton's doctrine of hypothesis nor the diverse senses in which he used the term. See Edwin A. Burtt, *The Metaphysical Foundations of Modern Science*, pp. 215–26; Cohen, *Franklin and Newton*, pp. 125–47.

68. IP, Essay 2, ch. 3, p. 89.

69. IP, Essay 1, ch. 3, p. 44. Stewart's view was less stringent. See CWDS, 3: *Elements*, pt. 2, ch. 4, sec. 4, p. 309.

70. IP, Essay 6, ch. 8, p. 702.

71. CWDS, 3: *Elements*, pt. 2, ch. 4, sec. 4, pp. 298–316.

72. IP, Essay 6, ch. 4, pp. 599–600; ibid., Essay 1, ch. 1, pp. 1–2. This too was a Lockean theme. See, e.g., Locke, *Essay*, Bk. 1, ch. 1, sec. 2.

73. Perry Miller, Introduction, pp. ix–xi.

74. Ibid., p. xi; Howard Mumford Jones, "The Influence of European Ideas in Nineteenth-Century America," p. 251.

75. George P. Schmidt, *The Old Time College President*, p. 122; Sydney E. Ahlstrom, "The Scottish Philosophy and American Theology," p. 261. The name later adopted, "Princeton College," will be used hereafter.

76. Ahlstrom, "Scottish Philosophy," pp. 267–68.

77. Miller, Introduction, p. ix. For an account of Brown, see [S. Gilman], "Cause and Effect," pp. 395–432.

78. Schneider, *American Philosophy*, p. 238.

79. [Gilman], "Cause and Effect," p. 395. See also "Stewart's Philosophy," pp. 360–78.

80. [Alexander H. Everett], "Stewart's Moral Philosophy," p. 214.

81. Emma Willard, "Universal Terms," p. 18.

82. [Everett], "Stewart's Moral Philosophy," p. 214.

83. Joseph Story, "Characteristics of the Age," p. 430.

84. "Brown's Philosophy," pp. 1–27.

85. [Andrew Preston Peabody], "Morell's History of Philosophy," p. 407.

86. Merle Curti, "The Great Mr. Locke," p. 108.

87. Beasley is quoted in Schneider, *American Philosophy*, p. 240; Schmidt, *Old Time College President*, pp. 122–23.

88. Curti, "Locke," pp. 110–13, 117.

89. Joel Barlow, *The Columbiad*, Bk. 9, p. 325.

90. William Wirt, *The Letters of the British Spy*, p. 245.

91. Stephen Simpson, *The Working Man's Manual*, p. 160. For a similar appeal by Richard Hildreth, see Schneider, *American Philosophy*, p. 124.

92. Barnaby Googe, "Old Agricultural Works," p. 189.

93. David Ramsay, *A Review of the Improvements, Progress, and State of Medicine in the Eighteenth Century*, pp. 1–3; [Walter Channing], "Ancient Medicine," p. 219; James Maclurg, "On Reasoning in Medicine," pp. 241, 220–21; Samuel Adams, "A Historical Sketch of Medical Philosophy," p. 398.

94. Francis Andrew March, "The Relation of the Study of Jurisprudence to the Origin and Progress of the Baconian Philosophy," pp. 543–47. See also "Whether Law is a Science?" pp. 349–52, 368.

95. "Wordsworth," p. 71.

96. [Lyman Atwater], "Coleridge," p. 165.

97. Samuel A. Cartwright, *Essays*. A southern Presbyterian reviewer in 1851 found an appropriate aphorism from Bacon to warn South Carolina against independent secession ("Critical Notices," SPR, 4:452). A reviewer for the Yale *New Englander* in 1852 cited Bacon as "among the principal authors of modern democracy" for his championing of "reverence of man" ("Lord Bacon," p. 370).

98. See, e.g., J. G. Spurzheim, *A View of the Philosophical Principles of Phrenology*, p. 10. George Combe's *Lectures on Phrenology* open with a short paean to "the Baconian philosophy," pp. 16–21. See also James D. Green, "Claims of Phrenology to be Regarded as the Science of Human Nature," p. 181.

99. "Psychology," p. 349.

100. Samuel Tyler, *A Discourse of the Baconian Philosophy*, p. 16.

101. [Everett], "Lord Bacon," p. 300.

102. "Pestalozzi—Diffusion of Knowledge," pp. 118–34. See also "Useful Knowledge," p. 372; Arthur A. Ekirch, Jr., *The Idea of Progress in America, 1815–1860*, p. 106.

103. Henry Crane, *Literary Discourses*, p. 33, and see James D. Whelpley, "Letter on Philosophical Induction," p. 36.

104. "Modern Science—Inductive Philosophy," p. 377. The term "inductive philosophy" generally referred to the inductive technique in the larger complex of the Baconian Philosophy, although the two terms often were used synonymously.

105. "Short Notices," BRPR, 16:609. See also "H," "The Nineteenth Century," p. 458.

106. [John Leslie], "History of the Barometer," p. 187.

107. [Thomas Babington Macaulay], "Lord Bacon," pp. 1–103. This article, which was widely circulated in the American edition of the *Edinburgh Review*, was reprinted later the same year by the *Southern Literary Messenger*, pp. 9–21, 73–79, 190–96. See also W. S. Grayson, "Bacon's Philosophy and Macaulay's Criticism of It," pp. 177–83, which defends Bacon, and the reply by "E. T.," "Bacon's Philosophy and Macaulay's Criticism of It," pp. 382–86, which supports Macaulay. The very form of Macaulay's argument, which assumed "induction" to be an axiomatic procedure in all "investigation," revealed how deeply the age was committed to the inductive philosophy. Bacon's contribution, according to Macaulay, had been decisive for the development of inductive science, for he had provided the crucial motive—control of nature for practical benefit—that for the first time induced men to pursue induction with the rigor and precision upon which natural science depended.

108. "Whately's *Elements of Logic*," pp. 137–72; "Useful Knowledge," p. 388; "Spedding's *Complete Edition of the Works of Bacon*," p. 106; R. H. Forrester, *Anniversary Address Delivered before the American Literary Institute of Bethany College* . . . , pp. 9–10; Erasmus D. MacMaster, *A Discourse Delivered November 7th, 1838* . . . , pp. 22–23.

109. David Brewster, *Memoirs of the Life, Writings, and Discoveries of Sir Isaac Newton*, 2:400–406.

110. Grayson, "Bacon's Philosophy," p. 179.

111. John Playfair, *Dissertation Second, Exhibiting a General View of the Progress of Mathematical and Physical Science* . . . , p. 87. Cf. the extravagant praise heaped upon Bacon by James Mackintosh, "Stewart's *Introduction to the Encyclopaedia*," pp. 223–41. Edward Everett admitted that Bacon had espoused the alchemic search for "gold," but claimed that such minor "aberrations only served to set off the central achievement—the Inductive Philosophy—more clearly" (*An Address Delivered before the Literary Societies of Amherst College, August 25, 1835*, pp. 17–18).

112. John Frederick William Herschel, *A Preliminary Discourse on the Study of Natural Philosophy*. The first edition appeared in 1830. The *Discourse* also went through several American editions.

113. Dwight E. Stevenson, "The Bacon College Story," p. 10.

114. "A Review of the Principia of Newton," p. 240; Ralph Waldo Emerson, "Lord Bacon," p. 333; and "Bacon's Philosophy," pp. 22–52.

115. Everett, *Address*, p. 22.

116. Joseph Story, "Characteristics of the Age," p. 428. For other characteristic statements, see, e.g., Thomas Dick, *On the Improvement of Society by the Diffusion of Knowledge*, p. 16; Mark Hopkins, *An Address Delivered before the Society of Alumni of Williams College, August 16, 1843*, p. 10; Francis Wayland, *Discourse, Delivered at the Dedication of Manning Hall, of Brown University, February 4, 1835*, p. 8; "Fossil Remains," p. 78. The *Encyclopaedia Americana* in 1839 even claimed that Bacon had "clearly" anticipated Newton's discovery of gravitation (*Encyclopaedia Americana*, s.v. "Bacon").

117. Stevenson, "Bacon College Story," p. 11.

118. Quoted in Roy Park, *Hazlitt and the Spirit of the Age*, p. 15. James Marsh, who after 1829 championed Coleridge in America as an antidote to the prevailing empiricism, testified to the iron hold of Bacon upon the period by presenting Coleridge simply as a purer "Baconian" (James Marsh, Preliminary Essay, p. xliv). A similar tactic was employed by Grayson, "Bacon's Philosophy," p. 178.

119. "Stewart's Dissertation," pp. 45–46.

120. "Whately's *Logic*," pp. 148, 137–38; "Scotch School of Philosophy and Criticism," pp. 386–97; [Francis Bowen], "Wilson's Treatise on Logic," p. 387.

121. [Samuel Tyler], "Psychology," p. 236.

122. The only direct treatment is George H. Daniels's chapter on "The Reign of Bacon in America" in *American Science*, pp. 63–85. Neal C. Gillespie's *The Collapse of Orthodoxy*, a study of George Frederick Holmes, has called attention to the Baconian element in Holmes's thought. See also Ekirch, *Idea of Progress*, pp. 106–7; Russel Blaine Nye, *Society and Culture in America, 1830–1860*, p. 239.

CHAPTER 2

1. See Henry F. May, "The Recovery of American Religious History."

2. See, e.g., the occasional and truculent references in Perry Miller's *The Life of the Mind in America*, pp. 32, 65.

3. See Donald G. Tewksbury, *The Founding of American Colleges and Universities before the Civil War*, pp. 91–102 and passim; Frederick Rudolph, *The American College and University*, pp. 57–58; Ernest Trice Thompson, *Presbyterians in the South*, 1:235–73.

4. A recent and stimulating work is George M. Marsden, *The Evangelical Mind and the New School Presbyterian Experience*. In a fine study, Elwyn A. Smith has measured the Old School with the yardstick of recent social concern and found it wanting (*The Presbyterian Ministry in American Culture*, especially pp. 95–175).

5. Sidney E. Mead, *The Lively Experiment*, p. 127. Mead excepts only the Unitarians. Old School Presbyterians doubtless are included in his references to "scholastic orthodoxy."

6. Other factors, such as slavery, contributed to the division, but the basic issues were theological, and the most important of these was clearly the question of human ability. See Marsden, *Evangelical Mind*, pp. 7–87, and his summary of recent scholarly debate on pp. 250–51.

7. Sidney E. Mead has recently observed that Methodism, centered in a profoundly arminian version of revivalism, represented "the characteristic temper" of American Protestantism from the Second Awakening until the early twentieth century. See Mead, "Professor Sweet's Religion and Culture in America," pp. 42–44.

8. Smith, *Presbyterian Ministry*, p. 52.

9. L. A. Lowry, *An Earnest Search for Truth, in a Series of Letters from a Father to His Son*, pp. 66–67. For some characteristically affirmative Old School views of revivalism, see Melanchthon, "On Religious Experience," pp. 153–54; Samuel Miller, *The Importance of the Gospel Ministry*, p. 31; [Ezra Fisk], "Character of the Present Age," pp. 125–28. Charles Hodge held the revival of 1857–58 to be "the most remarkable event in the religious history of our country" (Hodge to Rev. J. N. Campbell, 5 May 1858, Gratz Collection).

10. See, e.g., Winthrop S. Hudson, *Religion in America*, pp. 165–66; Claude Welch, *Protestant Thought in the Nineteenth Century*, 1:201.

11. [Robert Jefferson Breckinridge], "Some Thoughts on the Development of the Presbyterian Church in the United States of America," pp. 317, 334. See also "Critical Notices," SPR 7:158: "How signally [the church] . . . has prospered since the painful separations of 1837, '38." In the same year Nathan L. Rice announced triumphantly: "It is a fact, not denied, that since the division the Old School Church has made much more rapid progress than the New School—thus affording an instructive comment upon the oft-repeated charge against the former, of holding to a *dead orthodoxy*" (*The Old and the New Schools*, p.vi).

12. Herman C. Weber, *Presbyterian Statistics Through One Hundred Years*, pp. 12–17, 39–169. Since the Old School was heavily represented in the South, much of the story is told in Thompson, *Presbyterians in the South*. The parochial school effort is described in Lewis Joseph Sherrill, *Presbyterian Parochial Schools, 1846–1870*.

13. The most theologically powerful journals, modeled on the heavy "quarterly reviews" of the day, were the *Princeton Review* (1825–84) and the *Southern Presbyterian Review* (1847–62). A near-complete listing of Old School periodicals may be found in Thompson, *Presbyterians in the South*, p. 598, and "Presbyterian Periodicals," in *Minutes of the General Assembly . . . 1851*, p. 185.

14. James Hastings Nichols, *Romanticism in American Theology*, p. 88.

15. Thomas Smyth, *Autobiographical Notes, Letters and Reflections*, p. 171.

16. George P. Schmidt, *The Old Time College President*, p. 29, refers to "the domination of higher education by the Presbyterians"; and see Randolph, *American College and University*, p. 57; Nichols, *Romanticism*, p. 1.

17. Lefferts Loetscher, *The Broadening Church*, p. 22; BRPR, *Index Volume from 1825 to 1868*, s.v. "Archibald Alexander."

18. James W. Alexander, *The Life of Archibald Alexander*, pp. 403–4.

19. See, e.g., Nathan L. Rice, *Ten Letters on the Subject of Slavery*; [Charles Hodge], "Slavery," pp. 268–305.

20. Rice, *Old and New Schools*, p. vi.

21. The Union Theological Seminary at Hampden-Sydney was established in 1824 and later removed to Richmond. The Theological Seminary in Columbia was established in 1829. See Thompson, *Presbyterians in the South*, pp. 274–85.

22. Theodore Dwight Bozeman, "Science, Nature and Society," p. 325, n. 77.

23. For evidence of occasional friction between the southern and the Princeton-dominated northern leadership, see Drury Lacy to James Henley Thornwell, 10 Nov. 1845, Thornwell Papers (SCL); Benjamin Morgan Palmer, *The Life and Letters of James Henley Thornwell*, pp. 289–90, 296.

24. Palmer, *Thornwell*, p. 281; G. Lewis, *Impressions of America and the American Churches*, p. 283; "The Inefficiency of the Pulpit," p. 83.

25. John H. Rice, *Historical and Philosophical Considerations on Religion*, p. 109; John H. Rice, "Report on the Course of Study to be Pursued in the Union Theological Seminary," p. 522.

26. Ashbel Green, "The Union of Piety and Science," pp. 17–18. See also Ashbel Green, "Introduction," p. 3. Green here argued that if religious doctrine be exhibited "in a careless or slovenly garb, it will not be likely to attract the attention and win the hearts of

that large and important portion of the community which consists of the young, the cultivated and the aspiring."

27. A typical case of imprecision on this point is Richard B. Hughes, "Old School Presbyterians," pp. 324–36. The author does not appear to sense any contradiction between his description of the "inflexible easternism" of the Presbyterians, which "limited their influence" and constituted a "failure of adjustment to the frontier milieu," and the plain indication of his research that they "influenced many of the social and intellectual leaders of the state; and as educators, they left a legacy out of all proportion to their numbers" (p. 336). See also Robert Ellis Thompson, A History of the Presbyterian Churches in the United States, pp. 70–71; William Garrett West, Barton Warren Stone, p. 51. A more adequate view is presented in Leonard Woolsey Bacon, A History of American Christianity, p. 292, and in Thompson, Presbyterians in the South, pp. 83, 188.

28. The phrase is Ahlstrom's; see "The Scottish Philosophy and American Theology," p. 268. See also Schmidt, Old Time College President, pp. 113, 121–23; Perry Miller, Introduction, p. ix: "The Presbyterian church made the Scottish doctrine virtually synonymous with Protestantism."

29. Alexander, Life of Alexander, pp. 177, 366; James Green, "Dr. Alexander on Mental Science," MSS notebook, FL. See also Archibald Alexander, Outlines of Moral Science.

30. Mathetes, "On the Nature of Virtue," p. 145.

31. James Henley Thornwell to George Frederick Holmes, 7 July 1857, Holmes Papers.

32. Francis L. Broderick, "Pulpit, Physics, and Politics," p. 45.

33. Samuel Miller, A Brief Retrospect of the Eighteenth Century, 2:377. See also Brooke Hindle, The Pursuit of Science in Revolutionary America, p. 89; John Witherspoon, Address to the Inhabitants of Jamaica, and Other West-India Islands, in Behalf of the College of New Jersey, p. 142.

34. Samuel Stanhope Smith to Ashbel Green, 12 Dec. 1792, Gratz Collection; William H. Hudnut III, "Samuel Stanhope Smith," p. 541; Rudolph, American College and University, p. 113.

35. Schmidt, Old Time College President, p. 216; Smith, Presbyterian Ministry, p. 112; Joseph H. Jones, The Life of Ashbel Green, pp. 420, 427–28; John Maclean, History of the College of New Jersey . . . , 2:195, and see 2:205, for a view of science in the Princeton curriculum during Green's presidency.

36. For the Princeton curriculum, see, e.g., Catalogue of the Officers and Students of the College of New Jersey for 1844–5, pp. 18–19. The scientific faculty is discussed in Thomas Jefferson Wertenbaker, Princeton, 1746–1896, p. 227. For the spreading Princeton influence, see, e.g., Donald Robert Come, "The Influence of Princeton on Higher Education in the South before 1825," pp. 370, 381.

37. Jones, Life of Green, pp. 145, 136, 205, 287; Samuel Miller, The Life of Samuel Miller, p. 469; Alexander, Life of Alexander, pp. 17, 36, 200, 382, 297, 540, 177, 685. James W. Alexander's biography reveals scientific interests rivaling those of his father. John Hall, ed., Forty Years' Familiar Letters of James W. Alexander, 1:21, 31, 74, 78, 80–81, 124, 205, 378; 2:117, 321, 333.

38. Charles Hodge to Hugh Hodge, 12 Oct. 1834, Hodge Papers, FL; A. A. Hodge, The Life of Charles Hodge, pp. 239, 68. Thomas Smyth of Charleston also "attended lectures at the medical college in Charleston for two years, and pursued the study privately" (T. Watson Street, "Thomas Smyth," p. 9). Smyth also held membership in the British and American Association for the Advancement of Science (Smyth, Autobiographical Notes, p. 267).

39. Ethel M. McAllister, Amos Eaton, p. 320. William B. Sprague was a trustee of the Institute from 1842 to 1865 (ibid., p. 398).

40. Annals of the American Pulpit, s.v. "Baxter, George"; ibid., "Matthews, John."

Henry Ruffner, Old Schooler and president of Washington College during the 1830s, urged members of the Franklin Society of Lexington in 1838 to cultivate the amateur study of "natural philosophy." It was in his view scandalous to consider "how large a proportion of our countrymen would rather attend a horserace, than listen to the most instructive lecture on science or . . . study the laws of nature" (Henry Ruffner, *Annual Address Delivered before the Franklin Society of Lexington*, pp. 9, 13).

41. Thomas Cary Johnson, *The Life and Letters of Robert Lewis Dabney*, p. 73. Dabney later developed a greater appreciation for the classics (ibid., p. 74, n. 8).

42. Hughes, "Old School Presbyterians," p. 325.

43. Quoted in Thompson, *Presbyterians in the South*, p. 212; Thornwell Jacobs, *The Life of William S. Plumer*, p. 46.

44. "Literary and Philosophical Intelligence," p. 183.

45. "Quarterly Scientific Intelligence," pp. 350–56, 526–31.

46. George P. Fisher, *The Life of Benjamin Silliman*, 2:14; John D. Holmfeld, "From Amateurs to Professionals in American Science," p. 27.

CHAPTER 3

1. Herbert W. Schneider, *A History of American Philosophy*, p. 247. See also Paul K. Conkin, *Puritans and Pragmatists*, p. 118.

2. Peter Gay, *The Enlightenment*. The subtitle of the first volume is *The Rise of Paganism*; see 1:xi, 212–422. For the secularity of science, see, e.g., 1:18, 309. Gay's *philosophes* admired Epicurus as the ultimate advocate of "science, and science alone, pitilessly destroying myths" (1:100).

3. Ibid., 1:121, 127–78.

4. Ibid., 1:212–422.

5. See, e.g., Franklin L. Ford, "The Enlightenment," p. 21. Concerning Gay's thesis, Ford remarks that "his emphasis on the 'paganism' of the Enlightenment has often seemed to me to be exaggerated, until I have paused to reflect that he writes, most of the time, quite explicitly about the French Enlightenment" (p. 21). Charles Coulston Gillispie has noted a clear difference between the French and British Enlightenment upon the issue of science and religion (*Genesis and Geology*, p. 31).

6. Martin E. Marty, *The Infidel*.

7. Thomas Cooper, *On the Connection between Geology and the Pentateuch, in a Letter to Professor Silliman*, pp. 74, 50. See also Cooper to Mahlon Dickerson, 13 Feb. 1826, "Letters of Dr. Thomas Cooper, 1825–1832," p. 727.

8. Frances Wright, *Course of Popular Lectures, as Delivered by Frances Wright*, p. 73.

9. Ibid., p. 22.

10. See, e.g., Lewis W. Green, *The Progressive Advancement and Ultimate Regeneration of Human Society*, pp. 23–24; Gardiner Spring, *The Power of the Pulpit*, p. 65. Spring was moderator of the Old School General Assembly in 1843.

11. Cotton Mather, *The Christian Philosopher*.

12. Ashbel Green was also a member of the American Philosophical Society (Joseph H. Jones, *The Life of Ashbel Green*, p. 480).

13. Samuel Miller, *A Brief Retrospect of the Eighteenth Century*, 1:411, 434.

14. Ibid., 1:372, 412.

15. Ibid., 1:202, 161.

16. Ibid., 1:10, 14, and the discussion of Reid on pp. 446–50.

17. Ibid., 1:110, 167, 174, iv; 2:442, 433.

18. Wilhelm Windelband, *A History of Philosophy*, 2:624.

19. Richard Hofstadter, *Anti-Intellectualism in American Life*, pp. 55–329 passim.

20. See, e.g., Edward W. Hooker, *Love to the Doctrines of the Bible an Essential Element of Christian Character*, p. 7. Hooker sponsored "a jealous care that the head and the heart shall go together."

21. William D. Kelley, *Characteristics of the Age*, p. 10. See also George Chapman, "Lecture on the Sciences as Applicable to Domestic Life," p. 187.

22. "V," "The March of Mind," pp. 154–56; Solomon, "The March of Mind," pp. 171–74.

23. John H. Rice, "Ministerial Character and Preparation Best Adapted to the Wants of the United States . . . ," pp. 209–10. Rice was moderator of the General Assembly in 1819. See also George Junkin, *The Bearings of College Education Upon the Welfare of the Whole Community*, p. 23. Junkin was moderator of the Old School General Assembly in 1844.

24. [Ezra Fisk], "Character of the Present Age," BRPR, 2:376. See also C. S. Venable, "Alexander Von Humboldt," p. 155.

25. Wright, "Parts of Knowledge," p. 73. See also Robert Dale Owen, "Galileo and the Inquisition."

26. "K," "The Rise and Progress of Popery," p. 472; [Fisk], "Character of the Present Age," BRPR, 2:377–78; James Henley Thornwell, *The Collected Writings of James Henley Thornwell*, 3:459. Thornwell was moderator of the Old School General Assembly in 1847.

27. John H. Rice, *Historical and Philosophical Considerations on Religion*, p. 33; [A. A. Porter], "The Unity of the Human Race," p. 359; [Benjamin M. Palmer], "Baconianism and the Bible," p. 245.

28. William S. Plumer, "Man Responsible for His Belief," p. 11. Plumer was moderator of the first Old School General Assembly in 1838. [Porter], "Unity of the Human Race," p. 359; George Junkin, *The Progress of the Age*, p. 12; R. C. Ketchum, "Testimony of Modern Science to the Unity of Mankind," p. 123.

29. Edward Everett, "The Uses of Astronomy," p. 627. For a characteristic formulation, see David Hoffman, *Legal Outlines*, pp. 17–20.

30. Miller, *Brief Retrospect*, 1:11.

31. Gilbert Morgan, *The Inaugural Address of the Rev. Gilbert Morgan . . .* , p. 9.

32. James Henley Thornwell, "Address Delivered to the Euphradian and Clariosophic Societies of the South Carolina College," Thornwell Papers (SCL).

33. James Green, "Dr. Alexander on Mental Science," MSS notebook, Alexander Papers (FL). See also, e.g., [James W. Alexander], "Immediate Perception," p. 205.

34. Nathan L. Rice, *Phrenology Examined, and Shown to be Inconsistent with the Principles of Phisiology* [sic], *Mental and Moral Science, and the Doctrines of Christianity*, p. 187.

35. John Witherspoon, *The Works of the Rev. John Witherspoon*, 3:278.

36. Robert J. Breckinridge, *The Knowledge of God, Objectively Considered . . .* , p. 324.

37. [Thomas Smyth], "Assurance—Witness of the Spirit, and the Call to the Ministry," p. 103.

38. The thought was associated with Reid ([Francis Andrew March], "Sir William Hamilton's Theory of Perception," p. 292). This general emphasis must be viewed within the shared framework of Anglo-American thought. See Walter E. Houghton, *The Victorian Frame of Mind, 1830–1870*, pp. 16–17.

39. Benjamin Silliman, *Elements of Chemistry*, 1:23.

40. Samuel Jackson, *Introductory Lecture to the Course of the Institutes of Medicine, in the University of Pennsylvania . . .* , p. 9.

41. See Perry Miller, *The Life of the Mind in America*, pp. 65, 319, 321, 326–27.

42. John Locke, *An Essay Concerning Human Understanding*, "Epistle to the Reader," p. xii.

43. John D. Godman, "The Beaver," p. 98. Godman was professor of anatomy at Rutgers University.

44. Joseph Henry, "Explanations and Illustrations of the Plan of the Smithsonian Institution," p. 306.

45. Adam Sedgwick, *A Discourse on Classical, Metaphysical, Moral, and Natural Studies*, p. 212.

46. Archibald Alexander, "Nature and Evidences of Truth," MSS oration, Alexander Papers (SL).

47. Thornwell, *Collected Writings*, 3:119.

48. Witherspoon, *Works*, 3:275.

49. Matthew Brown, "The Importance and Obligation of Truth," pp. 69, 72.

50. Green, "Alexander on Mental Science," p. 5; Plumer, "Man Responsible," p. 6. Undoubtedly the most ingenuous statement of this pervasive theme came not from a Presbyterian but from Episcopalian educator Silas Totten in 1848: "Truth is objective; that is, it exists independently of ourselves . . . so that what is true, is absolutely and independently true. . . . Truth is in itself independent and immutable, and may be defined to be the actual state and condition of things." (*The Analogy of Truth, in Four Discourses*, p. 8).

51. Leroy J. Halsey, *Address to the Alumni Society of the University of Nashville, on the Study of Theology as a Part of Science, Literature and Religion*, p. 10.

52. [James Clement Moffat], "Popular Education," p. 615.

53. Junkin, *Bearings of College Education*, p. 4; Halsey, *On the Study of Theology*, p. 10.

54. [Archibald Alexander], "Principle of Design in the Interpretation of Scripture," p. 409.

55. Benjamin M. Palmer, *The Love of Truth, the Inspiration of the Scholar*, pp. 15–16. Palmer was to be moderator of the first General Assembly of the Presbyterian Church in the Confederate States of America, which split from the central body in 1861.

56. "Philosophy Subservient to Religion. Essay 12," p. 213.

57. John T. L. Preston, "The Mind of Man, the Image of God," p. 234.

58. Thornwell, *Collected Writings*, 2:480.

59. Thomas Dick, *On the Improvement of Society by the Diffusion of Knowledge*, p. 87: "The Creator has implanted in the human mind a principle of curiosity, and annexed a pleasure to its gratification, to excite us to investigations of the wonders of creation." Thomas Chalmers, *On the Power, Wisdom, and Goodness of God . . .* , p. 250; Henry Lord Brougham, *A Discourse on the Objects, Advantages, and Pleasures of Science*, p. 119.

60. John C. Young, *Advantages of Enlarged Scientific and Literary Attainments*, p. 3.

61. Nathan L. Rice, *Phrenology Examined*, p. 187.

62. Palmer, *Love of Truth*, p. 14.

63. "Bacon's Philosophy," p. 44; William Ellery Channing, *Discourse at the Dedication of Divinity Hall*, p. 501.

64. Joseph LeConte, "On the Science of Medicine and the Causes Which Have Retarded Its Progress," p. 474.

65. R. B. McMullen, *Truth the Foundation of Genuine Liberty*, p. 4.

66. Francis W. Pickens, *Science and Truth*, p. 3.

67. George Tucker, "The Progress of Philosophy, and Its Influence on the Intellectual and Moral Character of Man," p. 409; see also pp. 410–11.

68. [Walter Channing], "Ancient Medicine," p. 219.

69. Benjamin Silliman, "Introductory Remarks," p. 7. See also Peter Browne, "Hints to Students of Geology," p. 162; James D. Whelpley, "Letter on Philosophical Induction," p. 36; Denison Olmsted, *Letters on Astronomy . . .* , p. 137.

70. Miller, *Brief Retrospect*, 1:202.

71. Tucker, "Progress of Philosophy," p. 410; Dick, *Improvement of Society*, p. 54; Olmsted, *Letters on Astronomy*, pp. 16, 137.

72. The natural-history background is sketched in William Martin Smallwood and Mabel Sarah Coon Smallwood, *Natural History and the American Mind*, pp. 130–353, passim. Gulian C. Verplanck, *On the Importance of Scientific Knowledge to the Manufacturer and Practical Mechanic*, pp. 261–94.

73. Francis Wayland, *Discourse, Delivered at the Dedication of Manning Hall . . .* , p. 16; A[lonzo] Potter, "Preliminary Observations," p. xvii; [Willard Phillips], "Hedge's Logick," p. 84. See also Olmsted, *Letters on Astronomy*, pp. 166–67.

74. Mathetes, "On the Nature of Virtue," p. 145.

75. "Short Notices," BRPR, 23:696. The work in question was Eleazar Lord, *The Epoch of Creation*.

76. John Frederick William Herschel, *A Preliminary Discourse on the Study of Natural Philosophy*, pp. 102, 104; Palmer, "Baconianism and the Bible," p. 238. Palmer explicitly repudiated taxonomic interpretations of physical science (p. 233). See also Richard S. Gladney, "Natural Science and Revealed Religion," p. 449.

77. James Henley Thornwell, "Lecture Second," MSS in Thornwell Papers (SCL). Emphasis mine. See also Lewis W. Green, *Inaugural Address, Delivered before the Board of Trustees of Hampden-Sydney College, January 10th, 1849*, p. 22.

78. The quote is from Thomas Chalmers, *Institutes of Theology*, 1:358. Emphasis mine. Herschel, *Preliminary Discourse*, p. 102, limits the term "general fact" to the early stages of generalization. See also [George Ide Chace], "The Persistence of Physical Laws," p. 174.

79. "Philosophy Subservient to Religion. Essay 1," p. 65; "Philosophy Subservient to Religion. Essay 10," p. 21; [James W. Alexander], "Connection between Philosophy and Revelation," pp. 382–83.

80. George H. Daniels, *American Science in the Age of Jackson*, p. 69. Tyler himself claimed of the *Discourse* that "its circulation has been extensive, its notices in periodicals almost universal," and that it had received "the commendations of the first men of our country" (Tyler to George Frederick Holmes, 7 Aug. 1854, Holmes Papers).

81. I have used the fuller second edition: Samuel Tyler, *A Discourse on the Baconian Philosophy*; Samuel Tyler, "On Philosophical Induction."

82. Samuel Tyler to John Miller, 8 Oct. 1849, Miller Papers. The South Caroliniana Library of the University of South Carolina has letters from Tyler to Thornwell; the Firestone Library of Princeton University has letters from Tyler to Hodge. Samuel Tyler to "Carey & Hart," 20 Oct. 1843, Gratz Collection; Samuel Tyler to Charles Hodge, 12 Sept. 1859, Hodge Papers (FL); James Henley Thornwell to Robert J. Breckinridge, 27 Oct. 1855, in Benjamin M. Palmer, *The Life and Letters of James Henley Thornwell*, p. 388.

83. "Critical Notices," SPR, 11:676; "Short Notices," BRPR, 16:319; "Short Notices," BRPR, 16:609–10; "Short Notices," BRPR, 19:125–26; "Short Notices," BRPR, 30:735; "Critical Notices," SPR, 11:676.

84. [Samuel Tyler], "Balfour's Inquiry," pp. 327–48; [Samuel Tyler], "The Baconian Philosophy," pp. 350–77; [Samuel Tyler], "Psychology," pp. 227–50; [Samuel Tyler], "The Influence of the Baconian Philosophy," pp. 481–506.

85. Tyler, *Discourse*, p. 167.

86. Samuel Tyler to George Frederick Holmes, 2 Oct. 1854, Holmes Papers. Tyler indicated he had attempted in the *Discourse* to "rescue" induction from its degradation "into mere observation and classification."

87. Herschel, *Preliminary Discourse*, p. 102. Tyler's formulation reveals a close dependence on this passage (*Discourse*, p. 160).

88. TRPW, 2:701, 311–13. For characteristic later expressions of the view, see "Calumnies Against Oxford," p. 161: "The logic of Aristotle is particularly hostile to inductive science. By turning the mind to the syllogistic method, it becomes a very powerful obstruction to that knowledge which is derived, by induction, from experience and observation"; [J. Brazer], "Chalmer's Evidences of Christianity," pp. 365–66. At least one Old Schooler accepted this view. See Erasmus D. MacMaster, *A Discourse Delivered November 7th, 1838 . . .* , p. 9.

89. Alexander Campbell Fraser, *Archbishop Whately and the Restoration of the Study of Logic*; Wilbur Samuel Howell, *Eighteenth-Century British Logic and Rhetoric*, pp. 700–706; "Whately's *Elements of Logic*"; "Scotch School of Philosophy and Criticism," pp. 386–97; [Francis Bowen], "Wilson's Treatise on Logic," pp. 386–88.

90. [Samuel Tyler], "Elements of Logic," pp. 294–311.

91. Richard Whately, *Elements of Logic*, pp. 30–34.

92. Ibid., p. 182; Tyler, *Discourse*, p. 168. Cf. CWDS, 2: *Outlines of Moral Philosophy*, sec. 2, p. 7.

93. Samuel Tyler to George Frederick Holmes, 7 Aug. 1854, Holmes Papers.

94. Tyler, *Discourse*, pp. 169–72, 174, 177.

95. [Lyman Atwater], "Mill's System of Logic," p. 88; [Benjamin M. Palmer], "Narrative of a Mission to the Jews," p. 52.

96. Palmer, *Life and Letters of Thornwell*, p. 537; James Henley Thornwell, "To the President of South Carolina College," MSS report, dated 28 Nov. 1838, Thornwell Papers (SCL).

97. James Henley Thornwell, "Logic," MSS lecture, undated, p. 16, Thornwell Papers (SCL); James Henley Thornwell, "Lecture—Syllogism," MSS lecture, undated, p. 22, Thornwell Papers (SCL). Internal evidence reveals that this lecture was prepared during Thornwell's tenure as professor of metaphysics at the college during the 1838–39 academic year. The final quote is from Thornwell, "Logic," p. 15.

98. Thornwell, *Collected Writings*, 3:83; James Henley Thornwell, "Lecture First," MSS lecture, undated, Thornwell Papers (SCL).

CHAPTER 4

1. Edward A. Washburn, "Parallel between the Philosophical Relations of Early and Modern Christianity," p. 54.

2. Richard Hofstadter, *Anti-Intellectualism in American Life*, pp. 148–49; John H. Rice, Introduction, p. 6: "There are now in the world multitudes, who associate with the name of philosophy, ideas of infidelity and atheism."

3. [Thomas Babington Macaulay], "Lord Bacon," p. 5; "Remarks on a Late Review of Lord Bacon," p. 505.

4. [Edward Everett], "Character of Lord Bacon," pp. 300, 336.

5. Ralph Waldo Emerson, *Lord Bacon*, p. 323. See the similar account in "Lord Bacon," NE, 10:333–74.

6. Samuel M. Hopkins, "Religious Character of Lord Bacon," p. 132; "Shelley," p. 276.

7. A Provincial Protestant, "The Christian Religion Vindicated from the Charge of Being Hostile to Knowledge," p. 169; [Benjamin M. Palmer], "Baconianism and the Bible," p. 245; R. C. Smith, *The Educator of Youth*, p. 15; [Joseph Atkinson], "Moral Aesthetics," p. 52; [Lewis W. Green], "The Harmony of Revelation, and Natural Science: With Especial Reference to Geology.—Number 1," p. 93.

8. "Lord Bacon's Confession of Faith," pp. 241–47; [Benjamin M. Palmer], "The Relation between the Works of Christ, and the Condition of the Angelic World," p. 46; Nathan L. Rice, "Moral Effects of Christianity," p. 591; [William S. Plumer], "Life of Socrates," p. 246.

9. Rice, Introduction, p. 6; Samuel Miller, *Letters on Unitarianism*, pp. 108–9. Newton did in fact espouse an anti-Trinitarian view of Christianity. See John Dillenberger, *Protestant Thought and Natural Science*, p. 125.

10. Rice, "Moral Effects," p. 591.

11. Perry Miller, *The Life of the Mind in America*, p. 7.

12. William Maclure, *Opinions on Various Subjects, Dedicated to the Industrious Producers*, 1:55.

13. Hugo A. Meier, "Technology and Democracy, 1800–1860," pp. 623, 634; Thomas Cooper, *The Introductory Lecture of Thomas Cooper . . .*, p. 90; "Observations on the Rise and Progress of the Franklin Institute," p. 67. See also Brooke Hindle, *The Pursuit of Science in Revolutionary America*, p. 190.

14. Cooper, *Introductory Lecture*, pp. 3, 90–96, 99, 171; Thomas Cooper,

Introductory Lecture, On Chemistry . . . , pp. 7–9, 14; Maclure, *Opinions*, 1:48–57; Meier, "Technology and Democracy," pp. 618–40.

15. Albert Post, *Popular Freethought in America, 1825–1850*, pp. 33–38, 46–50, 115, 172; C. A. Browne, "Some Relations of the New Harmony Movement to the History of Science in America," p. 483; J. Percy Moore, "William Maclure—Scientist and Humanitarian," p. 239. Post shows the popularity of Paine, Voltaire, Ethan Allen, and other Enlightenment radicals among the freethinkers. He concludes that "in all essentials the freethinkers . . . were the intellectual heirs of the Enlightenment." (Post, *Popular Freethought*, p. 226).

16. Richard S. Westfall, *Science and Religion in Seventeenth Century England*; Dillenberger, *Protestant Thought*, pp. 104–32. The phrase is Dillenberger's (ibid., p. 104).

17. Basil Willey, *The Eighteenth Century Background*, p. 136.

18. Quoted in Charles Edwin Clark, "Science, Reason, and an Angry God," p. 353. See also Charles Coulston Gillispie, *Genesis and Geology*, p. 31.

19. Dillenberger, *Protestant Thought*, pp. 137–38, 152–53.

20. See John C. Greene, "Objectives and Methods in Intellectual History," p. 70 n.: "It is interesting to observe how many of the ablest American scientists . . . [in antebellum America] were evangelical in their faith and believers in the plenary inspiration of the Bible." In 1856, Edward Hitchcock and Mark Hopkins delivered major addresses on the relations between science and religion "according to previous arrangement, during the recent session of the American Associaton for the Advancement of Science, in Albany" ("Short Notices," BRPR, 29:158). For additional indication of the religious character of antebellum science, see, e.g., Conrad Wright, "The Religion of Geology," pp. 338–39, 342–43; Merle Curti, *The Growth of American Thought*, pp. 313–14.

It is of utmost importance to keep in view the British background of American thought in this as in most areas. Howard Mumford Jones has pointed out that "when we trace this [scientific] theism to its source, we are usually led to post-Napoleonic Britain" ("The Influence of European Ideas in Nineteenth-Century America," p. 257). See also Miller, *Life of the Mind*, p. 276. An indispensable study revealing the role of doxology in British science of the period is Gillispie, *Genesis and Geology*.

21. [John Davis], "An Address to the Linnaean Society of New England . . . ," p. 323.

22. This is continuous with the eighteenth-century ideal of science as "aesthetic contemplation" (Miller, *Life of the Mind*, pp. 276–77).

23. [T. Watkins], "Hayden's Geological Essays," p. 135; [C. T. Jackson], "Geology &c. of Massachusetts," p. 425; [I. Ray], "Decandolle's Botany," p. 35. See also Henry A. Miles, *On Natural Theology as a Study in Schools*, p. 8.

24. "Motion, the Natural State of Matter," p. 151. Herschel's *Preliminary Discourse* depicted science as "an endless source of pure and exciting contemplations" (John Frederick William Herschel, *A Preliminary Discourse on the Study of Natural Philosophy*, p. 15).

25. Edward Everett, "Uses of Astronomy," p. 623. Mrs. Almira Lincoln, in her *Familiar Lectures on Botany*, p. 16, presented the subject as a stimulus of "the most pure and delightful emotions" and of "a greater love and reverence for the deity." This view was also strongly represented in the popular diffusion-of-knowledge literature on science. See, e.g., Henry Lord Brougham, *A Discourse on the Objects, Advantages, and Pleasures of Science*, pp. 33–120; Thomas Dick, *On the Improvement of Society by the Diffusion of Knowledge*, pp. 82, 86–87, 92–93.

26. Jones, "Influence of European Ideas," p. 257; George H. Daniels, *American Science in the Age of Jackson*, pp. 53–54.

27. James Dwight Dana, "Science and Scientific Schools," p. 350. And see "Biblical Commentary," pp. 30–31; Edward Hitchcock, "First Anniversary Address before the Association of American Geologists . . . ," p. 275; Lewis W. Green, *The Progressive Advancement and Ultimate Regeneration of Human Society*, pp. 29–30; [Theophilus

Parsons], "The Tendencies of Modern Science," p. 97; Washburn, "Early and Modern Christianity," pp. 54–55.

28. George P. Fisher, *The Life of Benjamin Silliman*, 1:82–83, 95, 372, 386; 2:4, 23.

29. Edward Lurie, *Louis Agassiz*, p. 51. Agassiz leaned toward Unitarianism after coming to America.

30. For instance, Bruno A. Casile has observed that in contrast to earlier practice, "no writer of a zoology textbook in America between 1846 and 1860 neglected in his preface to make a special point of the religious value of science" (cited in George H. Daniels, "The Process of Professionalization in American Science," p. 163, n. 47). Two important antebellum scientists, Elias Loomis and Denison Olmsted, each had two years of theological training (Daniels, *American Science*, pp. 87, 133).

31. Henry D. Rogers, "Address Delivered at the Meeting of the Association of American Geologists and Naturalists . . . ," p. 278. The Hitchcock quote is from Daniels, *American Science*, p. 52. See also A. A. Gould, "An Address in Commemoration of Professor J. W. Bailey, Late President of the A.A.A.S.," p. 153; and James D. Whelpley, "Second Letter on Philosophical Analogy," p. 33: "The whole purpose of science, being to form a true and perfect idea of the universe . . . such as may satisfy the aspiration of Reason to understand the wisdom of the Creator in his work."

32. James D. Dana, "On American Geological History," p. 330. See also James D. Dana, "Agassiz's Contributions to the Natural History of the United States," p. 203; James D. Dana, "Science and Scientific Schools," p. 352.

33. Joseph LeConte, "Morphology and Its Connection with Fine Art," p. 108; Joseph LeConte, "On the Science of Medicine and the Causes Which Have Retarded Its Progress," p. 467; Joseph LeConte, "Lectures on Coal," p. 119.

34. Walter F. Cannon recently has pointed out the thorough integration of theological concepts into John Frederick William Herschel's view of the meaning and aims of science ("John Herschel and the Idea of Science," pp. 226–27). See also Herschel, *Preliminary Discourse*, p. 4, and L. Pearce Williams, *Michael Faraday*, p. 63. An admirable short sketch of the pattern is provided by John C. Greene, "Science and Religion," pp. 50–69.

35. The doctrinaire interests of Lewis Feuer, which make inconceivable any positive historical correlation between religion and science, have resulted in a seriously falsified view of antebellum science in his "The Scientific Intellectual in the United States," esp. pp. 351–69.

36. Lewis W. Green, *Regeneration of Human Society*, pp. 29–30.

37. "Remarks on the Study of Natural Philosophy," p. 262; "Philosophy Subservient to Religion. Essay 1," p. 65.

38. For the general pattern of protest within Anglo-American science, see, e.g., Herschel, *Preliminary Discourse*, p. 10; Brougham, *Objects, Advantages, and Pleasures of Science*, pp. 75, 128–30.

39. Benjamin M. Palmer, *The Love of Truth, the Inspiration of the Scholar*, p. 38. The scientist, thought Palmer, was likewise not the exploiter but "the Priest of nature" (Palmer, *The Influence of Religious Belief Upon National Character*, p. 8). See also J. R. Blake, "Popular Objections to Science," pp. 206–10; LeConte, "Morphology," pp. 108–9.

40. [Atkinson], "Moral Aesthetics," p. 38.

41. Both Reid and Stewart taught natural theology as a portion of their responsibilities in moral philosophy. Their published discussions of the meaning of science are dominated by a doxological understanding of research as discovery of Divine plan and purpose. See, e.g., IP, Essay 6, ch. 6, p. 668: "Every discovery we make in the constitution of the material . . . system becomes a hymn of praise"; CWDS, 6, pp. 63-64, 113.

42. Westfall, *Science and Religion*, pp. 50, 69; Dillenberger, *Protestant Thought*, pp. 114, 115, and passim; Daniels, *American Science*, p. 144.

43. Elizabeth Cary Agassiz, *Louis Agassiz*, p. 393.

44. "The Christian Religion Vindicated from the Charge of Being Hostile to

Knowledge," p. 227. The faith in design was deeply embedded in eighteenth-century Presbyterian thought. See, e.g., Jonathan Dickinson, *The Reasonableness of Christianity, in Four Sermons*, pp. 7, 23. For the Puritan background, see Perry Miller, *The New England Mind*, pp. 207, 225–26.

45. E. F. Rockwell, "The Alphabet of Natural Theology," pp. 429, 420. See also E. F. Rockwell, *Inaugural Address of the Rev. E. F. Rockwell, Professor of Natural Science . . . ,* p. 17: "When studying His works, we are looking into His mind."

46. [E. P. Rogers], "Reflections Upon Heaven," p. 170.

47. William Paley, *Natural Theology*, p. 423. This famous British work, first published in 1802, was a book-length elaboration of the themes of design and care. It went through several American editions in the antebellum era and was widely used as a college text. See Wendell Glick, "Bishop Paley in America," pp. 347–54.

48. Mrs. Phelps, *Botany for Beginners*, p. 10.

49. [Green], "Revelation, and Natural Science. Number 1," p. 95; *The Works of Creation Illustrated*, p. 259.

50. An annotated English translation of Laplace's *Mecanique Celeste* had been made available by Nathaniel Bowditch in 1829–30. See "Astronomy of Laplace," AQR, 5:310–42; "A Few Words on Astronomy," pp. 109–15.

51. "Astronomy of Laplace," AQR, 7:258. Samuel Miller praised Laplace in his *A Brief Retrospect of the Eighteenth Century*, 1:62.

52. Miller, *New England Mind*, p. 173.

53. John C. Young, *Advantages of Enlarged Scientific and Literary Attainments*, p. 5. See also Palmer, *Love of Truth*, p. 13.

54. Joseph H. Jones, *The Attainments of Men in Secular and Religious Knowledge, Contrasted*, p. 32; "Short Notices," BRPR, 25:325; C. S. Venable, "Alexander Von Humboldt," pp. 153–74. And see [Samuel Tyler], "Cosmos, by Alexander Von Humboldt," pp. 382–97.

55. James Henley Thornwell, "Oration," MSS address, Thornwell Papers (SCL).

56. [Green], "Revelation and Natural Science. Number 1," p. 101.

57. James Henley Thornwell, *The Collected Writings of James Henley Thornwell*, 1:64.

58. Rockwell, "Alphabet of Natural Theology," p. 429.

59. Palmer, *Love of Truth*, p. 16.

60. Curti, *Growth of American Thought*, p. 299.

61. [William Tudor], "On Geological Systems," p. 211.

62. "Philosophy Subservient, Essay 1," p. 65. See also [Archibald Alexander], "The Bible, a Key to the Phenomena of the Natural World," p. 105; [James W. Alexander], "Evils of an Unsanctified Literature," pp. 67, 71.

63. R. H. Forrester, *Anniversary Address Delivered before the American Literary Institute of Bethany College, November 10, 1842*, p. 11; Alexander T. McGill, *Individual Responsibility*, pp. 7–8.

64. [Charles Woodruff Shields], "The Positive Philosophy of Auguste Comte," p. 20; Rice, "Moral Effects," p. 583. See also Stuart Robinson, "Difficulties of Infidelity," p. 541; [James Read Eckard], "The Logical Relations of Religion and Natural Science," p. 577.

65. John C. Greene, *The Death of Adam*, p. 23; H. S. Thayer, ed., *Newton's Philosophy of Nature*, p. 4. For a characteristic nineteenth-century statement of atomism, see Herschel, *Preliminary Discourse*, p. 37.

66. Edwin A. Burtt, *The Metaphysical Foundations of Modern Science*, p. 239.

67. Greene, *Death of Adam*, pp. 11–24.

68. Ibid., p. 19; Hugo Friedrich, *Europäische Aufklärung*, p. 65; Cotton Mather, *The Christian Philosopher*, p. 289. And see Samuel Davies, *Sermons on Important Subjects*, 1:272.

69. William B. Sprague, *Lectures Illustrating the Contrast between True Christianity*

and Various Other Systems, p. 12; Jones, *Attainments of Men*, p. 17; Nathan L. Rice, *The Influence of Christianity on the Progress of Science*, p. 5; Robert C. Breckinridge, *The Knowledge of God, Objectively Considered . . .*, p. 333.

70. Benjamin M. Palmer, "Sermon Upon the Doctrine of a Special Providence," MSS sermon, Palmer Papers. See also R. C. Ketchum, "Testimony of Modern Science to the Unity of Mankind," p. 115.

71. Jacob J. Janeway, *The Internal Evidence of the Holy Bible . . .*, p. 169. Presbyterian pronouncements on this subject consistently associate atoms, apart from an externally imposed Divine rule, with chaos. For a later American attack upon this assumption, see Edward H. Madden, *Chauncey Wright*, p. 77.

72. Ashbel Green, *Lectures on the Shorter Catechism of the Presbyterian Church in the United States of America*, 1:216; [Green], "Revelation and Natural Science. Number 1," p. 97.

73. "Short Notices," BRPR, 24:142; Joseph LeConte, *Inaugural Address Delivered in the State House, Dec. 1, 1857*, p. 27. See also Thomas A. Hoyt, "The Astronomical Argument against Christianity," p. 516. Hoyt accused naturalistic astronomers of depicting a universe in which "innumerable and stupendous masses of matter wheel along their endless courses amid the silence of death."

74. Cortlandt Van Rensselaer, untitled MSS notebook from a course of physics at Yale College taught by Denison Olmsted, dated 1827, Van Rensselaer Papers.

75. Some characteristic passages are: "On the Origin of the Soul," p. 285; "Philosophy Subservient, Essay 1," p. 65; James Green, "Dr. Alexander on Mental Science," MSS notebook dated 1837, Alexander Papers (FL); Henry Ruffner, "The Middle State of Man," MSS treatise, undated, p. 24, Ruffner Papers; George Junkin, *An Apology for Collegiate Education*, p. 20.

76. "On the Origin of the Soul," p. 286. Reid had argued that human and Divine will was the only conceivable model of "power" in nature. Material itself had no inherent "active power"; atoms were "guided as a horse is by his rider" (Reid to Lord Kames, 16 Dec. 1780, TRPW, 1:59).

77. Ruffner, "Middle State of Man," p. 32. Daniel Walker Howe has found Harvard Unitarians of the antebellum period "fascinated with the theme of spirit triumphing over matter" (*The Unitarian Conscience*, p. 42).

78. Green, *Shorter Catechism*, 1:215; John Matthews, *The Divine Providence Displayed in the Works of Providence and Grace*, p. 30.

79. Miller, *Brief Retrospect*, 1:110; 2:28. The quote is from George Harmon Knowles, "The Religious Ideas of Thomas Jefferson," p. 200.

80. A Countryman, "On the Tendency of Doctrines Maintained by Some Modern Physiologists," pp. 482–83.

81. [Lyman Atwater], "Compte's Positive Philosophy," p. 68; Edward Hitchcock, *The Highest Use of Learning*, p. 19.

82. Joseph H. Jones, *Man Moral and Physical*, pp. 13–31.

83. The best account is John D. Davies, *Phrenology, Fad and Science*.

84. Nathan L. Rice, *Phrenology Examined, and Shown to be Inconsistent with the Principles of Phisiology [sic], Mental and Moral Science, and the Doctrines of Christianity*, p. 10. Rice claimed, "There is scarcely a village in the east or west, whose inhabitants have not been entertained by an itinerating phrenologist" (p. 10).

85. McGill, *Individual Responsibility*, p. 8.

86. See William Stanton, *The Leopard's Spots*, pp. 24–183.

87. Matthew Boyd Hope was shocked at Agassiz's suggestion that the gospel is directed only to the white species ("Professor Bachman on the Unity of the Human Race," p. 314).

88. [Albert B. Dod], "Vestiges of Creation," p. 535. See also [A. A. Porter], "The Unity of the Human Race," p. 377. James W. Alexander wrote a laudatory Introductory Notice to J. L. Cabell's *The Testimony of Modern Science to the Unity of Mankind*.

89. Justus Liebig, *Animal Chemistry, or Organic Chemistry in Its Applications to*

Physiology and Pathology; John W. Draper, *A Treatise on the Forces which Produce the Organization of Plants*. For a critical contemporary review of both works by a respected American Presbyterian scientist, see [Asa Gray], "The Chemistry of Vegetation," pp. 156–95.

90. See, e.g., "On the Vitality of Matter," pp. 54–62; E. B. Hunt, "On the Nature of Forces," pp. 237–49; Joseph Henry, "On the Conservation of Force," pp. 32–41.

91. T. V. Moore, "The Ethnological Objection," p. 423; "Short Notices," BRPR, 24:144–45.

92. LeConte, "Science of Medicine," p. 464; LeConte, *Inaugural*, p. 27; Rice, *Phrenology Examined*, p. 183; Rockwell, "Alphabet of Natural Theology," p. 421; Thornwell, *Collected Writings*, 1:183.

93. "Short Notices," BRPR, 17:345–47; Breckinridge, *Knowledge of God*, p. 335.

94. LeConte, *Inaugural*, p. 27.

95. Gillispie, *Genesis and Geology*, p. 149, and see pp. 149–83. Francis Bowen in 1849 correctly guessed the author to be Robert Chambers ("Recent Theories in Geology," pp. 256–69).

96. Samuel St. John, *Elements of Geology*, p. 117.

97. [Dod], "Vestiges of Creation," pp. 530, 533; Robinson, "Difficulties of Infidelity," p. 542.

98. Most of the problems are touched upon by Wright, "Religion of Geology,"; George H. Daniels, *Science in American Society*, pp. 206–22; and Greene, "Science and Religion," pp. 56–68. Indispensable background is furnished by Gillispie, *Genesis and Geology*, and Francis C. Haber, *The Age of the World*.

99. [George Howe], "Nott's Lectures," p. 441.

100. Richard S. Gladney, "Natural Science and Revealed Religion," p. 450.

101. [Matthew Boyd Hope], "Apologetics," p. 252.

102. W. C. Dana, "A Reasonable Answer to the Sceptic," p. 391; [William Channing], "American Medical Botany," p. 345; William Blackwood, *An Address Delivered at the Annual Meeting of the Missionary, Tract, and Education Society of the Theological Seminary at Princeton . . . ,*" p. 11.

103. Ethel M. McAllister, *Amos Eaton*, pp. 180–210; Daniels, *Science in American Society*, pp. 160–66; "Audubon's Ornithology, First Volume," p. 343; and see Hitchcock, "Anniversary Address," p. 271. Donald Zochert's "Science and the Common Man in Ante-Bellum America," a study of scientific interests and themes in Milwaukee newspapers from 1837 to 1843, reports a "vigorous, sustained interest in science" throughout the period.

104. Agassiz, *Louis Agassiz*, pp. 411–12, 444, 535; Fisher, *Life of Silliman*, 1:340, 347, 350, 363, 370; Lurie, *Louis Agassiz*, pp. 129–36. Curti relates the vogue in scientific lectures after about 1830 to "a nationwide enthusiasm for science" (*Growth of American Thought*, p. 318).

105. "Critical Notices," SPR, 3:682; [Palmer], "Baconianism and the Bible," pp. 226–27; Richard S. Gladney, "Natural Science and Revealed Religion," p. 449. Cf. Benjamin Silliman, *Elements of Chemistry*, 1:21: "It would, in this age, be as disrespectable for any person claiming to have received a liberal education . . . to be ignorant of the great principles and the leading facts of chemical as of mechanical philosophy." And see Miller, *Life of the Mind*, p. 309.

106. Rice, *Phrenology Examined*, p. 16.

107. [Porter], "Unity of the Human Race," pp. 359–62.

108. [Matthew Boyd Hope], "Relation between Scripture and Geology," p. 390. See also Rice, *Phrenology Examined*, pp. 27, 30; George [Howe], "The Unity of the Race," pp. 124–66.

109. Gladney, "Natural Science," p. 451. See also "Short Notices," BRPR, 23:556.

110. James A. Lyon, "The New Theological Professorship—Natural Science in Connexion with Revealed Religion," pp. 185–86; [Porter], "Unity of the Human Race," pp. 359, 361; Charles Hodge to S. J. Prince, 16 Feb. 1863, Gratz Collection; "Short Notices," BRPR, 23:556.

CHAPTER 5

1. [Mrs. John Ware], "Hugh Miller and Popular Science," p. 455.

2. Samuel Tyler simply assimilated Baconianism and sublimity. See [Tyler], "The Baconian Philosophy," p. 490: "[The] Baconian Philosophy is preeminently sublime."

3. [D. S. Hill], "Religion and Mathematics," p. 35.

4. Richard Hofstadter, *Anti-Intellectualism in American Life*, p. 277; Margaret W. Rossiter, "Benjamin Silliman and the Lowell Institute," p. 624; Daniel Boorstin, *The Lost World of Thomas Jefferson*, pp. 111, 131; Richard H. Shryock, *Medicine and Society in America, 1660–1860*, p. 129; George H. Daniels, *American Science in the Age of Jackson*, pp. 138–43. Joseph Henry incorporated into the early program of the Smithsonian Institution a requirement "that 'all unverified speculations' must be rejected" (Hunter Dupree, *Science in the Federal Government*, p. 82).

5. See, e.g., [T. Watkins], "Hayden's Geological Essays," p. 136; "Natural History," FJ, 1:17; "V," "The March of Mind," p. 154; James D. Whelpley, "Letter on Philosophical Induction," p. 35; Josiah Holbrook, "Remarks," p. 23. Confronted with the competing Huttonian and Wernerian geologies during his European trip of 1805–6, Benjamin Silliman held himself "aloof from entire committal to either theory, or to any theory, except one derived directly from the facts" (George P. Fisher, *The Life of Benjamin Silliman*, 1:170).

6. Daniels, *American Science*, p. 138; Shryock, *Medicine and Society*, p. 129; Ethel M. McAllister, *Amos Eaton*, p. 289. Cf. Walter E. Houghton, *The Victorian Frame of Mind, 1830–1870*, p. 112.

7. [S. Gilman], "Brown's Philosophy of Mind," p. 9.

8. Samuel Miller, *A Brief Retrospect of the Eighteenth Century*, 2:3. See also [Lyman Atwater], "Butler's Lectures on Ancient Philosophy," p. 263.

9. Herbert W. Schneider, *A History of American Philosophy*, p. 209; William H. Hudnut III, "Samuel Stanhope Smith," p. 550. Smith, who became president of the college in 1794, promptly assigned readings in Reid to his classes in moral philosophy (Elwyn A. Smith, *The Presbyterian Ministry in American Culture*, p. 90).

10. [Charles Hodge], "The General Assembly," p. 483. Robinson was a devoted disciple of Thornwell.

11. Samuel Stanhope Smith, *An Essay on the Causes of the Variety of Complexion and Figure in the Human Species*, pp. 3, 19, 50; Samuel Stanhope Smith, *Lectures on the Evidences of the Christian Religion*, p. 333.

12. Miller, *Brief Retrospect*, 1:165, 174, 202; [Ashbel Green], "Penn's Geology," p. 222; A Countryman, "On the Tendency of Doctrines Maintained by Some Modern Physiologists," p. 483.

13. See, e.g., Maxwell McDowell, "On Craniological Physiology," p. 144; J. Horwitz, "Cosmogony of Moses," p. 563.

14. [William S. Plumer], "Life of Socrates," p. 254.

15. [A. A. Porter], "The Unity of the Human Race," p. 367. Thornwell, a follower of Agassiz in geology, was convinced that "the Mosaic narrative contradicts not a single fact of descriptive geology. All that she reports of the shape of the earth, its minerals and fossils, its marks of convulsions and violence,—all these *facts* may be fully admitted, and yet not a line of Moses be impugned. It is only when the geologist proceeds to the causes of his facts, and invents hypotheses to explain them, that any inconsistency takes place" (James Henley Thornwell, *The Collected Writings of James Henley Thornwell*, 3:71).

16. [William J. Clark], "Prichard's Natural History of Man," p. 160; [Benjamin M. Palmer], "Baconianism and the Bible," p. 244; [Matthew Boyd Hope], "Relation between Scripture and Geology," p. 390.

17. [Charles Hodge], "The Unity of Mankind," p. 107. As in the sources, the terms "theory," "hypothesis," "speculation," and "metaphysics" will be used here inter-

changeably unless specified otherwise. See also "Philosophy Subservient to Religion. Essay 10," p. 24.

18. Nathan L. Rice, *Phrenology Examined . . .* , p. 28. See also [Albert B. Dod], "Vestiges of Creation," p. 527. Yet a writer in Breckinridge's *Baltimore Literary and Religious Magazine* in 1835 gave approval to phrenology on the grounds that it was "a doctrine of facts collected from observation and induction" ("J. P. C.," "Phrenology," p. 271). See also Nathan L. Rice's similar assault upon mesmerism (*Mesmerism*, pp. 256–57).

19. "Short Notices," BRPR 18:356; [Albert B. Dod], "Phrenology," p. 302. Phrenology also was perceived as a threat to the firmly unitary psychology to which the Old School subscribed. See, e.g., James Henley Thornwell, "Lecture Fifth," MSS lecture, pp. 17–18, Thornwell Papers (SCL); [Charles Hodge], "Finney's Lectures on Theology," p. 248.

20. Lewis W. Green, "The Harmony of Revelation and Natural Science . . . Number 1," p. 106.

21. [Dod], "Vestiges of Creation," p. 536; John B. Adger, "Inaugural Address on Church History and Church Polity," p. 150; James Henley Thornwell, "Lecture— Syllogism," MSS lecture, p. 22, Thornwell Papers (SCL). That a hypothesis may *precede* investigation was, however, not commonly admitted. See [James Read Eckard], "Religion and Natural Science," p. 582: "*Sooner* or *later* in our investigations we shall need to form a supposition, or hypothesis." The normal idea was that a hypothesis must emerge from prior contact with data. South Carolina scientist R. T. Brumby wrote in the *Southern Presbyterian Review* that a follower of "the true Baconian philosophy . . . collects and cautiously collates facts, from which conclusions necessarily follow" ("Footprints of the Creator," p. 118). And see [Clark], "Prichard's Natural History," pp. 159–60.

22. CWDS, 2: *Elements*, pt. 1, ch. 6, sec. 5, p. 403.

23. [Hope], "Scripture and Geology," p. 387.

24. [Dod], "Vestiges of Creation," p. 538. The *Vestiges* was generally received in the Anglo-American world as a thoroughgoing transgression of the inductive philosophy. See, e.g., [Adam Sedgwick], "Natural History of Creation," pp. 2, 85; "A Theory of Creation," pp. 437, 439.

25. Richard S. Gladney, "Natural Science and Revealed Religion," p. 449, emphasis mine. See also Edwin Cater, "Geological Speculation, and the Mosaic Account of Creation," p. 535: "Hypothesis can only be of value when it is made to hold a subordinate place, but it is a remorseless tyrant when we allow it . . . mastery."

26. Gardiner Spring, *The Power of the Pulpit*, p. 73. This was a common idea in antebellum intellectual literature. See, e.g., John Augustine Smith, *The Mutations of the Earth*, p. 17.

27. Thornwell, *Collected Writings*, 3:219–20; [S. J. Cassels], "The Philosophy of Life," p. 76; Nathan L. Rice, *Inaugural Address*, p. 33.

28. [Hodge], "Unity of Mankind," p. 106.

29. [Porter], "Unity of the Human Race," p. 367.

30. [Hodge], "Unity of Mankind," p. 149. Similarly, Lyman Atwater protested against the incongruity of the phrenological effort to determine the nature of the immaterial mind by studying the material of the brain ("Moral Insanity," pp. 353, 356–57).

31. T. V. Moore, "The Ethnological Objection," pp. 447–48; [Matthew Boyd Hope], "Apologetics," p. 286.

32. [Matthew Boyd Hope], "Professor Bachman on the Unity of the Human Race," pp. 315–16; Lewis W. Green, *Inaugural Address, Delivered before the Board of Trustees of Hampden-Sydney College, January 10th, 1849*, p. 22.

33. Moore, "Ethnological Objection," p. 451; [Hodge], "Unity of Mankind," p. 149; Thornwell, *Collected Writings*, 4:403.

34. [Palmer], "Baconianism and the Bible," p. 251; [Hodge], "Unity of Mankind," pp. 104–5. See also "Review and Criticism," p. 241. This reviewer of the *Annual of Scientific Discovery* took issue with the claim that the polygenist issue was " 'wholly a scientific

one,'—a very unscientific statement, unless 'scientific,' includes scriptural."

35. [Elias P. Ely], "Remarks on Independence of Thought, Addressed to Candidates for the Ministry," p. 365; Thornwell, "Lecture First," MSS lecture, pp. 13–14, Thornwell Papers (SCL).

36. Ashbel Green, "The Union of Piety and Science," p. 8; [William S. Plumer], "Revivals of Religion," p. 115.

37. IP, Essay 2, ch. 4, p. 105; ibid., Essay 2, ch. 8, p. 148; ibid., Essay 2, ch. 14, p. 217. CWDS, 1:287–89.

38. See, e.g., "A Series of Discourses on the Christian Revelation, Viewed in Connexion with the Modern Astronomy, by Sir Thomas Chalmers," p. 341; "Sir Isaac Newton," p. 655.

39. Joseph H. Jones, *The Attainments of Men in Secular and Religious Knowledge, Contrasted*, p. 11. See also Richard Foster Jones, *Ancients and Moderns*, p. 231. In 1820 the *Evangelical and Literary Magazine* contrasted Thomas Cooper's "rash" materialistic speculations with the "child-like" approach of Newton ("Review," p. 72).

40. [Palmer], "Baconianism and the Bible," p. 243. See also [Lyman Atwater], "Hickok's Rational Cosmology," p. 349; Samuel Tyler, *A Discourse of the Baconian Philosophy*, pp. 160–61; George Junkin, *The Progress of the Age*, p. 12.

41. [Thomas Smyth], "The Province of Reason, Especially in Matters of Religion," p. 292. Francis Wayland, Baptist moral philosopher and president of Brown University, had argued in his *Discourse, Delivered at the Dedication of Manning Hall, of Brown University, February 4, 1835*, p. 10, that the Baconian Philosophy was nothing other than an application to nature of the biblical principle of humility.

42. [James W. Alexander], "Connection between Philosophy and Revelation," pp. 382–83.

43. [Hope], "Scripture and Geology," p. 390; Cater, "Geological Speculation," p. 536.

44. [Porter], "Unity of the Human Race," p. 362. Joseph Henry, a devout Old School layman whose association with the Princeton theologians has been noted, wrote in 1865 that "the highest generalizations of science, . . . are yet but approximations to truth, provisionally adopted, and continually subject to modification and restatement" (Fisher, *Benjamin Silliman*, 2:330).

45. Moore, "Ethnological Objection," p. 416; Nathan L. Rice, *The Signs of the Times*, p. 114.

46. [Palmer], "Baconianism and the Bible," p. 228. For an extreme formulation, see [Eckard], "Religion and Natural Science," pp. 580–82. Eckard contended that owing to the difficulty of canvassing and coordinating all relevant facts, "physical science must ever be to a large degree uncertain."

47. Lewis W. Green, "Harmony of Revelation," p. 109.

CHAPTER 6

1. Thomas A. Hoyt, "Astronomical Argument Against Christianity," p. 515. This idea was widespread among defenders of doxological science. See, e.g., Thomas Dick, *On the Improvement of Society by the Diffusion of Knowledge*, p. 245; Mark Hopkins, *Influence of the Gospel in Liberalizing the Mind*, pp. 5–6.

2. William Blackwood, *An Address Delivered at the Annual Meeting of the Missionary, Tract, and Education Society of the Theological Seminary at Princeton . . .* , p. 24. See also James Henley Thornwell, *The Collected Writings of James Henley Thornwell*, 3:220: "Christianity has nothing to fear from true science"; George D. Baxter, "Theology," MSS notes from Charles Hodge's course in theology at Princeton Seminary, dated 1861–62, p. 84, Hodge Papers (PHS): *"we need have no fear of the truth."*

3. See, e.g., [Charles Woodruff Shields], "The Positive Philosophy of Auguste Comte"; [Matthew B. Grier], "The Positive Philosophy of Auguste Comte."

4. [Benjamin M. Palmer], "Baconianism and the Bible," pp. 251–52; J. R. Blake, "Popular Objections to Science," p. 220.

5. Ashbel Green, *Lectures on the Shorter Catechism of the Presbyterian Church in the United States of America*, p. 173. John F. W. Herschel had assured Presbyterian readers of his *Discourse* that conflict between science and religion was impossible because "truth can never be opposed to truth" (*A Preliminary Discourse on the Study of Natural Philosophy*, p. 9).

6. See, e.g., R. C. Ketchum, "Testimony of Modern Science to the Unity of Mankind," p. 118; [Palmer], "Baconianism and the Bible," p. 245; [Joseph Atkinson], "Moral Aesthetics," p. 52; N[athan] L. Rice, *Address of the Reverend N. L. Rice before the Miami Union Literary Society of the Miami University*, p. 5.

7. See, e.g., Gardiner Spring, *The Power of the Pulpit*, p. 73; James A. Lyon, "The New Theological Professorship," pp. 185–86.

8. W. C. Dana, "A Reasonable Answer to the Sceptic," p. 391.

9. Ashbel Green, "Strictures on Modern Geology," p. 17–18. In 1851, A. A. Porter also declared his determination to "welcome *truth*, come whence, or where, or how it may" ("The Unity of the Human Race," p. 362).

10. [Palmer], "Baconianism and the Bible," p. 251; [Charles Hodge], "The Unity of Mankind," p. 106; [George Howe], "The Secondary and Collateral Influences of the Sacred Scriptures," p. 108; Richard S. Gladney, "Natural Science and Revealed Religion," p. 450; E. F. Rockwell, *Inaugural Address of Rev. E. F. Rockwell, Professor of Natural Science, before the Board of Trustees of Davidson College, N.C., August 13, 1851*, pp. 11–15.

11. "Short Notices," BRPR, 23:556. See also T. V. Moore, "Inspiration of the Scriptures," p. 282. Cf. Green, "Strictures on Modern Geology," pp. 9, 19.

12. [Palmer], "Baconianism and the Bible," pp. 229, 251.

13. [Lewis W. Green], "Harmony of Revelation and Natural Science . . . Number 1," p. 94.

14. See, e.g., Ira V. Brown, "Watchers for the Second Coming," p. 451; Timothy Smith, *Revivalism and Social Reform*, pp. 151–53, 157–58, 176–77, 221–22, 225–37; Perry Miller, *The Life of the Mind in America*, pp. 79–80, 91; Ernest Lee Tuveson, *Redeemer Nation*, pp. 52–90; Robert T. Handy, *A Christian America*, p. 34.

15. See, e.g., Samuel Stanhope Smith, *Lectures on the Evidences of the Christian Religion*, p. 396; Thomas Dick, *The Christian Philosopher*, p. 329. Dick's immensely popular volume went through a score of American editions. See also George Junkin, *The Progress of the Age*, pp. 23–24; Leonard Woods, Jr., "Christianity and Philosophy," p. 483; Nathan L. Rice, *The Signs of the Times*, pp. 13–14; "The New Earth," p. 16; William B. Sprague, *A Sermon Addressed to the Second Presbyterian Congregation, Albany . . .*, pp. 27–28; [J. L. Wilson], "The Certainty of the World's Conversion," p. 438.

16. Edward Lurie, *Louis Agassiz*, pp. 46–62, 205; John C. Greene, *The Death of Adam*, pp. 125–30. A clear contemporary account of Agassiz's version of catastrophism may be read in James Dwight Dana, "On American Geological History," pp. 305–34.

17. A good general account, although neglecting the role of Agassiz, is in George H. Daniels, *Science in American Society*, pp. 211–22. For the later period, see, e.g., George I. Chace, "Of Spirit and the Constitution of Spiritual Beings," p. 635; Edward Hitchcock, *The Religion of Geology and Its Connected Sciences*, pp. 68, 165–66, 170; Dana, "American Geological History," pp. 306–7; Joseph LeConte, *Inaugural Address Delivered in the State House, Dec. 1, 1857*, p. 22.

18. For a typical appropriation, see [Howe], "Secondary and Collateral Influences," p. 109. Horace Bushnell also adopted the scheme (*Nature and the Supernatural*, pp. 76–82, 202–7).

19. Blake, "Popular Objections," p. 225; James Henley Thornwell, "Miracles," pp. 200–201. See the similar formulation in [Green], "Harmony of Revelation . . . Number 1," p. 97.

20. Lewis W. Green, *The Progressive Advancement and Ultimate Regeneration of Human Society*, p. 5; Rockwell, *Inaugural Address*, p. 9.

21. [Green], "Harmony of Revelation . . . Number 1," pp. 96–97.

22. Ibid., p. 96; [Green], "Harmony of Revelation. . . . Number 3," pp. 462–63, 473. The earlier essay cited is Green, *Regeneration of Human Society*, pp. 25, 29. For references to Agassiz, see [Green], "Harmony of Revelation. . . . Number 2," pp. 304, 306, 311.

23. [E. F. Rockwell], "The Final Destiny of Our Globe," pp. 129–30, 141–42, 144.

24. Ibid., pp. 143, 147. I have been unable to locate critical reactions to their work.

25. For some characteristic expressions, see [Willard Phillips], "Hedge's Logick," p. 82; [Thomas Babington Macaulay], "Lord Bacon," p. 72; "Benefits of the Reformation on the Happiness of Man"; Thomas Smith Grimke, *An Address on the Character and Objects of Science*, p. 30; John Williamson Nevin, "Human Freedom," p. 415; Edward Everett, *An Address Delivered before the Literary Societies of Amherst College, August 25, 1835*, p. 8.

26. John H. Rice, *Historical and Philosophical Considerations on Religion*, pp. 30–32. See also Samuel Miller, *The Life of Samuel Miller*, p. 322.

27. Philip Lindsley, *A Plea for the Theological Seminary at Princeton, New Jersey*, p. 11. The expression also occurs in Grimke, *Character and Objects of Science*, p. 30.

28. George Junkin, "The College a Religious Institution," p. 90. See also "On the Reciprocal Influence of Literature and Religion," pp. 11–12. At least one expositor reserved for Calvin the right of "re-enthroning injured reason" (S. A. Mutchmore, *Thought and Action*, p. 5).

29. Nathan L. Rice, *The Influence of Christianity on the Progress of Science*, p. 13.

30. Green, *Regeneration of Human Society*, p. 20.

31. [James W. Alexander], "Modern Miracles and Wonders," p. 348; Erasmus D. MacMaster, *A Discourse Delivered November 7th, 1838 . . .* , p. 15.

32. Green, *Regeneration of Human Society*, p. 32; Elisha P. Swift, "The Charge," p. 11; R. H. Morrison, *The Inaugural Address of the Rev. R. H. Morrison . . .* , p. 15; "The Influence of the Reformation on the American Revolution," pp. 510–11; James Henley Thornwell, "Address Delivered to the Euphradian and Clariosophic Societies of the South Carolina College, December 3, 1839," MSS oration, p. 22, Thornwell Papers (SCL).

33. [Matthew Boyd Hope], "Apologetics," p. 260. See also A. B. Van Zandt, "The Necessity of a Revelation," p. 53.

34. [Ezra Fisk], "Character of the Present Age," BRPR, 2:376; Nathan L. Rice, *The Signs of the Times*, pp. 66, 112; Thornwell, *Collected Writings*, 3:184, 220.

35. [W. T. Hamilton], "The Character of Moses," p. 515. Moses traditionally was believed to be the author of the first five books of the Old Testament.

36. [James Read Eckard], "The Logical Relations of Religion and Natural Science," p. 588. For similar references to Solomon, see Nathan L. Rice, "Moral Effects of Christianity," p. 582; William S. Plumer, *Earnest Hours*, p. 23.

37. R. B. McMullen, *Truth the Foundation of Genuine Liberty*, p. 15, and see p. 14. Rice, "Moral Effects," p. 582; [Green], "Harmony of Revelation . . . Number 1," p. 96.

38. Robert J. Breckinridge, "The General Internal Evidence of Christianity," p. 336. See also S. J. P. Anderson, *The Influence of the Bible on Liberty*, p. 5; [Palmer], "Baconianism and the Bible," p. 250.

39. Breckinridge, "General Internal Evidence," p. 336; T. V. Moore, "Inspiration of the Scriptures," p. 283.

40. [E. F. Rockwell], "The Phenomena of Freezing Water in the Book of Job," pp. 254–55. See also J. Horwitz, "Cosmogony of Moses," pp. 546, 566; *The Works of Creation Illustrated*, pp. 94–95.

41. [Palmer], "Baconianism and the Bible," p. 230.

42. [Macaulay], "Lord Bacon," p. 72.

43. Samuel Tyler, *Discourse of the Baconian Philosophy*, pp. 410–17, 15.

44. Rice, *Address of the Rev. N[athan] L. Rice*, p. 5. Tyler's *Discourse* had appeared the preceding year.

45. Rice, "Moral Effects," p. 591.

46. Ibid., pp. 584–85. See also Van Zandt, "Necessity of a Revelation," p. 53.

47. Presbyterians generally held that religious doctrine acted as "electricity" to mental effort. See, e.g., "The Injury Done to Religion by Ignorant Preachers," p. 601; [S. C. Pharr], "On Mental Development," p. 206; George Junkin, *Progress of the Age*, p. 10. This was an ultimate response to the charge leveled by "infidelity" that Christianity stifled mental action. Cf. William Maclure, *Opinions on Various Subjects, Dedicated to the Industrious Producers*, 1:79, 175.

48. Rice, "Moral Effects," pp. 591–92; Rice, *Progress of Science*, p. 10.

49. Rice, "Moral Effects," pp. 592–93. See also Thornwell, *Collected Writings*, 1:500–501.

50. Rice, "Moral Effects," pp. 592–93.

51. [Palmer], "Baconianism and the Bible," pp. 244–45, 247–48.

52. Ibid., pp. 248–49. James Read Eckard was to argue in 1860 that the "foundation axiom of inductive science" was the lawful regularity of nature, and that this had been inculcated by the biblical emphasis on the "uniformity of natural operations as being secured by the character of God" ("Religion and Natural Science," pp. 586–89).

53. [Palmer], "Baconianism and the Bible," p. 250. And see Tyler, *Discourse*, p. 41: "The evangelical theology and the Baconian philosophy . . . are parts of one great system of thought."

54. Lewis W. Green, *Inaugural Address, Delivered before the Board of Trustees of Hampden-Sydney College, January 10th, 1849*, p. 21. And see Nathan L. Rice, *Signs of the Times*, pp. 63–68.

55. [Eckard], "Religion and Natural Science," p. 601.

CHAPTER 7

1. For some characteristic passages, see "S. B. H.," "On the Importance of Sound Learning in the Gospel Ministry," pp. 260–71; John H. Rice, "Ministerial Character and Preparation Best Adapted to the Wants of the United States, and of the World in the Nineteenth Century," p. 214; [Charles Hodge], "Public Education," pp. 370–410; [Benjamin M. Palmer], "A Plea for Doctrine as the Instrument of Sanctification," pp. 35–36.

2. Ashbel Green, "The Union of Piety and Science," pp. 14–15; Nicholas Murray, "The Ministry We Need," p. 11.

3. [William S. Plumer], "Polemic Theology," pp. 184–85. See also John H. Rice to Leonard Woods, 12 Nov. 1848, in William Maxwell, ed., *A Memoir of the Rev. John H. Rice*, p. 364.

4. [Lewis W. Green], "The Harmony of Revelation and Natural Science: With Especial Reference to Geology.—Number 1," p. 106.

5. A Baconian Biblist, *A Practical View of the Common Causes of Inefficiency in the Christian Ministry of the Congregational and Presbyterian Churches of the United States*, p. 19. See also Thomas Scott, *The Bible a Revelation from God*, p. 41; [James W. Alexander], "Attractions of the Cross," p. 175.

6. "On Christianity Considered as a Practical System," p. 113.

7. The primary literature on the subject is much too immense to catalogue here. See, e.g., [James W. Alexander and Albert B. Dod], "Transcendentalism"; [Charles Hodge], "The Latest Form of Infidelity"; [Lyman Atwater], "Coleridge"; [James W. Alexander], "Life of Hegel"; James Henley Thornwell, *The Collected Writings of James Henley Thornwell*, 3:9–182; "Objections to the German Transcendental Philosophy," pp. 328–43; [S. N. Stanfield], "Scripturalism and Rationalism," pp. 271–84.

8. John H. Bocock, "The Instructed Scribe," p. 120.

9. W. G. Howard, "Mysteries of the Bible," p. 626. See also "W. J. T.," "The Mind, Its Powers and Results," p. 662. This author named Bacon and Newton as the highest exemplars of "mind." See also "Natural History," AQR, 1:459; Samuel Tyler, *A Discourse of the Baconian Philosophy*, p. 22.

10. William Ellery Channing, *Discourse at the Ordination of the Rev. E. S. Gannett, Boston, 1824*, p. 368; Channing, *Discourse at the Ordination of the Rev. F. A. Farley, Providence, R.I., 1828*, p. 461. By 1860, James Dwight Dana was declaring the present age "the Age of Mind" ("Anticipations of Man in Nature," p. 296).

11. Alexander T. McGill, *Individual Responsibility*, p. 11.

12. William Ellery Channing, *Discourse at the Dedication of the Second Congregational Unitarian Church, New York*, p. 428. See also Andrews Norton, *A Statement of Reasons for Not Believing the Doctrines of Trinitarians, Concerning the Nature of God and the Person of Christ*, pp. 32–33.

13. See, e.g., John H. Rice, "A Discourse Delivered before the Literary and Philosophical Society of Hampden Sydney College . . . ," p. 59; [John William Yeomans], "Physical Theory of Another Life," p. 131; Ashbel Green, "The Word of God the Guide of Youth," p. 95; [Lyman Atwater], "The True Barrier Against Ritualism and Rationalism," p. 702; Robert J. Breckinridge, *The Knowledge of God Objectively Considered . . .* , pp. 285–90.

14. Leroy J. Halsey, "The Work of Education," p. 45.

15. [Hodge], "Public Education," p. 399; "The Covenants," p. 331. See also [John Hall], "Mental Cultivation," p. 472; William B. Sprague, *Lectures Illustrating the Contrast between True Christianity and Various Other Systems*, p. 7.

16. S. B. Wylie, "Prayer, a Reasonable Duty," p. 97; [Yeomans], "Another Life," p. 123; Benjamin M. Palmer, *The Love of Truth, the Inspiration of the Scholar*, p. 17. This was a common idea of the time, by no means restricted to Presbyterian circles. See, e.g., Edward Hitchcock, *The Religion of Geology and Its Connected Sciences*, pp. 509–11. Hitchcock was sure "the Christian philosopher shall be permitted to resume the study of science in a future world, with powers of investigation enlarged . . . and all obstacles removed" (p. 511).

17. James Henley Thornwell, "Address Delivered to the Euphradian and Clariosophic Societies of the South Carolina College," MSS oration, p. 35, Thornwell Papers (SCL).

18. Mathetes, "On the Nature of Virtue," p. 146.

19. "A Critical Disquisition on Romans, V, 18," p. 50; Archibald Alexander, *Evidences of the Authenticity, Inspiration, and Canonical Authority of the Holy Scriptures*, p. 14; Samuel Miller, *Letters on Unitarianism*, p. 195.

20. John H. Rice, Introduction, p. 7; Ashbel Green, "Guide of Youth," p. 95; Gardiner Spring, *The Bible Not of Man*, p. 305.

21. A good example from our period is "An Attempt to Prove that There is a Future and Eternal State of Rewards and Punishments, in a Few Letters. Letter 6," p. 157: "In moral results causation is just as uniform and inevitable as in natural. Gravitation does not act more uniformly and certainly, than all the laws of morals." For background see Russel B. Nye, *The Cultural Life of the New Nation, 1776–1830*, pp. 17, 58.

22. Some typical expressions from the general literature are: R. H. Forrester, *Anniversary Address Delivered before the American Literary Institute of Bethany College, November 10, 1842*, p. 17; Henry Williams, *The Intellectual Progress and Destiny of Mankind*, pp. 13–16; Francis W. Pickens, *Science and Truth*, pp. 4–6; Silas Totten, *The Analogy of Truth, in Four Discourses*, pp. 8–9; Samuel Jackson, *Introductory Lecture to the Course of the Institutes of Medicine, in the University of Pennsylvania, Delivered October 12, 1855*, pp. 9–15. For the Old School adoption of this pattern, see, e.g., Archibald Alexander, "Nature and Evidences of Truth," pp. 1–34, MSS in Alexander Papers (SL); Jacob J. Janeway, "On the Importance and Practical Influence of Revealed Truth," pp. 9–10; Robert J. Breckinridge, "Some Thoughts on the Development of the Presbyterian Church in the United States of America," p. 328; Benjamin M. Palmer, untitled MSS sermon outline on Proverbs 9:10, Palmer Papers; George Junkin, *An Address on Truth*, pp. 10–12.

23. Stuart Robinson, "Difficulties of Infidelity," p. 546.

24. Sprague, *True Christianity*, p. 79.

25. The massive literature produced by writers on the Evidences is matched by a massive neglect of the subject by religious historians. To judge from the primary remains, the Evidences occupied a central place in the main structure of Anglo-American Protestant theology from the early eighteenth to the mid-nineteenth centuries. Yet the most significant scholarly treatment this writer has been able to find is a sketchy nine pages in John Dillenberger's *Protestant Thought and Natural Science*, pp. 38–47. See also Conrad Wright, *The Beginnings of Unitarianism in America*, p. 426; Leslie Stephen, *English Thought in the Eighteenth Century*, 1:77, 165–68, 351–55. The Evidences had been the mainstay of the British anti-Deist writers of the eighteenth century, whose work was a central source of Presbyterian theology in our period. See, e.g., *Plan of the Theological Seminary of the Presbyterian Church, at Princeton, New Jersey*, p. 18.

26. Archibald Alexander, *Evidences*; Spring, *The Bible Not of Man*; Jacob J. Janeway, *The Internal Evidence of the Holy Bible*; William H. Ruffner, ed., *Lectures on the Evidences of Christianity, Delivered at the University of Virginia, 1850–51*. See also Samuel Stanhope Smith's earlier *Lectures on the Evidences of the Christian Religion* (1809).

27. [A. A. Porter], "The Power of the Pulpit," p. 284.

28. Aaron W. Leland, "On the Proper Agency of Reason in Matters of Religion," p. 288; Alexander, *Evidences*, p. 89. Leland was later a professor in the Theological Seminary in Columbia, S.C.; he served as moderator of the Old School General Assembly in 1850.

29. A second category of Evidences, denominated "Internal," related the existential cogency of the Bible, its "moral fitness and beauty," its "astonishing power of searching and penetrating the heart," its "power to soothe and comfort" (Alexander, *Evidences*, pp. 189–90). The most popular text on the Evidences in early nineteenth-century America was Anglican theologian William Paley's *Evidences of Christianity*.

30. James Henley Thornwell, "Miracles," p. 249.

31. "Christ's Presence with the Preachers of the Gospel, a Proof of His Divinity," p. 282. See also Alexander, *Evidences*, p. 65.

32. Henry Ruffner, "Miracles, Considered as an Evidence of Christianity," pp. 64, 100. See also Sprague, *True Christianity*, p. 200.

33. See, e.g., Alexander, *Evidences*, pp. 130–68; Alexander T. McGill, "Prophecy," pp. 109–40.

34. Breckinridge, *Knowledge of God*, p. xi. In the more distant background was the tendency in sixteenth- and seventeenth-century Protestant scholasticism to "regard the Bible as objective information" (see Dillenberger, *Protestant Thought*, p. 59).

35. "Review," p. 539. See also [Thomas Smyth], "The Province of Reason, Especially in Matters of Religion," pp. 274–75. Samuel Miller took special umbrage at Unitarian charges that orthodox Christians were "narrow-minded . . . enemies of liberal thinking . . . and the weak slaves of system and authority" (Miller, *Letters on Unitarianism*, p. 104). And see George Junkin, *The Progress of the Age*, p. 18.

36. Mathetes, "On the Nature of Virtue," p. 147.

37. John Hall, ed., *Forty Years' Familiar Letters of James W. Alexander*, 1:55; Alexander, *Evidences*, title of chapter one. The passage may be intended as a sarcastic play upon a similar and well-known passage from Hume's *An Enquiry Concerning Human Understanding*, sec. 12, pt. 3, p. 689.

38. [Lyman Atwater], "Classification and Mutual Relation of the Mental Faculties," p. 62. S. C. Pharr noted that the apostles were not gullible to the personal claims of Christ. They "did not yield their assent till they were convinced by . . . *evidence* that could not be controverted" ("The Resurrection of Jesus," p. 250). Cf. Charles Coulston Gillispie, *Genesis and Geology*, p.32.

39. [Plumer], "Polemic Theology," p. 190; Sprague, *True Christianity*, p. 90; James Henley Thornwell, *The Collected Writings of James Henley Thornwell*, 2:501.

40. Thornwell, *Collected Writings*, 3:199–200. See also E. S. Ely, "Some Articles of

Faith in Which Antitrinitarians and Trinitarians Accord," p. 69; [Smyth], "Province of Reason," pp. 290–91.

41. "A Series of Discourses on the Christian Revelation, Viewed in Connexion with the Modern Astronomy, by Sir Thomas Chalmers," p. 343; Lewis W. Green, *Inaugural Address, Delivered before the Board of Trustees of Hampden-Sydney College, January 10th, 1849*, p. 17.

42. A good example of this thought is "Discussions of Some Important Questions in Theology. Number 1 . . . ," p. 53. See also Charles Hodge, *Systematic Theology*, 1:1–17; George Junkin, "Narrative of the State of Religion," p. 401.

43. [Archibald Alexander], "Symington on the Atonement," p. 211; Miller, *Letters on Unitarianism*, pp. 73–76; Nathan L. Rice, *God Sovereign and Man Free*, p. vi.

44. Scott, *The Bible a Revelation*, p. 36.

45. "The Bible, and Not Reason, the Only Certain and Authoritative Source of Our Knowledge, Even of the Knowledge of God," p. 347. See also Thornwell, *Collected Writings*, 3:188.

46. [James W. Alexander], "Connection between Philosophy and Revelation," p. 384.

47. [Stanfield], "Scripturalism and Rationalism," p. 276; [S. J. Cassels], "The Unity of the Human Race," p. 598; [Smyth], "Province of Reason," p. 291. See also James Henley Thornwell, "Lecture First," MSS lecture, p. 13, Thornwell Papers (SCL).

48. J. D. Morell, *The Philosophy of Religion*, pp. 192, 26.

49. J. S. Lamar, *The Organon of Scripture*, pp. 191, 176, 26, iii.

50. Perry Miller, *The New England Mind*, pp. 341, 191.

51. Leonard Woods, Jr., "Christianity and Philosophy," p. 674.

52. B. B. Smith, "Theology a Strictly Inductive Science," pp. 89, 94.

53. Laurens P. Hickok, "Christian Theology as a Science," pp. 457–87.

54. Totten, *Analogy of Truth*, p. 28.

55. Thomas Chalmers, *Institutes of Theology*, 1:375, 377.

56. "Chalmers on the Inductive Method in Theology and the Nature of Christian Theology," pp. 210–11; J. M. Manning, "The Theology of Dr. Chalmers," pp. 477–519. See also Samuel Harris, "The Harmony between Natural Science and Theology," p. 3: "Though the Baconian philosophy is the boast of modern times, its principles of reasoning are recognized in the Bible as really as in the Novum Organon."

57. William Lindsay Alexander, *Christ and Christianity*, p. 3.

58. Samuel Miller, *Infant Baptism Scriptural and Reasonable*, p. 32. See also Willis Lord, *The Federal Character of Adam and the Imputation of His Sin*, pp. 1–16; Ashbel Green, *Lectures on the Shorter Catechism of the Presbyterian Church in the United States of America*, 1:146–52.

59. [Robert J. Breckinridge and Andrew B. Cross], "An Attempt to Prove That There Is a Future and Eternal State of Rewards and Punishments, in a Few Letters. Letter 4," p. 67.

60. Hodge, *Systematic Theology*, 1:1–3.

61. Green, *Shorter Catechism*, 1:132, 113.

62. "The Influence of the Bible in Improving the Understanding," p. 206. See also [Asa Colton], "Thoughts on the Character of Christian Ministers," p. 283: "A thorough acquaintance with the inductive mode of seeking truth, is a most important element in the first Aphorism of Lord Bacon's *Novum Organum* [i.e., "Man . . . can do and understand so much . . . only as he has observed in fact"], be not so digested as to pervade his whole mental system, he rejects an essential principle in all his inquiries for truth." The same thought is expressed in [William J. R. Taylor], "Man, Moral and Physical," p. 321.

63. "The Covenants," p. 388; "Spirit of the Papacy," p. 455; Spring, *The Bible Not of Man*, p. 233; George Junkin, *Inaugural Address of Dr. Junkin*, pp. 27–29; Palmer, *Love of Truth*, p. 19; A. B. Van Zandt, "The Necessity of a Revelation," pp. 27, 32.

64. Benjamin Morgan Palmer, "Doctrine of the Fall of Man Established by the Universal Prevalence of Suffering and Death," MSS sermon, dated 8 March 1843, Palmer Papers.

65. The best summary of the subject in English is the Introduction to John W. Beardslee III, ed., *Reformed Dogmatics*.

66. Leonard J. Trinterud, *The Forming of an American Tradition*, pp. 39–52.

67. Ernest Trice Thompson, *Presbyterians in the South*, 1:545–46; Sydney E. Ahlstrom, *A Religious History of the American People*, pp. 464–65.

68. [Lyman Atwater], "Recent Works on Mental Philosophy," p. 74; Breckinridge, *Knowledge of God*, p. 522.

69. Lewis W. Green, *The Progressive Advancement and Ultimate Regeneration of Human Society*, pp. 5–7; Jacob J. Janeway, *Inaugural Address, Delivered before the Directors of the Western Theological Seminary . . .* , pp. 64–65.

70. Perry Miller has spoken of a "revolt against religious formalism" in the period (*The Life of the Mind in America*, p. 59).

71. Leroy J. Halsey, *Address to the Alumni Society of the University of Nashville . . .* , p. 19. For background, see Winthrop S. Hudson, *Religion in America*, pp. 122–24.

72. See, e.g., Morton White, *Science and Sentiment in America*, pp. 14–16; John Herman Randall, Jr., *The Making of the Modern Mind*, pp. 261–62.

73. A Baconian Biblist, *Common Causes of Inefficiency*.

74. Janeway, *Inaugural Address*, pp. 64–65. Pervasive hostility toward system was an important background factor heightening the Old School's fidelity to doctrinal tradition. See, e.g., [Palmer], "A Plea for Doctrine," p. 33: "That a deeply seated prejudice exists, in many parts of the Church against the systematic exposition of the doctrines of the Bible, is too obvious a fact to be questioned."

75. [James W. Alexander], "On the Use and Abuse of Systematic Theology," pp. 171, 180, 174–75.

76. Hickok, "Christian Theology," p. 473; Lamar, *Organon of Scripture*, pp. 140, 150–51, 173.

77. [Alexander], "Systematic Theology," pp. 183, 185, 187; Halsey, *Address to the Alumni Society*, pp. 19–20. Halsey held that "standards of doctrine . . . are to be received not as infallible oracles, but only so far as they are found to agree with the Bible" (p. 20).

78. John H. Rice, "Report on the Course of Study to be Pursued in the Union Theological Seminary," pp. 518–19.

79. "Flatt's Dissertation on the Deity of Christ," p. 42; [Asa Colton], "Advancement of Society," p. 313.

80. B. M. Smith, *An Inaugural Discourse by the Rev. B. M. Smith, Professor of Oriental Literature in Union Theological Seminary . . .* , pp. 27, 32; [James Read Eckard], "The Logical Relations of Religion and Natural Science," p. 601; [George Howe], "The Secondary and Collateral Influences of the Sacred Scriptures," p. 108; [Thomas Smyth], "On the Trinity," pp. 71–72; Nathan L. Rice, *Address of the Reverend N. L. Rice before the Miami Union Literary Society of the Miami University*, p. 5.

81. [Benjamin M. Palmer], "Baconianism and the Bible," p. 243.

82. Charles Hodge was moderator of the Old School General Assembly in 1846; Thornwell in 1847. By 1861 the late-blooming Old School *Danville Quarterly Review* was finding it "strange that the recognition of theology as a science should not have suggested long ago the idea of presenting it in a form analogous to that which true science herself . . . has adopted" ("The Relation Which Reason and Philosophy Sustain to Revelation," p. 27).

83. Tyler, *Discourse*, pp. 372, 417. Tyler had argued in the *Princeton Review* that "the Baconian philosophy is not confined to physical nature. Bacon expressly says that his method of investigation is intended to be applied to all the sciences" ("The Influence of the Baconian Philosophy," p. 493).

84. Thornwell, *Collected Writings*, 3:200; see also 1:25–26.

85. Ibid., 1:582.

86. [Charles Hodge], "Professor Park's Sermon," p. 648.

87. Hodge, *Systematic Theology*, 1:1–3, 9–17.

88. [James W. Alexander], "Education for the Ministry," p. 589.

89. [James W. Alexander], "Connection between Philosophy and Revelation," p. 405.

90. Hodge, *Systematic Theology*, 1:18.

91. See Ernest R. Sandeen, *The Roots of Fundamentalism*, pp. 114–31.

92. Ashbel Green, "Address Delivered to the Theological Students of the Princeton Seminary . . . ," p. 543.

93. Benjamin M. Palmer, "Sermon Upon the Doctrine of a Special Providence," MSS sermon, p. 6, Palmer Papers. For a characteristic expression from the general literature, see Edward Everett, *An Address Delivered before the Literary Societies of Amherst College, August 25, 1835*, p. 22.

94. [James W. Alexander], "Emmons' Works," p. 540.

95. [Charles Hodge], "Finney's Lectures on Theology," pp. 237, 243.

96. J. R. Blake, "Popular Objections to Science," p. 223; Green, *Regeneration of Human Society*, pp. 7, 26; Thornwell, *Collected Writings*, 3:203.

97. "Discussions of Some Important Questions in Theology," pp. 54–55.

98. [Smyth], "On the Trinity," p. 71.

99. Ibid., pp. 71–72.

CHAPTER 8

1. Timothy L. Smith, *Revivalism and Social Reform*.

2. Elwyn A. Smith, *The Presbyterian Ministry in American Culture*, pp. 105–6, 143–44.

3. William James, *The Varieties of Religious Experience*, p. 469.

4. See beginning of Chapter 1; John C. Greene, "Objectives and Methods in Intellectual History," pp. 59, 71.

5. David Brewster, *Memoirs of the Life, Writings, and Discoveries of Sir Isaac Newton*, 2:400–406.

6. William Whewell, *The Philosophy of the Inductive Sciences, Founded Upon Their History*, 1:62–77; 2:26–94, 226–51.

7. Edward H. Madden, *Chauncey Wright*, pp. 59–66.

8. Alvar Ellegard, "The Darwinian Theory and Nineteenth-Century Philosophies of Science," pp. 362–93.

9. Charles Hodge, *What is Darwinism?* p. 177.

10. Newman Smyth, *Old Faiths in New Light*, excerpted in H. Shelton Smith, Robert T. Handy, and Lefferts Loetscher, *American Christianity*, 2:266; Shailer Mathews, *The Faith of Modernism*, p. 16.

11. Ian Barbour, *Issues in Science and Religion*, pp. 126, 104.

12. [Charles Hodge], "Introductory Lecture," p. 90. For corroborating passages in Hodge, see [his] "Regeneration, and the Manner of Its Occurrence," p. 261; "The Latest Form of Infidelity," pp. 32–37; "Thornwell on the Apocrypha," p. 274; and *Systematic Theology*, 1:129. Ernest R. Sandeen's comment that "it is with the external not the internal" that Princetonian Old Schoolers dealt is a substantial exaggeration, as applied to the antebellum development (*The Roots of Fundamentalism*, p. 118).

13. Spring, *Bible Not of Man*, p. 152.

14. Sandeen, *Roots of Fundamentalism*, pp. 103–31, 168–70, 172; Sydney E. Ahlstrom, ed., *Theology in America*, p. 47.

15. H. Shelton Smith, "The Church and the Social Order as Interpreted by James Henley Thornwell," p. 116.

16. The story of southern Presbyterianism since the Civil War is told in vols. 3 and 4 of Ernest Trice Thompson, *Presbyterians in the South*.

17. The New School church resulting from the 1837 excision had itself ruptured into northern and southern sections over the slavery issue in 1857.

18. The best general account is in Lefferts Loetscher, *The Broadening Church*.

19. See Robert T. Handy, *A Christian America*; Martin E. Marty, *Righteous Empire*.

Bibliography

PRIMARY SOURCES

Manuscript Collections

COLUMBIA, SOUTH CAROLINA
University of South Carolina,
South Caroliniana Library
James Henley Thornwell
Papers
DURHAM, NORTH CAROLINA
Duke University, Perkins
Library
George Frederick Holmes
Papers
MONTREAT, NORTH CAROLINA
Historical Foundation of the
Presbyterian and Reformed
Churches Library
Benjamin Morgan Palmer
Papers
Henry Ruffner Papers
James Henley Thornwell
Papers

PHILADELPHIA, PENNSYLVANIA
Historical Society of Pennsyl-
vania
Simon Gratz Collection
PHILADELPHIA, PENNSYLVANIA
Presbyterian Historical Society
Charles Hodge Papers
Cortlandt Van Rensselaer
Papers
PRINCETON, NEW JERSEY
Princeton Theological Seminary,
Speer Library
Archibald Alexander Papers
PRINCETON, NEW JERSEY
Princeton University, Firestone
Library
Archibald Alexander Papers
Charles Hodge Papers
John Miller Papers

Books and Pamphlets

Alexander, Archibald. *Evidences of the Authenticity, Inspiration, and
Canonical Authority of the Holy Scriptures*. Philadelphia, 1836.
───── . *Outlines of Moral Science*. New York: Charles Scribner, 1852.

Alexander, James W. Introductory Notice to *The Testimony of Modern Science to the Unity of Mankind*, by J. L. Cabell. New York: Robert Carter & Bros., 1859.

———. *The Life of Archibald Alexander*. New York: Charles Scribner, 1854.

Alexander, William Lindsay. *Christ and Christianity*. New York: Carlton & Phillips, 1854.

Anderson, S. J. P. *The Influence of the Bible on Liberty: An Address before the Union Society of Hampden Sydney College, Sept. 18, 1845*. Richmond: H. K. Ellyson, 1845.

Bacon, Francis. *The Great Instauration*. In EPBM.

———. *Novum Organum*. In EPBM.

A Baconian Biblist. *A Practical View of the Common Causes of Inefficiency in the Christian Ministry of the Congregational and Presbyterian Churches of the United States*. Philadelphia: William Stavely, 1830.

Barlow, Joel. *The Columbiad*. Washington City, 1825.

Beattie, James. *The Works of James Beattie*. Vol. 4, *An Essay on the Nature and Immutability of Truth*. Philadelphia, 1809.

Blackwood, William. *An Address Delivered at the Annual Meeting of the Missionary, Tract, and Educational Society of the Theological Seminary at Princeton, New Jersey, April 20, 1852, On Nature and Revelation*. Philadelphia: W. S. Martien, 1852.

Breckinridge, Robert J. "The General Internal Evidence of Christianity." In LEC.

———. *The Knowledge of God, Objectively Considered, Being the First Part of Theology Considered as a Science of Positive Truth, Both Inductive and Deductive*. New York: Robert Carter & Bros., 1858.

Brewster, David. *Memoirs of the Life, Writings, and Discoveries of Sir Isaac Newton*. Vol. 2. Edinburgh: Thomas Constable & Co., 1855.

Brougham, Henry Lord. *A Discourse on the Objects, Advantages, and Pleasures of Science*. In OUSL.

Bushnell, Horace. *Nature and the Supernatural*. New York: Charles Scribner's Sons, 1877.

Capen, Nahum. *Reminiscences of Dr. Spurzheim and George Combe*. New York: Fowler & Wells, 1881.

Cartwright, Samuel A. *Essays, Being Inductions from the Baconian Philosophy, Proving the Truth of the Bible and the Justice and Benevolence of the Decree Dooming Canaan to be Servant of Servants*. Vidalia, Miss., 1843.

Catalogue of the Officers and Students of the College of New Jersey for 1844–5. Princeton, 1845.

Chalmers, Thomas. *Institutes of Theology*. Vol. 1. New York: Harper & Bros., 1849.

————. *On the Power, Wisdom, and Goodness of God, as Manifested in the Adaptation of External Nature, to the Moral and Intellectual Constitution of Man*. New York: Harper & Bros., 1851.

Channing, William Ellery. *Discourse at the Dedication of Divinity Hall*. In DRM.

————. *Discourse at the Ordination of the Rev. E. S. Gannett, Boston, 1824*. In DRM.

————. *Discourse at the Ordination of the Rev. F. A. Farley, Providence, R.I., 1828*. In DRM.

————. *Discourse at the Dedication of the Second Congregational Unitarian Church, New York, 1826*. In DRM.

Combe, George. *Lectures on Phrenology*. 3d ed. New York: Fowler & Wells, 1856.

Cooper, Thomas. *The Introductory Lecture of Thomas Cooper, Esq., Professor of Chemistry at Carlisle College, Pennsylvania*. Carlisle, Pa., 1812.

————. *Introductory Lecture, on Chemistry, Delivered at the College of South Carolina, in Columbia, January, 1820*. Columbia, 1821.

————. *On the Connection between Geology and the Pentateuch, in a Letter to Professor Silliman*. Boston, 1837.

Crane, Henry. *Literary Discourses*. New York: Edward H. Fletcher, 1853.

Davies, Samuel. "Sermon 72." In *Sermons on Important Subjects*. Vol. 1. New York: Saxton & Miles, 1842.

Dick, Thomas. *The Christian Philosopher: Or, the Connexion of Science with Philosophy and Revelation*. 8th ed. Philadelphia: Edward C. Biddle, 1844.

————. *On the Improvement of Society by the Diffusion of Knowledge*. Glasgow: William Collins, 1860.

Dickinson, Jonathan. *The Reasonableness of Christianity, in Four Sermons*. Boston, 1732.

Draper, John W. *A Treatise on the Forces Which Produce the Organization of Plants*. New York: Harper & Bros., 1844.

Emerson, Ralph Waldo. "Lord Bacon." In *The Early Lectures of Ralph Waldo Emerson*. Edited by Stephen E. Whicher and Robert E. Spiller. Vol. 1. Cambridge: Harvard University Press, 1959.

Everett, Edward. *An Address Delivered before the Literary Societies of Amherst College, August 25, 1835*. Boston: Russell, Shattuck & Williams, 1835.

Forrester, R. H. *Anniversary Address Delivered before the American Literary Institute of Bethany College, November 10, 1842*. Bethany, 1842.

Green, Ashbel. *Lectures on the Shorter Catechism of the Presbyterian Church in the United States of America. Addressed to Youth*. Vol. 2. Philadelphia, 1841.

————. "The Union of Piety and Science." In *Discourses Delivered in the College of New Jersey*. Philadelphia, 1822.

————. "The Word of God the Guide of Youth." In ibid.

Green, James D. "Claims of Phrenology to be Regarded as the Science of Human Nature." Appendix B in *Reminiscences of Dr. Spurzheim and George Combe*, by Nahum Capen. New York: Fowler & Wells, 1881.

Green, Lewis W. *Inaugural Address, Delivered before the Board of Trustees of Hampden-Sydney College, January 10th, 1849*. Pittsburgh, 1849.

————. *The Progressive Advancement and Ultimate Regeneration of Human Society: An Address before the Erodelphian Society of Miami University, August 10th, 1842*. Pittsburgh, 1842.

Grimke, Thomas Smith. *An Address on the Character and Objects of Science: And, Especially, The Influence of the Reformation on the Science and Literature, Past, Present and Future, of Protestant Nations*. Charleston, 1827.

Hall, John, ed. *Forty Years' Familiar Letters of James W. Alexander*. 2 vols. New York, 1860.

Halsey, Leroy J. *Address to the Alumni Society of the University of Nashville, on the Study of Theology as a Part of Science, Literature and Religion*. Nashville, 1841.

Herschel, John Frederick William. *A Preliminary Discourse on the Study of Natural Philosophy*. New York and London: Johnson Reprint Corp., 1966.

Hitchcock, Edward. *The Highest Use of Learning: An Address Delivered at His Inauguration to the Presidency of Amherst College*. Amherst, 1845.

————. *The Religion of Geology and Its Connected Sciences*. Boston: Phillips, Sampson & Co., 1855.

Hodge, Charles. *Systematic Theology*. Vol. I. New York: Charles Scribner's Sons, 1921.

————. *What is Darwinism?* New York: Scribner, Armsborg, & Co., 1874.

Hoffman, David. *Legal Outlines*. Baltimore, 1856.

Hooker, Edward W. *Love to the Doctrines of the Bible an Essential Element of Christian Character*. Philadelphia, 1835.

Hopkins, Mark. *An Address Delivered before the Society of Alumni of Williams College, August 16, 1843*. 2d ed. Boston, 1843.

————. *Influence of the Gospel in Liberalizing the Mind: An Address Delivered before the Porter Rhetorical Society, of the Theological Seminary, at Its Anniversary, Sept. 5, 1837*. Andover, 1837.

Hume, David. *An Enquiry Concerning Human Understanding*. In EPBM.

Jackson, Samuel. *Introductory Lecture to the Course of the Institutes of*

Medicine, in the University of Pennsylvania, Delivered October 12, 1855. Philadelphia, 1855.

Janeway, Jacob J. *Inaugural Address, Delivered before the Directors of the Western Theological Seminary, in the First Presbyterian Church, on Friday, October 17, 1828.* N.p., n.d.

————. *The Internal Evidence of the Holy Bible, or, the Bible Proved from Its Own Pages to be a Divine Revelation.* Philadelphia, 1845.

Jones, Joseph H. *The Attainments of Men in Secular and Religious Knowledge, Contrasted.* Philadelphia: Joseph M. Wilson, 1854.

————. *Man Moral and Physical: Or the Influence of Health and Disease on Religious Experience.* Philadelphia, 1860.

Junkin, George. *An Address on Truth.* N.p., n.d.

————. *An Apology for Collegiate Education: Being the Baccalaureate Address Delivered on Commencement Day of Washington College, June 18, 1851.* Lexington, Va., 1851.

————. *The Bearings of College Education Upon the Welfare of the Whole Community: The Baccalaureate in Miami University, Delivered August 10th, 1843.* Rossville, Ohio, 1843.

————. *Inaugural Address of Dr. Junkin.* In *Two Addresses Delivered at Oxford, Ohio, on Occasion of the Inauguration of Rev. Geo. Junkin as President of Miami University.* Cincinnati, 1841.

————. *The Progress of the Age: An Address Delivered before the Literary Societies of Washington College, June 17, 1851.* Philadelphia, 1851.

Kelley, William D. *Characteristics of the Age. An Address before the Linnaean Association of Pennsylvania College, September 18th, 1850.* Gettysburg, 1850.

Lamar, J. S. *The Organon of Scripture: Or, the Inductive Method of Biblical Interpretation.* Philadelphia: J. B. Lippincott & Co., 1860.

LeConte, Joseph. *Inaugural Address Delivered in the State House, Dec. 1, 1857.* Columbia, S.C., 1858.

Leland, Aaron W. "On the Proper Agency of Reason in Matters of Religion." In *The Southern Preacher: A Collection of Sermons from the MSS of Several Eminent Ministers of the Gospel, Residing in the Southern States.* Edited by Colin M'Iver. Philadelphia, 1824.

Lewis, G. *Impressions of America and the American Churches.* New York: Negro Universities Press, 1958.

Liebig, Justus. *Animal Chemistry, or Organic Chemistry in Its Applications to Physiology and Pathology.* Philadelphia: J. M. Campbell, 1843.

Lincoln, Mrs. Almira. *Familiar Lectures on Botany.* 2d ed. Hartford: H. and F. J. Huntington, 1831.

Lindsley, Philip. *A Plea for the Theological Seminary at Princeton, New Jersey.* 3d ed. Trenton, N.J., 1821.

Locke, John. *An Essay Concerning the Human Understanding.* London and New York: George Routledge & Sons, n.d.

Lord, Eleazar. *The Epoch of Creation.* New York: C. Scribner, 1851.

Lord, Willis. *The Federal Character of Adam, and the Imputation of His Sin.* Philadelphia, 1845.

Lowry, L. A. *An Earnest Search for Truth, in a Series of Letters from a Son to His Father.* Philadelphia, 1852.

McGill, Alexander T. *Individual Responsibility: An Address, before the Athenian and Philomathean Societies, of Indiana University.* Pittsburgh, 1846.

————. "Prophecy." In LEC.

Maclaurin, Colin. *An Account of Sir Isaac Newton's Philosophical Discoveries.* London, 1748.

Maclure, William. *Opinions on Various Subjects, Dedicated to the Industrious Producers.* Vol. 1. New-Harmony, Ind., 1831.

MacMaster, Erasmus D. *A Discourse Delivered November 7th, 1838, On the Occasion of the Author's Inauguration as President of Hanover College, Indiana.* Hanover, Ind., 1838.

McMullen, R. B. *Truth the Foundation of Genuine Liberty. An Address Delivered before the Alumni of the University of Alabama, July 13, 1858.* Tuscaloosa, Ala., 1858.

Marsh, James. Preliminary Essay to *Aids to Reflection,* by Samuel Taylor Coleridge. Edited by Henry Nelson Coleridge. London, 1838.

Mather, Cotton. *The Christian Philosopher.* Edited by Josephine K. Piercy. Gainesville, Fla.: Scholars' Facsimiles and Reprints, 1968.

Mathews, Shailer. *The Faith of Modernism.* New York: AMS Press, 1969.

Matthews, John. *The Divine Providence Displayed in the Works of Providence and Grace. In a Series of Letters from an Inquiring Friend.* Philadelphia, 1843.

Maxwell, William, ed. *A Memoir of the Rev. John H. Rice.* Richmond: R. I. Smith, 1835.

Miles, Henry A. *On Natural Theology as a Study in Schools. A Lecture Delivered before the American Institute of Instruction, at Its Annual Session, August, 1834.* Boston, 1840.

Miller, Samuel. *A Brief Retrospect of the Eighteenth Century.* 2 vols. New York, 1803.

————. *The Importance of the Gospel Ministry.* Princeton, 1827.

————. *Infant Baptism Scriptural and Reasonable: And Baptism by Sprinkling or Affusion the Most Suitable and Edifying Mode.* Philadelphia, 1835.

————. *Letters on Unitarianism: Addressed to the Members of the First Presbyterian Church, in the City of Baltimore.* Trenton, N.J., 1821.

Moore, T. V. "The Ethnological Objection: The Unity of the Human Race." In LEC.

———. "Inspiration of the Scriptures: Morell's Theory Tested and Refuted." In LEC.

Morell, J. D. *The Philosophy of Religion.* New York: Appleton & Co., 1849.

Morgan, Gilbert. *The Inaugural Address of the Rev. Gilbert Morgan, President of the Western University of Pennsylvania.* Pittsburgh, 1835.

Morrison, R. H. *The Inaugural Address of the Rev. R. H. Morrison, Pronounced at His Inauguration as President of Davidson College, North Carolina, August 2, 1838.* Philadelphia: William S. Martien, 1838.

Murray, Nicholas. "The Ministry We Need." In *Discourses at the Inauguration of the Rev. Alexander T. McGill.* Philadelphia, 1854.

Mutchmore, S. A. *Thought and Action: The Perfection of True Greatness, Illustrated in the Life and Character of John Calvin. An Address to the Graduates from the Chamberlain Literary Society of Centre College, Danville, Ky., Sept. 8, 1856.* Cincinnati, 1857.

Newton, Isaac. *Newton's Philosophy of Nature.* Edited by H. S. Thayer. New York and London: Hafner Publishing Co., 1953.

Norton, Andrews. *A Statement of Reasons for Not Believing the Doctrines of Trinitarians, Concerning the Nature of God and the Person of Christ.* 13th ed. Boston: American Unitarian Association, 1882.

Olmsted, Denison. *Letters on Astronomy, in Which the Elements of the Science are Familiarly Explained in Connection with Biographical Sketches of the Most Eminent Astronomers.* Rev. ed. New York: Harper & Bros., 1850.

Owen, Robert Dale. "Galileo and the Inquisition." In *Popular Tracts.* London, 1851.

Paley, William. *Evidences of Christianity.* New York: S. King, 1824.

———. *Natural Theology.* New York: American Tract Society, n.d.

Palmer, Benjamin Morgan. *The Influence of Religious Belief Upon National Character.* Athens, Ga., 1854.

———. *The Life and Letters of James Henley Thornwell.* Richmond: Whittet & Shepperson, 1875.

———. *The Love of Truth, the Inspiration of the Scholar. An Address Delivered before the Philomathean & Euphemian Literary Societies of Erskine College, at the Annual Commencement, August 9th, 1854.* Due West, S.C., 1854.

Pemberton, Henry. *A View of Sir Isaac Newton's Philosophy.* London, 1748.

Phelps, Mrs. *Botany for Beginners.* 2d ed. Hartford, 1833.

Pickens, Francis W. *Science and Truth. An Address before the Literary*

Societies of Erskine College, South Carolina, at the Annual Commencement, Held September 19, 1849. Fraziersville, S.C., 1849.

Plan of the Theological Seminary of the Presbyterian Church, at Princeton, New Jersey: Together With Its Constitution, Bye-Laws, &c. Princeton, 1838.

Playfair, John. Dissertation Second, Exhibiting a General View of the Progress of Mathematical and Physical Science, Since the Revival of Letters in Europe. N.p., n.d.

Plumer, William S. Earnest Hours. Richmond: Presbyterian Committee of Publication, 1869.

———. "Man Responsible for His Belief." In LEC.

Potter, A[lonzo]. "Preliminary Observations." In OUSL.

Ramsay, David. A Review of the Improvements, Progress, and State of Medicine in the Eighteenth Century. Charleston, 1801.

Reid, Thomas. A Brief Account of Aristotle's Logic. In TRPW, vol. 2.

———. Correspondence of Dr. Reid. In TRPW, vol. 1.

———. Essays on the Active Powers of the Human Mind. Cambridge, Mass.: M.I.T. Press, 1969.

———. Essays on the Intellectual Powers of Man. Cambridge, Mass.: M.I.T. Press, 1969.

———. An Inquiry into the Human Mind. Edited by Timothy Duggan. Chicago: University of Chicago Press, 1970.

———. "A Statistical Account of the University of Glasgow." In TRPW, vol. 1.

Rice, John Holt. Historical and Philosophical Considerations on Religion: Addressed to James Madison, Esq. Richmond, 1832.

Rice, N[athan] L. Address of the Reverend N. L. Rice before the Miami Union Literary Society of the Miami University. Cincinnati, 1845.

———. God Sovereign and Man Free. Cincinnati, 1850.

———. Inaugural Address. Inaugural Addresses at the Opening of the Presbyterian Theological Seminary of the North West, Chicago, Illinois. Philadelphia, 1860.

———. The Influence of Christianity on the Progress of Science: An Address Delivered before the Erodelphian Society of Miami University, June 25, 1851. Hamilton, Ohio, 1852.

———. Mesmerism: An Investigation of Its Mental and Physical Phenomena, and of Its Moral Tendencies. New York: Robert Carter & Bros., 1849.

———. "Moral Effects of Christianity." In LEC.

———. The Old and the New Schools. 2d ed. Cincinnati, 1853.

———. Phrenology Examined, and Shown to be Inconsistent with the Principles of Phisiology [sic], Mental and Moral Science, and the Doctrines of Christianity. New York: Robert Carter & Bros., 1849.

————. *The Signs of the Times*. St. Louis, 1855.

————. *Ten Letters on the Subject of Slavery*. St. Louis, 1855.

Robinson, Stuart. "The Difficulties of Infidelity." In LEC.

Robison, John. Introduction to *Elements of Chemistry*, by Joseph Black. Vol. 1. Edinburgh, 1802.

Rockwell, E. F. *Inaugural Address of Rev. E. F. Rockwell, Professor of Natural Science, before the Board of Trustees of Davidson College, N.C., August 13, 1851*. Salisbury, N.C., 1851.

Ruffner, Henry. *Annual Address Delivered before the Franklin Society of Lexington*. Richmond, 1838.

————. "Miracles, Considered as an Evidence of Christianity." In LEC.

Ruffner, William H., ed. *Lectures on the Evidences of Christianity Delivered at the University of Virginia, 1850–51*. New York: Robert Carter & Bros., 1856.

St. John, Samuel. *Elements of Geology*. 5th ed. New York: G. P. Putnam, 1851.

Scott, Thomas. *The Bible a Revelation from God*. Philadelphia: Presbyterian Board of Publication, n.d.

Sedgwick, Adam. *A Discourse on Classical, Metaphysical, Moral, and Natural Studies*. In OUSL.

Silliman, Benjamin. *Elements of Chemistry*. 2 vols. New Haven, 1830.

Simpson, Stephen. *The Working Man's Manual: A New Theory of Political Economy*. Philadelphia, 1831. Excerpt in *Social Theories of Jacksonian Democracy*, edited by Joseph L. Blau. Indianapolis: Bobbs-Merrill, 1954.

Smith, B. M. *An Inaugural Discourse by the Rev. B. M. Smith, Professor of Oriental Literature in Union Theological Seminary, Delivered Sept. 12, 1855*. Richmond, 1855.

Smith, John Augustine. *The Mutations of the Earth*. New York: Bartlett & Welford, 1846.

Smith, R. C. *The Educator of Youth. An Address, Delivered at the Annual Examination of the East Alabama Presbyterian High School*. Charleston, 1852.

Smith, Samuel Stanhope. *An Essay on the Causes of the Variety of Complexion and Figure in the Human Species*. Edited by Winthrop C. Jordan. Cambridge, Mass.: Harvard University Press, 1965.

————. *Lectures on the Evidences of the Christian Religion*. Philadelphia: Hopkins & Earle, 1809.

Smyth, Newman. *Old Faiths in New Light*. Excerpt in *American Christianity: An Historical Interpretation with Representative Documents*, by H. Shelton Smith, et al. Vol. 2. New York: Charles Scribner's Sons, 1963.

Smyth, Thomas. *Autobiographical Notes, Letters and Reflections*. Edited by Louis Cheves Stoney. Charleston, 1914.

Sprague, William B. *Lectures Illustrating the Contrast between True Christianity and Various Other Systems*. New York: D. Appleton & Co., 1837.

————. *A Sermon Addressed to the Second Presbyterian Congregation, Albany, September 5, 1858, On the Completion of the Atlantic Telegraph*. Albany, 1858.

Spring, Gardiner. *The Bible Not of Man*. New York, 1847.

————. *The Power of the Pulpit*. New York: Baker and Scribner, 1848.

Spurzheim, J. G. *A View of the Philosophical Principles of Phrenology*. 3d ed. London: Charles Knight, 1825.

Stewart, Dugald. *Account of the Life and Writings of Thomas Reid*. In TRPW, vol. 1.

————. *Dissertation: Exhibiting the Progress of Metaphysical, Ethical, and Political Philosophy, Since the Revival of Letters in Europe*. In CWDS, vol. 1.

————. *Elements of the Philosophy of the Human Mind*. In CWDS, vols. 2–4.

————. *Outlines of Moral Philosophy*. In CWDS, vol. 2.

Story, Joseph. "Characteristics of the Age." In *American Eloquence*. Vol. 2. New York: D. Appleton & Co., 1859.

Swift, Elisha P. "The Charge." In *Addresses Delivered at the Inauguration of William S. Plumer as Professor of Didactic and Pastoral Theology in the Western Theological Seminary*. Pittsburgh, 1854.

Thornwell, James Henley. *The Collected Writings of James Henley Thornwell*. Edited by John B. Adger. 4 vols. Richmond: Presbyterian Committee of Publication, 1871–73.

Totten, Silas. *The Analogy of Truth, in Four Discourses*. New York: Stanford & Swords, 1848.

Tyler, Samuel. *A Discourse of the Baconian Philosophy*. 2d ed. New York: Baker and Scribner, 1850.

Van Zandt, A. B. "The Necessity of a Revelation: The Condition of Man Without It." In LEC.

Veitch, John. *Memoir of Dugald Stewart, with Selections from His Correspondence*. In CWDS, vol. 10.

Verplanck, Gulian C. *On the Importance of Scientific Knowledge to the Manufacturer and Practical Mechanic*. In OUSL.

Wayland, Francis. *Discourse, Delivered at the Dedication of Manning Hall, of Brown University, February 4, 1835*. Providence: Marshall Brown & Co., 1835.

Whately, Richard. *Elements of Logic*. 9th ed. Louisville, Ky.: Morton & Groswold, 1854.

Whewell, William. *The Philosophy of the Inductive Sciences, Founded Upon Their History*. 2 vols. 2d ed. New York and London: Johnson Reprint Corp., 1967.

Williams, Henry. *The Intellectual Progress and Destiny of Mankind.* N.p., 1855.

Wirt, William. *The Letters of the British Spy.* 10th ed. New York, 1837.

Witherspoon, John. *Address to the Inhabitants of Jamaica, and Other West-India Islands, in Behalf of the College of New Jersey.* Philadelphia, 1772. Reprinted in *American Higher Education: A Documentary History,* edited by Richard Hofstadter and Wilson Smith. Vol. I. Chicago: University of Chicago Press, 1961.

————. *The Works of the Rev. John Witherspoon.* Vol. 3, *Lectures on Moral Philosophy.* Philadelphia, 1800.

The Works of Creation Illustrated. Philadelphia: Presbyterian Board of Publication, n.d.

Wright, Frances. *Course of Popular Lectures, as Delivered by Frances Wright.* New York, 1829.

Young, John C. *Advantages of Enlarged Scientific and Literary Attainments. An Address to the Senior Class, Delivered at the Commencement in Centre College, September 22d, 1831.* Danville, Ky., 1831.

Periodical Literature

Adams, Samuel. "A Historical Sketch of Medical Philosophy." ABR 2d ser. 11 (1844): 392–407.

Adger, John B. "Inaugural Address on Church History and Church Polity." SPR 12 (1859): 140–81.

[Alexander, Archibald]. "The Bible, a Key to the Phenomena of the Natural World." BRPR 1 (1829): 101–20.

[————]. "Principle of Design in the Interpretation of Scripture." BRPR 17 (1845): 409–28.

[————]. "Symington on the Atonement." BRPR 8 (1836): 201–33.

Alexander, James W. "Attractions of the Cross." BRPR 18 (1846): 158–75.

[————]. "Connection between Philosophy and Revelation." BRPR 17 (1845): 381–408.

[————]. "Education for the Ministry." BRPR 15 (1843): 587–604.

[————]. "Emmons' Works." BRPR 14 (1842): 529–61.

[————]. "Evils of an Unsanctified Literature." BRPR 15 (1843): 65–77.

[————]. "Immediate Perception." BRPR 31 (1859): 177–206.

[————]. "Life of Hegel." BRPR 20 (1848): 561–91.

[————]. "Modern Miracles and Wonders." BRPR 8 (1836): 348–62.

[————]. "On the Use and Abuse of Systematic Theology." BRPR 4 (1832): 171–90.

[————]; and Dod, Albert B. "Transcendentalism." BRPR 11 (1839): 37–101.

"Astronomy of LaPlace." AQR 5 (1829): 310–42.

"Astronomy of LaPlace." AQR 7 (1830): 255–79.

[Atkinson, Joseph]. "Moral Aesthetics: Or the Goodness of God in the Ornaments of the Universe." BRPR 24 (1852): 38–52.

[Atwater, Lyman]. "Butler's Lectures on Ancient Philosophy." BRPR 30 (1858): 261–79.

[————]. "Classification and Mutual Relation of the Mental Faculties." BRPR 32 (1860): 43–68.

[————]. "Coleridge." BRPR 20 (1848): 143–86.

[————]. "Compte's Positive Philosophy." BRPR 28 (1856): 59–88.

[————]. "Hickok's Rational Cosmology." BRPR 31 (1859): 305–59.

[————]. "Mill's System of Logic." BRPR 28 (1856): 88–112.

[————]. "Moral Insanity." BRPR 29 (1857): 345–75.

[————]. "Recent Works on Mental Philosophy." BRPR 27 (1855): 69–102.

[————]. "The True Barrier Against Ritualism and Rationalism." BRPR 26 (1854): 689–708.

"Audubon's Ornithology, First Volume." AJS 39 (1840): 343–57.

"Bacon's Philosophy." *Methodist Quarterly Review* 29 (1847): 22–52.

"Benefits of the Reformation on the Happiness of Man." SLM 4 (1838): 524–28.

"The Bible, and Not Reason, the Only Certain and Authoritative Source of Our Knowledge, Even of the Knowledge of God." SPR 7 (1854): 325–47.

"Biblical Commentary." AQR 20 (1836): 28–65.

Blake, J. R. "Popular Objections to Science." SPR 11 (1858): 206–10.

Bocock, John H. "The Instructed Scribe." *The Home, the School, the Church* 2 (1851): 112–22.

[Bowen, Francis]. "Recent Theories in Geology." NAR 69 (1849): 256–68.

[————]. "Wilson's Treatise on Logic." NAR 83 (1856): 382–402.

[Brazer, J.] "Chalmer's Evidences of Christianity." NAR 7 (1818): 364–400.

[Breckinridge, Robert J.] "Some Thoughts on the Development of the Presbyterian Church in the United States of America." SPR 2 (1848): 311–40.

[————; and Cross, Andrew B.] "An Attempt to Prove That There Is a Future and Eternal State of Rewards and Punishments, in a Few Letters. Letter 4." BLRM 2 (1836): 58–67.

Brown, Matthew. "The Importance and Obligation of Truth." CA 11 (1833): 69–75.

Browne, Peter. "Hints to Students of Geology." SLM 1 (1834): 162–63.

"Brown's Philosophy." AQR 4 (1828): 1–27.

[Brumby, R. T.] "Footprints of the Creator." SPR 5 (1851): 111–14.

"Calumnies Against Oxford." ER 16 (1818): 158–87.

[Cassels, S. J.] "The Philosophy of Life." SPR 7 (1853): 74–85.

[_____]. "The Unity of the Human Race." SPR 6 (1852): 572–601.

Cater, Edwin. "Geological Speculation, and the Mosaic Account of Creation." SPR 10 (1858): 534–73.

[Chace, George Ide]. "The Persistence of Physical Laws." NAR 81 (1855): 159–94.

[_____]. "Of Spirit and the Constitution of Spiritual Beings." BS 5 (1848): 633–50.

"Chalmers on the Inductive Method in Theology and the Nature of Christian Theology." NE 8 (1850): 203–19.

[Channing, Walter]. "Ancient Medicine." NAR 8 (1819): 217–53.

[Channing, William]. "American Medical Botany." NAR 6 (1818): 344–51.

Chapman, George. "Lecture on the Sciences as Applicable to Domestic Life." FJ 19 (1850): 187–93.

"The Christian Religion Vindicated from the Charge of Being Hostile to Knowledge. No. 2." VELM 1 (1818): 225–31.

"On Christianity Considered as a Practical System." VELM 5 (1822): 113–18.

"Christ's Presence with the Preachers of the Gospel, a Proof of His Divinity." VELM 4 (1821): 281–84.

[Clark, William J.] "Prichard's Natural History of Man." BRPR 21 (1849): 159–74.

[Colton, Asa]. "Advancement of Society." BRPR 3 (1831): 306–19.

[_____]. "Thoughts on the Character of Christian Ministers." BRPR (1831): 279–89.

A Countryman. "On the Tendency of Doctrines Maintained by Some Modern Physiologists." VELM 4 (1822): 480–84.

"The Covenants." BLRM 1 (1835): 327–33.

"A Critical Disquisition on Romans, V. 18." BLRM 6 (1840): 49–63.

"Critical Notices." SPR 3 (1850): 682–85.

"Critical Notices." SPR 4 (1851): 444–52.

"Critical Notices." SPR 7 (1853): 158.

"Critical Notices." SPR 11 (1859): 676.

Dana, James D. "Agassiz's Contributions to the Natural History of the United States." AJS, n.s. 25 (1858): 202–16.

_____ . "On American Geological History." AJS, n.s. 22 (1856): 305–34.

_____ . "Anticipations of Man in Nature." NE 17 (1859): 293–334.

_____ . "Science and Scientific Schools." American Journal of Education 2 (1856): 349–74.

Dana, W. C. "A Reasonable Answer to the Sceptic." SPR 11 (1858): 386–401.

Davis, John. "An Address to the Linnaean Society of New England, at

Their First Anniversary Meeting, at the Boston Athenaeum, June 14, 1815." NAR 1 (1815): 315–28.

"Discussions of Some Important Questions in Theology. Number 1. On the Submission of the Understanding Required in Scripture." VELM 2 (1819): 50–56.

[Dod, Albert B.] "Phrenology." BRPR 10 (1838): 279–320.

[_____]. "Vestiges of Creation." BRPR 17 (1845): 505–57.

"E. T." "Bacon's Philosophy and Macaulay's Criticism of It." SLM 29 (1859): 382–86.

[Eckard, James Read]. "The Logical Relations of Religion and Natural Science." BRPR 32 (1860): 577–608.

Ely, E. S. "Some Articles of Faith in Which Antitrinitarians and Trinitarians Accord." PM 1 (1821): 66–69.

[Ely, Elias P.] "Remarks on Independence of Thought, addressed to Candidates for the Ministry." BRPR 15 (1833): 359–69.

Encyclopaedia Americana. S.v. "Bacon." Philadelphia: Blanchard & Lea, 1853.

[Everett, Alexander H.] "History of Philosophy." NAR 18 (1824): 234–66.

[_____]. "Stewart's Moral Philosophy." NAR 31 (1830): 213–66.

[Everett, Edward]. "Character of Lord Bacon." NAR 16 (1823): 300–337.

_____ . "Uses of Astronomy." *American Journal of Education* 2 (1856): 606–28.

"A Few Words on Astronomy." FJ 22 (1838): 109–15.

[Fisk, Ezra]. "Character of the Present Age." BRPR 2 (1830): 372–89.

[_____]. "Character of the Present Age." BRPR 4 (1832): 115–31.

"Flatt's Dissertation on the Deity of Christ." BRPR 1 (1829): 9–71.

"Fossil Remains." AQR 1 (1827): 78–105.

Franklin, Benjamin. "Poor Richard, April 11, 1749." Vol. 3 in *The Papers of Benjamin Franklin.* Edited by Leonard W. Labaree. New Haven: Yale University Press, 1959.

[Gilman, S.] "Brown's Philosophy of Mind." NAR 19 (1824): 1–41.

[_____]. "Cause and Effect." NAR 12 (1821): 395–431.

Gladney, Richard S. "Natural Science and Revealed Religion." SPR 12 (1859): 443–67.

Godman, John D. "The Beaver." FJ 4 (1827): 98–104.

Googe, Barnaby. "Old Agricultural Works." *American Agriculturalist* 1 (1842): 189–90.

Gould, A. A. "An Address in Commemoration of Professor J. W. Bailey, Late President of the A. A. A. S." AJS, n.s. 25 (1858): 153–58.

[Gray, Asa]. "The Chemistry of Vegetation." NAR 60 (1845): 156–95.

Grayson, W. S. "Bacon's Philosophy and Macaulay's Criticism of It." SLM 29 (1859): 177–83.

Green, Ashbel. "Address Delivered to the Theological Students of the Princeton Seminary, N.J., at the Close of the Semi-Annual Examination in May, 1835." BRPR 7 (1835): 529–46.

[————]. "Introduction." CA 1 (1823): 1–3.

[————]. "Penn's Geology." CA 1 (1823): 222–30.

————. "Strictures on Modern Geology." CA 7 (1829): 17–22.

[Green, Lewis W.] "The Harmony of Revelation, and Natural Science; With Especial Reference to Geology.—Number 1." SPR 5 (1851): 93–111.

[————]. "The Harmony of Revelation and Natural Science—Number 2." SPR 5 (1851): 284–315.

Grier, Matthew B. "The Positive Philosophy of Auguste Comte." SPR 9 (1855): 202–24.

"H." "The Nineteenth Century." SLM 17 (1851): 457–67.

Hale, E. "Remarks on the Use of Theories in Science. An Address to the Boylston Medical Society of Harvard University, at the Annual Meeting in November 1822." *The New-England Journal of Medicine and Surgery* 12 (1822): 113–21.

[Hall, John]. "Mental Cultivation." BRPR 16 (1844): 463–77.

————. "The Harmony of Revelation and Natural Science—Number 3." SPR 5 (1851): 461–94.

Halsey, Leroy J. "The Work of Education." *The Home, The School, The Church* 9 (1859): 37–58.

[Hamilton, W. T.] "The Character of Moses." SPR 5 (1852): 504–35.

Harris, Samuel. "The Harmony between Natural Science and Theology." NE 10 (1852): 1–19.

Henry, Joseph. "Explanations and Illustrations of the Plan of the Smithsonian Institution." AJS, n.s. 6 (1848): 305–17.

————. "On the Conservation of Force." AJS, n.s. 30 (1860): 32–41.

Hickok, Laurens P. "Christian Theology as a Science." ABR, 3d ser. 1 (1845): 457–87.

[Hill, D. S.] "Religion and Mathematics." SPR 8 (1854): 27–53.

Hitchcock, Edward. "First Anniversary Address before the Association of American Geologists, at Their Second Anniversary Meeting, in Philadelphia, April 5, 1841." AJS 41 (1841): 232–75.

Hodge, Charles. "Finney's Lectures on Theology." BRPR 19 (1847): 237–72.

[————]. "The General Assembly." BRPR 24 (1852): 462–501.

————. "Introductory Lecture." BRPR 1 (1829): 73–98.

[————]. "The Latest Form of Infidelity." BRPR 12 (1840): 31–71.

[————]. "Professor Park's Sermon." BRPR 22 (1850): 642–74.

[————]. "Public Education." BRPR 1 (1829): 370–410.

[————]. "Regeneration, and the Manner of Its Occurrence." BRPR 2 (1830): 250–97.

[_____]. "Slavery." BRPR 8 (1836): 268–305.
[_____]. "Thornwell on the Apocrypha." BRPR 17 (1845): 268–82.
[_____]. "The Unity of Mankind." BRPR 31 (1859): 103–49.
Holbrook, Josiah. "Remarks." In *Scientific Tracts Designed for Instruction and Entertainment, and Adapted to Schools, Lyceums, and Families*. Vol. 1. Edited by Josiah Holbrook. Boston: Carter, Hendee, and Babcock, 1831.
[Hope, Matthew Boyd]. "Apologetics." BRPR 24 (1852): 250–94.
[_____]. "Professor Bachman on the Unity of the Human Race." BRPR 22 (1850): 313–28.
[_____]. "Relation between Scripture and Geology." BRPR 13 (1841): 368–94.
Hopkins, Samuel M. "Religious Character of Lord Bacon." ABR ed. ser. 3 (1847): 127–42.
Horwitz, J. "Cosmogony of Moses." BLRM 5 (1839): 525–67.
Howard, W. G. "Mysteries of the Bible." SLM 6 (1840): 624–28.
[Howe, George]. "Nott's Lectures." SPR 3 (1850): 426–90.
[_____]. "The Secondary and Collateral Influences of the Sacred Scriptures." SPR 7 (1853): 103–27.
[_____]. "The Unity of the Race." SPR 3 (1849): 124–66.
Hoyt, Thomas A. "The Astronomical Argument against Christianity." SPR 11 (1859): 513–31.
Hunt, E. B. "On the Nature of Forces." AJS, n.s. 18 (1854): 237–49.
"The Inefficiency of the Pulpit." SLM 24 (1857): 81–112.
"The Influence of the Bible in Improving the Understanding." VELM 7 (1824): 202–10.
"The Influence of the Reformation on the American Revolution." VELM 7 (1824): 504–14.
"The Injury Done to Religion by Ignorant Preachers." VELM 8 (1825): 587–607.
"J. P. C." "Phrenology." BLRM 1 (1835): 269–75.
[Jackson, C. T.] "Geology &c. of Massachusetts." NAR 42 (1836): 422–48.
Janeway, Jacob J. "On the Importance and Practical Influence of Revealed Truth." PM 1 (1821): 9–16.
Junkin, George. "The College a Religious Institution." *The Home, The School, The Church* 3 (1852): 75–92.
_____ . "Narrative of the State of Religion." In *Minutes of the General Assembly of the Presbyterian Church in the United States of America; A. D. 1844*. Philadelphia, 1844. Pp. 397–401.
"K." "The Rise and Progress of Popery." VELM 8 (1825): 472–75.
Ketchum, R. C. "Testimony of Modern Science to the Unity of Mankind." SPR 12 (1859): 115–30.
LeConte, Joseph. "Lectures on Coal." *Annual Report of the Board of*

Regents of the Smithsonian Institution . . . for the Year 1857.
Washington, 1858.
———. "Morphology and Its Connection with Fine Art." SPR 12
(1859): 83–114.
———. "On the Science of Medicine and the Causes Which Have
Retarded Its Progress." *Southern Medical and Surgical Journal* 6
(1850): 456–74.
[Leslie, John]. "History of the Barometer." ER 20 (1821): 169–202.
"Letters of Dr. Thomas Cooper, 1825–1832." *American Historical
Review* 6 (1901): 725–36.
"Literary and Philosophical Intelligence." CA 1 (1823): 183.
"Lord Bacon." NE 10 (1852): 333–74.
"Lord Bacon." SLM 4 (1838): 9–21, 73–79, 190–96.
"Lord Bacon's Confession of Faith." VELM 4 (1821): 241–47.
Lyon, James A. "The New Theological Professorship—Natural Science
in Connexion with Revealed Religion." SPR 12 (1859): 181–95.
[Macaulay, Thomas Babington]. "Lord Bacon." ER 65 (1837): 1–103.
McDowell, Maxwell. "On Craniological Physiology." BLRM 1 (1835):
138–45.
Mackintosh, James. "Stewart's *Introduction to the Encyclopaedia.*" ER
36 (1821): 220–41.
Maclurg, James. "On Reasoning in Medicine." *Philadelphia Journal of
the Medical and Physical Sciences* 1 (1820): 217–41.
Manning, J. M. "The Theology of Dr. Chalmers." BS 13 (1856):
477–519.
March, Francis Andrew. "The Relation of the Study of Jurisprudence to
the Origin and Progress of the Baconian Philosophy." NE 6 (1848):
543–48.
———. "Sir William Hamilton's Theory of Perception." BRPR 32
(1860): 273–307.
Mathetes. "On the Nature of Virtue." PM 1 (1821): 145–51.
Melanchthon. "On Religious Experience." VELM 1 (1818): 153–57.
"Modern Science—Inductive Philosophy." *Quarterly Review* 45 (1831):
374–407.
[Moffat, James Clement]. "Popular Education." BRPR 29 (1857):
609–35.
"Motion, the Natural State of Matter." AJS 16 (1829): 151–54.
"Natural History." AQR 1 (1827): 458–72.
"Natural History." FJ 1 (1826): 16–19.
Nevin, John Williamson. "Human Freedom." *American Review* 7
(1848): 406–18.
"The New Earth." NE 17 (1849): 1–16.
"Objections to the German Transcendental Philosophy." SPR 4 (1851):
328–43.

"Observations on the Rise and Progress of the Franklin Institute." FJ 1 (1826): 66–71.

"On the Origin of the Soul." VELM 4 (1821): 285–92.

"On the Vitality of Matter." AJS 15 (1829): 54–62.

[Palmer, Benjamin Morgan]. "Baconianism and the Bible." SPR 6 (1852): 226–53.

[_____]. "Narrative of a Mission to the Jews." SPR 1 (1847): 30–55.

[_____]. "A Plea for Doctrine as the Instrument of Sanctification." SPR 3 (1849): 32–53.

[_____]. "The Relation between the Works of Christ, and the Condition of the Angelic World." SPR 1 (1847): 34–63.

[Parsons, Theophilus]. "The Tendencies of Modern Science." NAR 72 (1851): 84–115.

[Peabody, Andrew Preston]. "Morell's History of Philosophy." NAR 68 (1849): 388–412.

"Pestalozzi—Diffusion of Knowledge." ER 47 (1828): 118–34.

[Pharr, S. C.] "On Mental Development." SPR 3 (1849): 200–210.

_____. "The Resurrection of Jesus." SPR 4 (1850): 243–56.

[Phillips, Willard]. "Hedge's Logick." NAR 4 (1816): 78–92.

"Philosophy Subservient to Religion. Essay 1." CA 5 (1827): 60–65.

"Philosophy Subservient to Religion. Essay 10." CA 6 (1828): 19–26.

"Philosophy Subservient to Religion. Essay 12." CA 6 (1828): 213–16.

[Plumer, William S.] "Life of Socrates." BRPR 23 (1851): 236–65.

[_____]. "Polemic Theology." SPR 2 (1848): 183–203.

[_____]. "Revivals of Religion." BRPR 6 (1834): 109–26.

[Porter, A. A.] "The Power of the Pulpit." SPR 2 (1848): 270–94.

[_____]. "The Unity of the Human Race." SPR 4 (1851): 357–81.

"Presbyterian Periodicals." *Minutes of the General Assembly of the Presbyterian Church of America; A. D. 1851*. Philadelphia, 1852.

Preston, John T. L. "The Mind of Man, the Image of God." SPR 11 (1858): 228–45.

A Provincial Protestant. "The Christian Religion Vindicated from the Charge of Being Hostile to Knowledge." VELM 1 (1818): 164–70.

_____. "The Christian Religion Vindicated from the Charge of Being Hostile to Knowledge. No. 2." VELM 1 (1818): 225–31.

"Psychology." BLRM 7 (1841): 348–57.

"Quarterly Scientific Intelligence." BRPR 24 (1852): 350–52, 526–31.

[Ray, I.] "Decandolle's Botany." NAR 38 (1834): 32–63.

"On the Reciprocal Influence of Literature and Religion." VELM 5 (1822): 11–15.

"The Relation Which Reason and Philosophy Sustain to the Theology of Revelation." *Danville Quarterly Review* 1 (1861): 24–53.

"Remarks on a Late Review of Lord Bacon." SLM 4 (1838): 499–505.

"Remarks on the Study of Natural Philosophy." VELM 1 (1818): 261–65.

"Review." VELM 10 (1827): 538–47.

"Review and Criticism." PM 1 (1851): 241.

"A Review of the Principia of Newton." AJS 11 (1826): 238–46.

Rice, John Holt. "A Discourse Delivered before the Literary and Philosophical Society of Hampden Sydney College, at Their Anniversary Meeting, on the 24th of Sept., 1824." VELM 8 (1825): 1–9, 57–65.

———. Introduction. VELM 1 (1818): 1–8.

———. "Ministerial Character and Preparation Best Adapted to the Wants of the United States, and of the World, in the Nineteenth Century." *Quarterly Journal of the American Education Society* 1 (1829): 209–16.

[———]. "Report on the Course of Study to be Pursued in the Union Theological Seminary." VELM 11 (1828): 513–26.

Rockwell, E. F. "The Alphabet of Natural Theology." SPR 10 (1857): 411–36.

[———]. "The Final Destiny of Our Globe." SPR 7 (1853): 127–50.

[———]. "The Phenomena of Freezing Water in the Book of Job." SPR 6 (1852): 254–59.

[Rogers, E. P.] "Reflections Upon Heaven." SPR 4 (1850): 165–77.

Rogers, Henry D. "Address Delivered at the Meeting of American Geologists and Naturalists, Held in Washington, May, 1844." AJS 47 (1844): 247–78.

"S. B. H." "On the Importance of Sound Learning in the Gospel Ministry." PM 2 (1822): 260–71.

"Scotch School of Philosophy and Criticism." *American Review* 2 (1845): 386–97.

[Sedgwick, Adam]. "Natural History of Creation." ER 82 (1845): 1–86.

"A Series of Discourses on the Christian Revelation, Viewed in Connexion with the Modern Astronomy, by Sir Thomas Chalmers." *Christian Monitor*, 2d ser. 2 (1817): 337–43.

"Shelley." AQR 19 (1836): 257–87.

[Shields, Charles Woodruff]. "The Positive Philosophy of Auguste Comte." BRPR 30 (1858): 1–27.

"Short Notices." BRPR 16 (1844): 319.

"Short Notices." BRPR 16 (1844): 609–10.

"Short Notices." BRPR 17 (1845): 345–47.

"Short Notices." BRPR 18 (1846): 354–58.

"Short Notices." BRPR 19 (1847): 125–26.

"Short Notices." BRPR 23 (1851): 554–57.

"Short Notices." BRPR 23 (1851): 696–98.

"Short Notices." BRPR 24 (1852): 141–46.

"Short Notices." BRPR 25 (1853): 324–26.

"Short Notices." BRPR 29 (1857): 158.

"Short Notices." BRPR 30 (1858): 735.

Silliman, Benjamin. "Introductory Remarks." AJS 1 (1818): 2–10.

"Sir Isaac Newton." VELM 5 (1822): 655.

Smith, B. B. "Theology a Strictly Inductive Science." LTR 2 (1835): 89–95.

[Smyth, Thomas]. "Assurance—Witness of the Spirit, and the Call to the Ministry." SPR 2 (1848): 99–133.

[_____]. "The Province of Reason, Especially in Matters of Religion." SPR 7 (1853): 274–93.

[_____]. "On the Trinity." SPR 8 (1854): 54–90.

Solomon. "The March of Mind." *Portland Magazine* 1 (1835): 171–74.

"Spedding's *Complete Edition of the Works of Bacon*." ER 106 (1857): 287–322.

"Spirit of the Papacy." BLRM 6 (1840): 454–57.

[Stanfield, S. N.] "Scripturalism and Rationalism." SPR 5 (1851): 271–84.

"Stewart's Dissertation." *Quarterly Review* 17 (1817): 39–72.

"Stewart's Philosophy." AQR 6 (1829): 360–78.

Taylor, William J. R. "Man, Moral and Physical." BRPR 32 (1860): 308–35.

"A Theory of Creation." NAR 60 (1845): 426–78.

Thornwell, James Henley. "Matthew 22:29." SPR 4 (1851): 498–527.

_____ . "Miracles." SPR 10 (1857): 161–201.

Tucker, George. "The Progress of Philosophy, and Its Influence on the Intellectual and Moral Character of Man." SLM 1 (1835): 405–21.

[Tudor, William]. "On Geological Systems." NAR 3 (1816): 209–12.

[Tyler, Samuel]. "The Baconian Philosophy." BRPR 12 (1840): 350–77.

[_____]. "Balfour's Inquiry." BRPR 8 (1836): 327–43.

[_____]. "Cosmos, by Alexander Von Humboldt." BRPR 24 (1852): 382–97.

[_____]. "Elements of Logic." AQR 22 (1837): 294–311.

[_____]. "The Influence of the Baconian Philosophy." BRPR 15 (1843): 481–506.

_____ . "On Philosophical Induction." AJS, n.s. 5 (1848): 319–21.

_____ . "Psychology." BRPR 15 (1843): 227–50.

"Useful Knowledge." *Westminster Review* 14 (1831): 365–94.

"V." "The March of Mind." SLM 1 (1834): 154–56.

Venable, C. S. "Alexander Von Humboldt." SPR 11 (1858): 153–74.

"W. J. T." "The Mind, Its Powers and Results." SLM 10 (1844): 662–66.

[Ware, Mrs. John]. "Hugh Miller and Popular Science." NAR 73 (1851): 448–73.

Washburn, Edward A. "Parallel Between the Philosophical Relations of Early and Modern Christianity." BS 8 (1851): 34–57.

[Watkins, T.] "Hayden's Geological Essays." NAR 12 (1821): 134–49.

"Whately's *Elements of Logic*." *Westminster Review* 9 (1828): 137–72.

Whelpley, James D. "Letter on Philosophical Induction." AJS, n.s. 5 (1848): 33–36.

————. "Second Letter on Philosophical Analogy." AJS, n.s. 5 (1848): 32–35.

"Whether Law is a Science?" *American Jurist and Law Magazine* 9 (1833): 349–70.

Willard, Emma. "Universal Terms." AJS 23 (1833): 18–28.

[Wilson, J. L.] "The Certainty of the World's Conversion." SPR 2 (1848): 427–41.

Woods, Leonard, Jr. "Christianity and Philosophy." LTR 1 (1834): 669–89.

"Wordsworth." AQR 20 (1836): 66–87.

Wylie, S. B. "Prayer, a Reasonable Duty." PM 1 (1821): 97–101.

[Yeomans, John William]. "Physical Theory of Another Life." BRPR 10 (1838): 119–40.

SECONDARY SOURCES

Books

Agassiz, Elizabeth Cary. *Louis Agassiz: His Life and Correspondence.* Boston: Houghton, Mifflin & Co., 1890.

Ahlstrom, Sydney E. *A Religious History of the American People.* New Haven: Yale University Press, 1972.

————, ed. *Theology in America: The Major Protestant Voices from Puritanism to Neo-Orthodoxy.* Indianapolis: Bobbs-Merrill, 1967.

Bacon, Leonard Woolsey. *A History of American Christianity.* New York: Charles Scribner's Sons, 1925.

Barbour, Ian. *Issues in Science and Religion.* New York: Harper & Row, 1966.

Beardslee, John W., III, ed. *Reformed Dogmatics.* New York: Oxford University Press, 1965.

Blakey, Robert. *A History of the Philosophy of Mind.* Vol. 4. London: 1850.

Boorstin, Daniel. *The Lost World of Thomas Jefferson.* New York: H. Holt, 1948.

Bryson, Gladys. *Man and Society.* Princeton: Princeton University Press, 1945.

Burtt, Edwin A. *The Metaphysical Foundations of Modern Science.* Rev. ed. Garden City, N.Y.: Doubleday & Co., 1932.

Butterfield, Herbert. *The Origins of Modern Science.* Rev. ed. N.p., G. Bell & Sons, 1957.

Cohen, I. Bernard. *Franklin and Newton.* Philadelphia: American Philosophical Society, 1956.

Collingwood, R. G. *The Idea of Nature*. Oxford: Oxford University Press, 1945.

Conkin, Paul K. *Puritans and Pragmatists: Eight American Thinkers*. New York: Dodd, Mead & Co., 1968.

Copleston, Frederick. *A History of Philosophy*. Vol. 5, *Hobbes to Hume*. Westminster, Md.: Newman Press, 1959.

Curti, Merle. *The Growth of American Thought*. 3d ed. New York: Harper & Row, 1964.

Daniels, George H. *American Science in the Age of Jackson*. New York: Columbia University Press, 1968.

―――― . *Science in American Society: A Social History*. New York: Alfred A. Knopf, 1971.

Davies, John D. *Phrenology, Fad and Science: A 19th-Century Crusade*. New Haven: Yale University Press, 1955.

Dillenberger, John. *Protestant Thought and Natural Science: A Historical Interpretation*. Nashville: Abingdon Press, 1960.

Dupree, Hunter. *Science in the Federal Government: A History of Policy and Activities to 1940*. Cambridge: Harvard University Press, 1957.

Ekirch, Arthur Alphonse, Jr. *The Idea of Progress in America, 1815–1860*. New York: Columbia University Press, 1944.

Fisher, George P. *The Life of Benjamin Silliman*. 2 vols. New York: Charles Scribner & Company, 1866.

Fraser, Alexander Campbell. *Archbishop Whately and the Restoration of the Study of Logic*. London, 1864.

―――― . *Thomas Reid*. Edinburgh: Oliphant & Ferrier, 1898.

Friedrich, Hugo. *Europäische Aufklärung*. München-Allach: Wilhelm Fink Verlag, 1967.

Gaustad, Edwin Scott. *A Religious History of America*. New York: Harper & Row, 1966.

Gay, Peter. *The Enlightenment: An Interpretation*. 2 vols. New York: Alfred A. Knopf, 1967–69.

Gillespie, Neal C. *The Collapse of Orthodoxy: The Intellectual Ordeal of George Frederick Holmes*. Charlottesville: University Press of Virginia, 1972.

Gillispie, Charles Coulston. *The Edge of Objectivity: An Essay in the History of Scientific Ideas*. Princeton: Princeton University Press, 1960.

―――― . *Genesis and Geology: A Study in the Relations of Scientific Thought, Natural Theology, and Social Opinion in Great Britain, 1790–1850*. Cambridge: Harvard University Press, 1951.

Grave, S. A. *The Scottish Philosophy of Common Sense*. Oxford: Oxford University Press, 1960.

Greene, John C. *The Death of Adam: Evolution and Its Impact on Western Thought*. Ames, Iowa: Iowa State University Press, 1959.

Haber, Francis C. *The Age of the World: Moses to Darwin*. Baltimore: Johns Hopkins Press, 1959.

Hall, A. Rupert. *From Galileo to Newton, 1630–1720*. New York: Harper and Row, 1963.

Handy, Robert T. *A Christian America: Protestant Hopes and Historical Realities*. New York: Oxford University Press, 1971.

Hindle, Brooke. *The Pursuit of Science in Revolutionary America*. Chapel Hill: University of North Carolina Press, 1956.

Hodge, A. A. *The Life of Charles Hodge*. New York: Charles Scribner's Sons, 1880.

Hofstadter, Richard. *Anti-Intellectualism in American Life*. Vintage Books. New York: Random House, 1963.

Hooykaas, R. *Religion and the Rise of Modern Science*. Edinburgh: Scottish Academic Press, 1972.

Houghton, Walter E. *The Victorian Frame of Mind, 1830–1870*. New Haven: Yale University Press, 1957.

Howe, Daniel Walker. *The Unitarian Conscience: Harvard Moral Philosophy, 1805–1861*. Cambridge: Harvard University Press, 1970.

Howell, Wilbur Samuel. *Eighteenth-Century British Logic and Rhetoric*. Princeton: Princeton University Press, 1971.

Hudson, Winthrop S. *Religion in America*. New York: Charles Scribner's Sons, 1965.

Jacobs, Thornwell. *The Life of William S. Plumer*. New York: Fleming H. Revell Co., 1918.

James, William. *The Varieties of Religious Experience*. Fontana Books. London: The Fontana Library, 1962.

Johnson, Thomas Cary. *The Life and Letters of Robert Lewis Dabney*. Richmond: Presbyterian Committee of Publication, 1903.

Jones, Joseph H. *The Life of Ashbel Green*. New York: Robert Carter and Bros., 1849.

Jones, Olin McKendree. *Empiricism and Intuitionism in Reid's Common Sense Philosophy*. Princeton: Princeton University Press, 1927.

Jones, Richard Foster. *Ancients and Moderns: A Study of the Scientific Movement in Seventeenth-Century England*. 2d ed. St. Louis: Washington University Press, 1961.

Laurie, Henry. *The Scottish Philosophy in Its National Development*. Glasgow: James Maclehose & Sons, 1902.

Loetscher, Lefferts. *The Broadening Church: A Study of Theological Issues in the Presbyterian Church Since 1869*. Philadelphia: University of Pennsylvania Press, 1954.

Lurie, Edward. *Louis Agassiz: A Life in Science*. Chicago: University of Chicago Press, 1960.

McAllister, Ethel M. *Amos Eaton: Scientist and Educator, 1776–1842*. Philadelphia: University of Pennsylvania Press, 1941.

Maclean, John. *History of the College of New Jersey, From Its Origin in 1746 to the Commencement of 1854.* 2 vols. Philadelphia: J. B. Lippincott & Co., 1877.

McCosh, James. *The Scottish Philosophy, Biographical, Expository, Critical, from Hutcheson to Hamilton.* New York: Robert Carter & Bros., 1875.

Madden, Edward H. *Chauncey Wright.* New York: Washington Square Press, 1964.

Marsden, George M. *The Evangelical Mind and the New School Presbyterian Experience: A Case Study of Thought and Theology in Nineteenth-Century America.* New Haven: Yale University Press, 1970.

Martin, Terence. *Instructed Vision: Scottish Common Sense Philosophy and the Origins of American Fiction.* Bloomington, Ind.: Indiana University Press, 1961.

Marty, Martin E. *The Infidel.* Cleveland: Meridian Books, 1961.

_____. *Righteous Empire: The Protestant Experience in America.* New York: Dial Press, 1970.

Mead, Sidney E. *The Lively Experiment.* New York: Harper & Row, 1963.

Metz, Rudolf. *A Hundred Years of British Philosophy.* New York: Macmillan, 1938.

Miller, Perry. *The Life of the Mind in America.* New York: Harcourt, Brace & World, 1965.

_____. *The New England Mind: The Seventeenth Century.* New York: Macmillan, 1939.

Miller, Samuel. *The Life of Samuel Miller.* Philadelphia: Claxton, Remsen & Haffelfinger, 1869.

Nichols, James Hastings. *Romanticism in American Theology: Nevin and Schaff at Mercersburg.* Chicago: University of Chicago Press, 1961.

Nye, Russel Blaine. *The Cultural Life of the New Nation, 1776–1830.* New York: Harper & Bros., 1960.

_____. *Society and Culture in America, 1830–1860.* New York: Harper & Bros., 1974.

Olson, Richard. *Scottish Philosophy and British Physics, 1750–1880.* Princeton: Princeton University Press, 1975.

Palmer, Benjamin Morgan. *The Life and Letters of James Henley Thornwell.* Richmond: Whittet & Shepperson, 1875.

Park, Roy. *Hazlitt and the Spirit of the Age: Abstraction and Critical Theory.* Oxford: Clarendon Press, 1971.

Parrington, V. L. *Main Currents in American Thought.* Vol. 2, *The Romantic Revolution.* New York: Harcourt, Brace & Co., 1927.

Petersen, Richard J. "Scottish Common Sense in America, 1768–1850:

An Evaluation of Its Influence." Ph.D. dissertation, The American University, 1963.

Post, Albert. *Popular Freethought in America, 1825–1850.* New York: Columbia University Press, 1943.

Randall, John Herman, Jr. *The Making of the Modern Mind.* Rev. ed. Boston: Houghton Mifflin Co., 1940.

Riley, I. Woodbridge. *American Philosophy: The Early Schools.* New York: Russell and Russell, n.d.

Rossi, Paolo. *Francis Bacon, From Magic to Science.* Chicago: University of Chicago Press, 1968.

Rudolph, Frederick. *The American College and University: A History.* Vintage Books. New York: Random House, 1962.

Sandeen, Ernest R. *The Roots of Fundamentalism: British and American Millennarianism, 1800–1930.* Chicago: University of Chicago Press, 1970.

Schmidt, George P. *The Old Time College President.* New York: Columbia University Press, 1935.

Schneider, Herbert W. *A History of American Philosophy.* New York: Columbia University Press, 1946.

Schofield, Robert E. *Mechanism and Materialism: British Natural Philosophy in an Age of Reason.* Princeton: Princeton University Press, 1970.

Segerstedt, Torgny T. *The Problem of Knowledge in Scottish Philosophy. Lunds Universitets Arsskrift,* vol. 31. Lund: C. W. K. Gleerup, 1935.

Sherrill, Lewis Joseph. *Presbyterian Parochial Schools, 1846–1870.* New Haven: Yale University Press, 1932.

Shryock, Richard H. *Medicine and Society in America, 1660–1860.* New York: New York University Press, 1960.

Smallwood, William Martin; and Smallwood, Mabel Sarah Coon. *Natural History and the American Mind.* New York: Columbia University Press, 1941.

Smith, Elwyn A. *The Presbyterian Ministry in American Culture: A Study in Changing Concepts, 1700–1900.* Philadelphia: Westminster Press, 1962.

Smith, H. Shelton; Handy, Robert T.; and Loetscher, Lefferts. *American Christianity: An Historical Interpretation with Representative Documents.* 2 vols. New York: Charles Scribner's Sons, 1965.

Smith, Timothy. *Revivalism and Social Reform: American Protestantism on the Eve of the Civil War.* Nashville: Abingdon Press, 1957.

Sprague, William B. *Annals of the American Pulpit.* Vols. 2–4. New York: Robert Carter & Bros., 1857–69.

Stanton, William. *The Leopard's Spots: Scientific Attitudes toward Race in America, 1815–1859.* Chicago: University of Chicago Press, 1960.

Stephen, Leslie. *English Thought in the Eighteenth Century*. Vol. 1. New York: Harcourt, Brace & World, 1962.

Sweet, William Warren. *The Story of Religion in America*. New York: Harper & Bros., 1950.

Tewksbury, Donald G. *The Founding of American Colleges and Universities before the Civil War*. New York: Teacher's College Bureau of Publications, 1932.

Thompson, Ernest Trice. *Presbyterians in the South*. Vol. 1. Richmond: John Knox Press, 1963.

Thompson, Robert Ellis. *A History of the Presbyterian Churches in the United States*. New York: Christian Literature Co., 1895.

Trinterud, Leonard J. *The Forming of an American Tradition*. Philadelphia: Westminster Press, 1949.

Tuveson, Ernest Lee. *Redeemer Nation: The Idea of America's Millennial Role*. Chicago: University of Chicago Press, 1968.

Weber, Herman C. *Presbyterian Statistics Through One Hundred Years*. N.p.: Presbyterian Board of Christian Education, 1927.

Welch, Claude. *Protestant Thought in the Nineteenth Century*. Vol. 1. New Haven: Yale University Press, 1972.

Werkmeister, W. H. *A History of Philosophical Ideas in America*. New York: Ronald Press, 1949.

Wertenbaker, Thomas Jefferson. *Princeton, 1746–1896*. Princeton: Princeton University Press, 1946.

West, William Garrett. *Barton Warren Stone: Early American Advocate of Christian Unity*. Nashville: Disciples of Christ Historical Society, 1954.

Westfall, Richard S. *Science and Religion in Seventeenth Century England*. New Haven: Yale University Press, 1958.

White, Morton. *Science and Sentiment in America: Philosophical Thought from Jonathan Edwards to John Dewey*. New York: Oxford University Press, 1972.

Whitehead, Alfred North. *Science and the Modern World*. New York: Macmillan, 1928.

Willey, Basil. *The Eighteenth Century Background: Studies on the Idea of Nature in the Thought of the Period*. London: Chatto & Windus, 1940.

————. *Nineteenth Century Studies: Coleridge to Matthew Arnold*. New York: Columbia University Press, 1949.

————. *The Seventeenth Century Background*. New York: Columbia University Press, 1934.

Williams, L. Pearce. *Michael Faraday*. New York: Basic Books, n.d.

Windelband, Wilhelm. *A History of Philosophy*. Vol. 2. New York: Macmillan, 1901.

Wright, Conrad. *The Beginnings of Unitarianism in America*. Boston: Starr King Press, 1955.

Articles and Essays

Ahlstrom, Sydney E. "The Scottish Philosophy and American Theology." CH 24 (1955): 257-72.

Annals of the American Pulpit. S.v. "George Baxter."

Annals of the American Pulpit. S.v. "John Matthews."

Biblical Repertory and Princeton Review. Index Volume from 1825–1868. S.v. "Archibald Alexander."

Bozeman, Theodore Dwight. "Science, Nature and Society: A New Approach to James Henley Thornwell." *Journal of Presbyterian History* 50 (1972): 307-25.

Broderick, Francis L. "Pulpit, Physics and Politics: The Curriculum of the College of New Jersey, 1794–1846." *William and Mary Quarterly,* 3d ser. 6 (1949): 42–68.

Brown, Ira V. "Watchers for the Second Coming: The Millenarian Tradition in America." MVHR 39 (1952): 441–58.

Browne, C. A. "Some Relations of the New Harmony Movement to the History of Science in America." *Scientific Monthly* 42 (1936): 483–97.

Bullough, Geoffrey. "Bacon and the Defence of Learning." In *Seventeenth Century Studies to Sir Herbert Grierson.* Oxford: Clarendon Press, 1938.

Caldwell, R. L. "Another Look at Thomas Reid." JHI 23 (1962): 546–49.

Cannon, Walter F. "John Herschel and the Idea of Science." JHI 22 (1961): 215–39.

Clark, Charles Edwin. "Science, Reason, and an Angry God: The Literature of an Earthquake." NEQ 38 (1965): 340–62.

Come, Donald Robert. "The Influence of Princeton on Higher Education in the South before 1825." *William and Mary Quarterly,* 3d ser. 2 (1945): 359–96.

Curti, Merle. "The Great Mr. Locke: America's Philosopher, 1783–1861." *Huntington Library Bulletin* 11 (1937): 107–51.

Daniels, George H. "The Process of Professionalization in American Science: The Emergent Period, 1820–1860." *Isis* 68 (1967): 151–66.

Dictionary of National Biography. S.v. "Thomas Reid," by Leslie Stephen.

Ellegard, Alvar. "The Darwinian Theory and Nineteenth-Century Philosophies of Science." JHI 18 (1957): 362–93.

Feuer, Lewis. "The Scientific Intellectual in the United States." In Lewis Feuer, *The Scientific Intellectual: The Psychological and Sociological Origins of Modern Science.* New York: Basic Books, 1963.

Ford, Franklin L. "The Enlightenment: Towards a Useful Redefinition." In *Studies of the Eighteenth Century,* edited by R. F. Brissenden. Canberra: Australian National University Press, 1968.

Glick, Wendell. "Bishop Paley in America." NEQ 27 (1954): 347–54.

Greene, John C. "Objectives and Methods in Intellectual History." MVHR 44 (1957): 58–74.

_____ . "Science and Religion." In *The Rise of Adventism*, edited by Edwin Scott Gaustad. New York: Harper & Row, 1974.

Hesse, Mary B. "Francis Bacon." In *A Critical History of Western Philosophy*, edited by D. J. O'Connor. London: Free Press of Glencoe, 1964.

Holmfeld, John D. "From Amateurs to Professionals in American Science: The Controversy over the Proceedings of an 1853 Scientific Meeting." *Philosophical Quarterly* 114 (1970): 22–36.

Hudnut, William H., III. "Samuel Stanhope Smith: Enlightened Conservative." JHI 17 (1956): 540–52.

Hughes, Richard B. "Old School Presbyterians: Eastern Invaders of Texas, 1830–1865." *Southwestern Historical Quarterly* 84 (1971): 324–36.

Jones, Howard Mumford. "The Influence of European Ideas in Nineteenth-Century America." *American Literature* 7 (1935): 241–73.

Knowles, George Harmon. "The Religious Ideas of Thomas Jefferson." MVHR 30 (1943): 187–204.

Larsen, Robert E. "The Aristotelianism of Bacon's *Novum Organum*." JHI 23 (1962): 435–50.

Laudan, L. L. "Thomas Reid and the Newtonian Turn of British Methodological Thought." In *The Methodological Heritage of Newton*, edited by Robert E. Butts and John W. Davis. Toronto: University of Toronto Press, 1970.

May, Henry F. "The Recovery of American Religious History." *American Historical Review* 70 (1964): 79–92.

Mead, Sidney E. "Professor Sweet's Religion and Culture in America: A Review Article." CH 22 (1953): 33–49.

Meier, Hugo A. "Technology and Democracy, 1800–1860." MVHR 43 (1957): 618–40.

Miller, Perry. Introduction. In *American Thought: Civil War to World War I*, edited by Perry Miller. New York: Holt, Rinehart and Winston, 1954.

Moore, J. Percy. "William Maclure—Scientist and Humanitarian." *Proceedings of the American Philosophical Society* 91 (1947): 239–49.

Prior, Moody E. "Bacon's Man of Science." JHI 15 (1954): 348–70.

Rossiter, Margaret W. "Benjamin Silliman and the Lowell Institute." NEQ 44 (1971): 602–26.

Sandeen, Ernest R. "The Princeton Theology: One Source of Biblical Literalism in American Protestantism." CH 31 (1962): 307–20.

Smith, H. Shelton. "The Church and the Social Order as Interpreted by
    James Henley Thornwell." CH 7 (1938): 115–24.
Smith, James Ward. "Religion and Science in American Philosophy." In
    The Shaping of American Religion, edited by James Ward Smith and
    A. Leland Jamison. Princeton: Princeton University Press, 1961.
Stevenson, Dwight E. "The Bacon College Story." *The College of the
    Bible Quarterly* 39 (1962): 7–56.
Street, T. Watson. "Thomas Smyth: Presbyterian Bookman." *Journal of
    the Presbyterian Historical Society* 37 (1859): 1–14.
Woozley, A. D. Introduction. In *Reid's Essays on the Intellectual Powers
    of Man*, edited by A. D. Woozley. London: Macmillan & Co., 1941.
Wright, Conrad. "The Religion of Geology." NEQ 14 (1941): 335–58.
Zochert, Donald. "Science and the Common Man in Ante-Bellum
    America." *Isis* 45 (1974): 448–73.

Index

Royal Society, the, 3
Ruffner, William H., 74

S

Schleiermacher, Friedrich, 135, 144
Science: influence upon the Scottish
    Philosophy, 6, 7, 8, 180 (n. 10); and
    classification, 62–63, 66; and "generali-
    zation," 15–16, 62–64, 66, 182 (n. 49),
    192 (n. 78); as utilitarian, 75–76, 82
Science and religion, xiii, xiv–xv, 39,
    49–51, 60, 71–175; inquiry *versus* re-
    ligion, 44–48
Scottish Realism, 4–30, 32, 37–38, 54–55,
    102–3; and "first principles," 7, 13, 181
    (n. 24); and "judgment," 10, 12, 54; and
    "ideas," 9
Senses, the, 10, 11, 54–55, 181 (n. 25)
Silliman, Benjamin, 43, 55, 61, 79, 98, 180
    (n. 11), 198 (n. 105), 199 (n. 5)
Slavery, 26, 36
Smith, Samuel Stanhope, 39–40, 102, 103,
    199 (n. 9)
Smyth, Thomas, 35, 55, 143, 159, 188 (n.
    38)
Sprague, William B., 139
Stewart, Dugald, 5–20, 22–23, 29, 38, 50,
    107, 195 (n. 41)

T

Thornwell, James Henley, 35, 38, 53, 58,
    63, 65, 69, 85, 107, 108, 110, 111, 121,
    140, 142, 153–55, 172, 190 (n. 26), 199
    (n. 15)
Transcendentalism, 135, 141, 143, 156,
    165, 170
Tyler, Samuel, 26–27, 30, 65–69, 128,
    130, 153

U

Unitarianism, 134–38, 141, 142, 156

V

Vestiges of the Natural History of Creation,
    95, 106, 107, 200 (n. 24)
Vital principle, the, 94, 108

W

Whately, Richard, 66, 68
Whewell, William, 4, 63, 166–67
Witherspoon, John, 32, 37, 39, 54, 57, 102
Woodrow, James, 168
Wright, Chauncey, 167, 197 (n. 71)
Wright, Frances, 47, 52, 76